THE HISTORY OF OUR LADY OF LOURDES CATHOLIC CHURCH, MILTON, WESTON-SUPER-MARE

80th ANNIVERSARY 1938 - 2018

Edited By

Geoff Thornton, Fr Alexander Redman,
Chris May, Sue Maguire, Mel Sarich,
Mary Studham and Tony Collyer

First published 2018 by The Independent Publishing Network, info@ipubnet.co.uk

Copyright © Our Lady of Lourdes Weston-super-Mare 2017.
28, Baytree Road, Milton, Weston-super-Mare, Somerset BS23 2PB

The moral right of the authors has been asserted.

All rights reserved. Without limiting the rights under copyright reserved above, no part of this publication may be reproduced, stored or introduced into a retrieval system, or transmitted in any form or by any means (electronic, mechanic, photocopying, recording or otherwise), without the prior written permission of both the copyright owner and the publisher of this book.

Copyright Material

Every effort has been made to trace the copyright holders of material quoted in this book. If application is made in writing to the publisher any omission will be included in future editions.

ISBN 978-1-78808-121-4

Printed and bound by Tasker Printers Ltd.
Unit 10, Lynx Crescent, Winterstoke Road, Weston-super-Mare, Somerset BS24 9DJ.

This book is dedicated to the Priests and Parishioners of Our Lady of Lourdes, past, present and future.

THE HISTORY OF OUR LADY OF LOURDES CATHOLIC CHURCH, MILTON, WESTON-SUPER-MARE

80th ANNIVERSARY 1938 - 2018

Contents

Foreword	Lord Cotter of Congresbury	vii
Preface - The Editors		ix
Chapter 1:	Setting us in an Historical Context	1
Chapter 2:	The Return of the Catholic Faith to Our Area	37
Chapter 3:	The Church of Our Lady of Lourdes in the Parish of Corpus Christi	101
Chapter 4:	The Parish of Our Lady of Lourdes	129
Bibliography		228

Foreword – by Brian Cotter, Lord Cotter of Congresbury

Dominic Cotter

Dr Michael Cotter (Father), Daniel Cotter (Grandfather) and Brian Cotter (later to be Lord Cotter of Congresbury) sitting on a bench on the promenade at Weston-super-Mare circa 1945.

In 1923 my grandfather Daniel Cotter gave a piece of land in Milton to Corpus Christi Parish to build a small Chapel-of-Ease at Baytree Road in Milton. He lived in Weston and was a parishioner at Corpus Christi Church.

Every year he travelled to Lourdes to assist the sick and lame hoping for a cure to their terrible ailments as well as to pray at the Shrine for his own intentions. This is probably why the little chapel was called Our Lady of Lourdes.

My father, Dr Michael Cotter was a Medical Doctor working in Barton Hill, Bristol, for a short while, where I was brought up, and then he worked in Greenford, Middlesex. When I left school, which was Downside in Somerset, I did my National Service. After this I worked in a small plastics company in Farnborough, occasionally liaising with the MoD. I then started up my own business in plastics, until I was selected to be Member of Parliament for the Liberal Democrat Party. There were three seats with vacancies at the time and I tried all three, the last being successful, the vacancy at Weston-super-Mare, where I had visited my grandfather many times when I was a boy. What a strange turn of events!

I was accused or at least suspected of having had nothing to do with Weston, so that to prove this was not the case, I searched through all my belongings and found the photograph above, the only one I could find with my grandfather and father with me on Weston promenade. I included this in my advertising leaflets.

Chris and Jan Simpson

Brian and Eyleen Cotter at one of Our Lady of Lourdes' Annual Dinners.

Eyleen and I took residence in Congresbury so that I could easily get to Parliament and be in my constituency. I was the first Non-Conservative Member of Parliament for Weston for over 70 years. I was elected in 1997 and held my seat until 2005, when I lost it to the Conservatives. In 2006, I was recommended to the House of Lords for my work for the Party.

Eventually we moved into a flat in Weston from where I travel to the House of Lords to work during the week, returning home to Weston for the weekends.

Another coincidence is that if I look out of my window here I can see where my grandfather's house used to be. I overlook it.

The final extraordinary experience was an invitation I received to write the Foreword of this book, The History of Our Lady of Lourdes Catholic Church, Milton, Weston-super-Mare for its 80th anniversary - the very church that my grandfather helped to create by donating the land on which it stands. Writing this Foreword completes a wonderful association for my family with Our Lady of Lourdes at Milton, and a great personal honour for me.

Brian Cotter

Preface – by the Editors

The original idea of writing a history of our parish came from the Parish Council, when they were discussing ways of marking the beginning of the Third Christian Millennium, the Holy Year of Jubilee, 2000 AD. It was believed to be good for us to know "where we had come from" as we were beginning another chapter of our history. As scripture says:

> "This shall be put on record for a future generation, and a people yet to be born shall praise God."
>
> Psalm 102

Although the new millennium was rapidly approaching, there seemed to be a lack of enthusiasm for the work it would involve; the year 2000 came and went. Geoff found someone to put the draft book, as it was, into WORD and added some more details; he also spoke with Tony Inganni. The resources at that time were vastly inferior to what is available now, both in the libraries and on the internet. Much later, Geoff discussed the book again, this time with Fr Martin and Sue Maguire, and the initial work and handwritten notes were then passed to Chris May for typing and setting out. Mel Sarich and Mary Studham also became interested and contacted Tony Collyer. Thus, work began again with fresh enthusiasm!

The new Parish Priest, Fr Alexander Redman, is extremely interested in history, especially Church history and the tradition of the Catholic Church, and was determined that we should write the history of our parish, continuing from where Geoff Thornton left it. Since those days, Geoff has retired as our choir master and historian, although he is still interested in what we are doing, and what a wonderful start he gave us.

In 1858, St Bernadette had visions of the Blessed Virgin Mary and St Joseph's Church was built; 80 years later Our Lady of Lourdes' Church was built and in 2018, 80 years further on again this history is due - an interesting symmetry. In the time of Jesus, the number 40 held a rich symbolism for Israel: Jesus fasted for 40 days and 40 nights in the wilderness; the Israelites wandered for 40 years in the desert; Moses spent 40 days and 40 nights on Mount Sinai before he was privileged to receive the Word of God; there are the Forty Martyrs of England and Wales, quite apart from the symmetry above and its significance to the world at large, our church was consecrated by our third Parish Priest, Bishop Mervyn Alexander, exactly 40 years after it was built. Moreover, it will be another 40 years from that date until its 80th Anniversary in 2018.

We could not have contemplated the work involved without the help many of our eager parishioners and friends: Napoleon Almazan, Brian Austin, Richard Austin (numerous pictures), Sisilah Baker, Anita and Frank Bailey, Maricris Magbanua, Sheila Berry, Annette Board, Fr John Brennan (the former Diocesan Archivist for Art and Architecture), Michael Brealey (Archivist of La Retraite), Sonia Briffitt, Joseph Burke, Jeanette Carter, Douglas Chamberlain, Fr Peter Clarke of the Ordinariate, Joan Dunne (née Petheram), Mgr Richard Dwyer, Jo Gaer (Corpus Christi), Fr Wieslaw Garbacz, Janet Greaney, Brian Griffin, Canon J A Harding (Diocesan Archivist), Gill Hogarth the Diocesan Assistant Archivist, Tony Horry (Kewstoke Family History Society),

Sue Inganni, Mgr Gabriel Leyden, Sr Pauline Mahony of La Retraite, John Martell, Deacon Tom Moffat, Angela Morley, Ken and Monica Morrison, Maria O'Sullivan, Peter Ottley, Graham Payne (WSM Family History Society), David Pluck. Louise Pople, Fr Martin Queenan for extensive discussions, Kathleen Reynolds, Trisha Roberts, Tracey Robinson, Sue Ryall (Kewstoke Family History Society), John Sach, Kathie Savage, Chris and Jan Simpson, Roderick and Angela Sleep, Barbara Smith, Maureen Spicer (née Fay), Mike Tedstone (St Paul's, Kewstoke), Betty Terrell, Paul Turner, Gillian Wall and Phyllis Wilson.

We are greatly indebted to Philippa Taylor of the Free Library Enquiry Centre in Taunton for researching the census data and the income data, and helping us find out more about the fate of the putative Pittoni picture; the staff in the Frederick Wood Room of Weston-super-Library for all their help and encouragement; Roderick Sleep for travelling around the district to photograph some of the local churches; Chris May for photographing the picture the *Adoration of the Shepherds in the Stable at Bethlehem* in Chipping Campden; to Sue Maguire for photographing the church and its grounds; to John Sach for digitally remastering some of the older photographs; to Chris and Janet Simpson for donating two large boxes of archives; to Ken and Monica Morrison for their archives; to Fr Martin Queenan for finding some older archives amongst his belongings; and to Viv Young for the more recent archives.

This group of archives means that the Parish is blessed with details of Parish Council Meetings and AGMs from 1965 to 1986, with a gap until 1990, followed by a few AGMs to 1994. This is followed by details of Parish Council Meetings, Parish Pastoral Council Meetings and AGMs from 1995 to 2006, additionally we have details of these meetings from 2010 to present. We also have financial details covering most of these periods. Geoff Thornton had few if any of these archives available to him when he started the process prior to the year 2000.

We should like to thank La Retraite for a copy of *La Retraite: Origins and Growth* from which we have gained information about Canon Barron and his work with the Sisters of La Retraite before the First World War and allowing us to reproduce two key paragraphs and photographs, and to our own Diocesan archivists, Canon John Harding and Gill Hogarth for giving us copyright permission form the Clifton Diocese Archives at Alexander House.

We should like to give great thanks to the Weston Mercury and Somerset Herald for their kindness in giving us copyright permission to publish many of their photographs of events taken over the years at Our Lady of Lourdes. Our thanks also to the photographer, Mark Atherton, for sourcing the photographs. Without these pictures, the book would be greatly inferior.

We are greatly indebted to the parishioners in general for their help and interest. It is dangerous to name people in an acknowledgement for fear of forgetting some great kindness. We hope that we have included everyone who gave assistance in whatever way, but if we have forgotten someone we beg pardon, and hope they take consolation in that there may be many saints in Heaven of whom we are totally unaware.

This book could not have been produced had it not been for the kind donation of money by the person or persons unknown who felt strongly that it should be published.

The Lord's Prayer

Our Father, who art in heaven, hallowed be thy name; thy kingdom come; thy will be done on earth as it is in heaven; give us this day our daily bread; and forgive us our trespasses, as we forgive those who trespass against us; and lead us not into temptation; but deliver us from evil.

Amen

David Pluck

The Sacred Heart of Jesus

CHAPTER 1 - SETTING US IN AN HISTORICAL CONTEXT

The Glastonbury Legend - Cradle of Christianity

To begin our history, we start with the Phoenicians and Romans who had been in commerce with England for years before the birth of Jesus, carrying on a thriving trade in the West Country. Legends attribute visits by Joseph of Aramithaea to places in Somerset, including Glastonbury where he is reputed to have built the first Christian Church. For this he may have used the busy port of Opopille (Uphill) to follow a route made by many traders and travellers before him and later used by pilgrims along the Mendip Hills to Glastonbury and Wells. Legend suggests that Jesus Himself may have joined Joseph of Arimathaea on such a visit. The famous English historian, St Bede (672 AD – 735 AD) makes no mention of this but St Gildas (516 AD) does.

After Jesus died, a legend tells that Joseph of Aramithaea with a company of followers returned to Britain. He brought with him the cup used by Jesus at the Last Supper, the Holy Grail, which contained two drops of blood from Jesus' side when He was hanging on the cross. Joseph was granted land at Glastonbury by the local king. When Joseph arrived at Glastonbury he stuck his thorn staff into the ground. It rooted and burst into bloom. In the grounds of what became Glastonbury Abbey was planted a cutting from that first tree, where it continued to bloom every year at Christmas time. A thorn tree still survives in the Abbey grounds, of a variety native to the Holy Land, which does bloom annually around Christmas time.

Joseph was claimed to have established the first church in England at Glastonbury, backed up by archaeological evidence suggesting a very early church there. Some legends have that Joseph buried the Holy Grail at the foot of Glastonbury Tor, from which a spring of blood gushed from the ground. The Chalice Well is situated at the base of the Tor from which the water issuing forth has a noticeable reddish tinge from the iron content in it.

Other legends suggest that the church founded by Joseph of Aramithaea lasted for many years, eventually becoming a monastery, where one of the first abbots was St Patrick, who was born in the West Country.

More evidence of Christianity arises from a discovery in 1991, when an amulet said by experts to be dated from the 4th or early 5th century AD was discovered at Shepton Mallet in a grave in the Roman settlement nearby. It is about 2 inches long in the shape of a cross with the symbols Chi Rho (Greek letters referring to Christ) inscribed on it.

Three British Bishops attended the Council of Arles in France in 314 AD, where they joined their fellow bishops in sending a letter of filial homage and obedience to the Pope. All this indicates that there were pockets of Christianity about the country, particularly in the West Country, before the arrival of St Augustine in 597 AD. Moreover, there are numerous Monastic foundations dating from Anglo-Saxon times and the Middle Ages, with men like Aldhelm of Malmesbury and Dunstan of Glastonbury and later of Canterbury, who emerged as religious leaders during a period of substantial religious and cultural achievement.

There is archaeological evidence that the Romans occupied the Mendip Hills, where there were lead and silver mines. With water levels being higher than today, the sea covered the land as far as Congresbury and almost as far as Street and Glastonbury, such that

Opopille would be one of the few ways to approach Glastonbury from the west. The Romans used various points on the Mendips and Roneck (Steep Holm - holm is a Scandinavian, and hence Viking - word for island) and Echni (Flat Holm) for warning beacons, and for signalling to the Welsh coast. Opopille would lie in an excellent position for signalling across the River Severn and as a light house to guide seafarers safely into port.

Early Saints associated with the area

Trying to discern the fact from the legend of the early saints is as clear as the amorphous mists over the Somerset Levels and Moors. After the Romans left the Island of Ronech (Steep Holm), there is no archaeological evidence for any occupation until the stories associated with St Gildas (the s is silent), who was a 5th/6th century northern chieftain's son. Legends associated with this saint are heavily embellished with miraculous events, some of them not befitting of a saint. He had a stormy temperament as testified by some of the events that happened to him during his journeys as a well-travelled monk. His main claim to fame was that he wrote the first history of Britain. This contained twenty-six chapters and was called "Liber Querulus De Exidio Britanniae (Lament over the Destruction of Britain)", which was more of a rant about the evils of the day than a history. In keeping with his alleged anger, tradition holds that after a row with King Arthur, Gildas flung the pages mentioning the king from Ronech into the sea, thus washing him out of history. This history was based on hearsay, tradition and memory, because there were few written documents on which he could base his work.

It is believed that Gildas was born about 476 AD. After the Romans left, during which there had been peace between the quarrelsome chieftains due to the strict and vicious Roman rule, various tribal disputes broke out again, and during one of them Gildas with his family had to flee to Wales – around 506 AD. His wife died the following year, whereupon Gildas tonsured his head, leading the ascetic life of a monk. Later, after making some particularly vitriolic comments about a few of the Welsh chieftains, his brother and sons had to make a hasty withdrawal from Wales.

Gildas made a journey to Rome, and, on returning, he stopped off on the Islet of Rhuis in Southern Brittany, where he obtained a grant of land on which to found a monastery in about 520 AD. From Rhuis he returned to Britain in search of recruits for his new community. From this era, the legends around St Gildas and Ronech begin. Legends suggested that he spent seven years on Ronech in solitude, or he may have travelled around Britain again looking for his future monks, some of whom may have spent time with him on Ronech as his novices. For two or three years, he was at Llancarfan Monastery in South Wales with his friend St Cadoc, who was Abbot of Llancarfon Monastery about 527 – 9 AD. During that short stay, he may have joined his friend by withdrawing each year to a place of retreat during the season of Lent, returning to the Monastery by Palm Sunday in preparation for Holy Week.

Some early accounts tell that St Gildas and St Cadoc spent Lent on Echni (Flat Holm), which was in the ancient boundary of Llancarfan Monastery. It was reported that whereas St Cadoc preferred Echni, which of the islands was the more hospitable, St Gildas favoured the more rugged cliffs and solitude of Ronech. No remains of an oratory have been found on either of the two islands. Both saints would have been familiar with the port of Opopille.

Gildas died at Rhuis on 29th January 570 AD. His body was placed in a boat and allowed to drift, at his request. Three months later, on 11th May, men from Rhuis found the boat in a creek with the body of Gildas still intact. They took his body back to Rhuis and buried it there.

Lifris of Llancarfan wrote the story of St Cadoc shortly before 1086. Llancarfan did not survive the Norman Conquest, being dissolved about the time of the Doomsday Book. Cadoc was born in Monmouthshire around 497 AD. An angel announced his birth, summoning the hermit Meuthi to baptise and teach him. A Holy well sprung up for his baptism and afterwards flowed with wine and milk. Cadoc is believed to have been baptised at Cathmail (Cadfael). Eventually Cadoc was sent away to be educated by Tathyw at his monastery at Caerwent, where Cadoc became a monk and a priest.

He founded the first monastery at Llancarfan, the "Church of the Stags", Vale of Glamorgan, before going to study in Ireland for three years. Returning to Wales, he found the monastery in ruins. He forced the monks back to manual labour, dragging timber from the woods for reconstruction. Two stags came into the open to help them, which is said to be why the stream there is called the Nant Carfan, the Stag Brook.

Then he continued his studies under a teacher of rhetoric from Italy, Bachan or Pachan, before travelling to Scotland, where he founded a monastery at Cambuslang. His influence back at Llancarfan helped it to become one of the chief monasteries in South Wales. Later he settled in Brittany on an island on the Etel River, now called the L'Ile de Cado, where he built an oratory, funded a monastery and devoted himself to spreading the Gospel. There are chapels dedicated to him at Belz, at Locoal-Mendon in Morbihan and at Gouesnac'h in Finistère. He was asked to cure the deaf there. His name is also the basis of some thirty Breton place-names.

Moving on to more concrete historical facts, and temporarily away from the marshes of Somerset, after the Council of Hertford (673 AD), Theodore, Archbishop of Canterbury, began an era of ecclesiastical reorganisation throughout Britain. During the division of the whole country into ecclesiastical parishes, Wessex was placed under two dioceses, Winchester and Sherborne. Opopille was in the latter. In later reorganisation, the Diocese of Wells was formed (909 AD). In 1088 AD, this diocese became the Diocese of Bath, and later still the Diocese of Bath and Glastonbury (1192), eventually changing in 1219 to the Diocese of Bath and Wells. These dates are useful in giving approximate dates for undated documents.

The Norman Churches

After the victory of William Duke of Normandy over King Harold Godwinson at the Battle of Hastings in 1066, followed by the aftermath of the subjugation of Britain to Norman rule, William instigated a census of the wealth of Britain in the Doomsday Book (1086). This book provides a wonderful snapshot of Britain in the 11th century, and it is from this time we focus our development of the history of the Catholic Church in and around Weston-super-Mare. The Table at the end of the Chapter taken from the Doomsday Book shows the relative wealth of each area mentioned in the text.

The second project that William initiated was to establish many religious houses to atone for the slaughter at the Battle of Hastings. Many wealthy landowners, Norman barons, rewarded for their fealty, followed his example, creating many small churches and, as their wealth increased, priories of their own. In return for the patronage of the king, the newly rich landowners, employed the brethren to offer regular prayers for their patrons, their patrons' antecedents, and successors. In the environs of Weston there were, and in some cases still are, those churches still in use: the Church of St Nicholas at Uphill (1080); the Church of St Martin at Worle (1125 - 50); the Church of St Paul at Kewstoke (12th century); the Church of St Augustine at Locking (mentioned in 1262 – although probably earlier); the Church of St Mary at Berrow (1017 - 27); the Church of St Bridget at Brean (13th century); and the Parish Church of Weston, St John the Baptist (1226); and much later two priories were gradually built, St Michael's Priory on Steep Holm (1189 - 99) and Worspring (Woodspring) Priory (ca 1210).

In many cases the churches to be described were originally built on or close to wooden Saxon churches, which were later rebuilt in stone in the Norman style with its typical pointed Norman arches. Between the dates 1377 and 1547, a large proportion of these Norman churches were rebuilt or had parts added to them, in the Perpendicular style (often called the Perpendicular Gothic style) - so called because of the emphasis on vertical lines. This Perpendicular style is the third and longest lasting phase of English Gothic architecture, following the Early English and the Decorative periods. Some of the towers in the churches of Somerset are claimed to be amongst the best examples of Perpendicular Gothic architecture in the land.

The Doomsday Book states that Opopille was owned by Serlo de Burci, a Norman Baron, who was granted extensive lands in the West Country. Under his lordship four knights were granted rights to work the land at Opopille and Christon. Each knight was granted a quarter share. The land had originally been held from King Edward the Confessor possibly by the wealthy Alwaker (Ewias or Ewacre) family. There was a mill on the top of Opopille and the Church of St Nicholas.

Some of the measurements of Serlo de Burci's land are not in units that have much meaning to us now, but some have. A hide of land is judged to be about 240 acres, with a plough-team as half that area. The Doomsday Book entry states that four Knights hold land belonging to Serlo de Burci. Alwaker (Ewacre, Ewias) held it from King Edward the Confessor and paid Danegold for six hides and a half. There is land for ten plough-teams. In the Manor, there are four plough-teams, with one serf and seven villeins, and four boors with three plough-teams. There are seventy acres of meadow and a hundred acres of pasture. It was then and is now worth six pounds (1086 AD).

Before going on, it is interesting to examine the employment conditions of these various classes: serfs were workmen who were the absolute property of the Lord of the Manor and could be sold like any other form of property; villeins were a higher class of workman who belonged to the local manor and had no freedom; boors were the highest class of workman labouring on the estate. This changed dramatically after the Black Death, which decimated the population, and gave the workers greater bargaining power.

The Church of St Nicholas at Uphill

The name Uphill was probably derived from Hubba's Pill, a pill being a small creek where Hubba was a Viking who regularly visited the area. An alternative theory is that Opopille might mean "the place upon the pill" or "the place upon the hill". Much of this period of Uphill was researched by Dr William Clifford, the third Catholic Bishop of

Clifton. In those days, the lower parts of Opopille were marshy and washed by the sea, so that the dwellings were positioned farther up the hill than those of today. Even so, bearing coffins to the graveyard and regular attendance at Holy Mass must have been arduous.

As Opopille was a small, busy port, it seems appropriate for St Nicholas, who has associations with sailors and seafaring, to be chosen as the patron saint for the church. Some parts of this little Norman church have been dated to 1080, and it is believed that it was consecrated in 1129. Like many of the other churches in the surroundings, later changes to the architecture are of the Perpendicular Gothic style.

The three stunning figures behind the altar represent from left to right, St Andrew, the risen Christ and St Nicholas. The two pictures beneath the tower represent King Alfred and St Gildas.

The known list of rectors can be traced back to 1318 to John de Gidding. In 1197, there is a record of a dispute between the rectors of Banwell and Uppepull (Uphill) because the latter buried the bodies of freemen under the jurisdiction of Chicheston (Christon) in Uppepull cemetery. The Black Death struck Uppepull in 1349, when in that year two rectors Rog. Tylie, and Joh. Muleward, in close succession, were followed by a gap. In 1496, there are records of two wills: one was the record of a gift to the Parish Church of Uppepull; the other by Sir Richard West requested burial within the chancel of the blessed Nicholas of Uphill. The patrons of the living include the Longet family (reign of Edward I (1272 -1307), Philip de Lung (1318), Thomas Cheddre Esquire, who was associated with Cheddar (1441), and King Henry VII (1498).

Chris May   Church of St Nicholas in Uphill

Chapter 1

In 1333, Bishop Ralph of Shrewsbury announced that he would be visiting the Churches of Blaedon, Uphull, Weston and the Chapel of Pokerston (Puxton). This Register of his to the Dean of Axbridge is kept at Wells. The next entry, dated 1334, to the Rectors of Bleodon and Uphhulle, and their chaplains, orders them to announce that false jurors have fallen under the sentence of greater excommunication. In another entry, by Walter Bursey to Sir Thomas Lord of Berkelee, he quit claims for ever (withdraws) the right of the Isle of Stepelholme to his lands of Upphall and Crucheston (Christon). This loss of income would hit the finances of the Canons of Stepholm severely.

In 1536, the Dissolution of the Monasteries ended Catholicism in Britain. From then Catholics had to celebrate the Holy Mass in secret. Thereafter the parishioners of the Church of St Nicholas celebrated in the Anglican rite.

The new Church of St Nicholas was consecrated in 1844. After that, services were conducted in each church on alternate Sundays, until the church on the hill eventually fell into severe disrepair, despite some effort of restoration. Three years later, the south window nearest the west end was walled up; the archway between the body of the church and the tower was walled up; the partition between the chancel and the tower into the belfry was taken down; the present chancel door near the east end visible only from the outside was walled up; and repair was made to the chancel roof and tower. After this the little church was only used for burials. Finally, in 1864, part of the roof was removed. Thereafter further work was carried out on the church to preserve it to its current state. The old Norman Church of St Nicholas is now in the care of the Churches Conservation Trust and is still opened occasionally, especially at Christmastime.

The Church of St Martin at Worle

Asgar (Edgar) owned the area around Worle before the Norman conquest. Afterwards the land belonged to Walter de Douwai (Douai) from the King. In 1086, the Doomsday Book entry for Worle states that it paid tax for 6½ hides with land for 15 plough-teams. The Lord of the Manor owned 15 plough-teams, 5 slaves, 22 villagers and 3 small holders with 9 plough-teams. There were 50 acres of meadow, and pasture of 13 furlongs by 2 furlongs. The value was £10 but now only £7. The reason for this fall in value may have been caused by one of the sons of Harold Godwinson, who in 1067 suddenly crossed over from Ireland with a fleet of warships, sailed up the Avon, despoiling all the neighbourhood. Having failed in his attack on Bristol the aggressors retired to Somerset and continued plundering. Much later, Worle became the property of William de Courtenay, and after his death in the reign of Henry III (1216 – 1272) went to his relative, Sir Vitalis Engayne, whose sons gave it to the Prior and Canons of Worspring, which later went to Henry Engayne.

The name Worle is possibly formed from the Old English wor + leah meaning a wood or clearing frequented by grouse, or perhaps "moor meadow". In around 1210, William de Courtenay inherited the land at the death of his father, Robert. It was William's idea to give the land to Worspring for a priory.

The Church of St Martin in Worle was built between 1125 – 50. Some rebuilding was carried out in the 14th and 15th centuries, with major restoration and extension in 1870. The first recorded vicar was Alias of Coleshull in 1325. In 1347, the Vicar of Worle, John de Stodelegh, died and the following year the Black death claimed John le Hayward,

Robert Geffray, and William Hareforde – the three of them within a month. The land and the church remained under the custodianship of Worspring until the Dissolution of the Monasteries. It is still in full use as an Anglican Church.

Chris May   Church of St Martin in Worle

The Church of St Paul at Kewstoke

The ancient manors of Woodspring, Kewstoke and Milton are described in the Doomsday Book in the following way:

> "Gilbert FitzTurold holds from the King Chiwestock, and Osbern from him. Edric held it in the time of King Edward, and paid Danegold for one hide and a half. There is land for twelve plough-teams which are in the demesne; and two slaves and two boors, and twenty acres of pasture, and ten acres of copsewood. Formerly worth twenty shillings, now thirty shillings."

Chapter 1

The Exeter Doomsday Book adds that at Kewstoke there were five wild brood-mares, indomitae equae, and fifteen goats.

In the 11th century, Kewstoke was called Chiwstock, which, 200 years later during the reign of King Edward I (1272 - 1307), had become Kewstock. In the first year of his reign, it is recorded that the six daughters of Geffrey Vassell held half a knight's fee in Kewstock. In about 1291, in the records of the ecclesiastical taxation of England and Wales ordered by Pope Nicholas IV "Ecclia de Kystok" is valued at £5, 6s. 8d. when it was the property of Worspring Priory.

There are three theories explaining the origin of the name Chiwstock. One suggestion is that it comes from the Celtic word "Kewch, the name for a boat and stoke being derived from "stock" or landing place. This suggests that in ancient times the early Britons constructed a landing stage, driving in sticks (or piles) to fasten their boats after crossing the River Severn. The second theory is that the word "stock" or "stoke" simply meant a holy meeting place. It may also mean 'stockade'.

The third theory involves a hermit, St Kew (a 6th century saint), who is reputed to have lived in a cave at the top of a small gorge above the church and, using a stick or in Anglo Saxon "stocc", descended some steps named after her.

The landward approach to Kewstoke in ancient times, was via St Kew's Steps - now usually referred to as Monk's Steps, of which there are about 100. For those travelling from the sea to the church to pray before going up St Kew's steps to the interior, or for those approaching the church from the landside, descending past St Kew's cave to reach the church, either way formed a pilgrims' trail.

From the Sea-board of Mendip　　　　　　　　　　*Chris May*

Monk's Steps at Kewstoke in 1900　　　　　　　　　In 2017

Chapter 1

As the legend recalls, St Kew (Cywa or Ciwa) the Virgin was a Welsh girl from Gwent, where she founded a church at Llangwicke (Llangiwa) and travelled through Glastonbury (Glastening), founding a church at Kewstoke on the way to Lannohou (St Kew) in Cornwall (Cerniw) to see her brother, Dochau. Her brother would not admit her until she had rid the region of a man-eating bear or boar. She is said to have tamed the creature, which then became her companion – a more recent tradition says that she inspired the locals to hunt it down and kill it. Ciwa was then allowed to build herself a small hermitage and chapel near her brother's, but she wisely chose a safer site more protected from wild animals. She died on February 8th (year unknown). The village of St Kew in Cornwall grew up around her church. The memory of St Kew is preserved in the East window of the Church of St Kew in North Cornwall, where she is portrayed in the company of a wild boar. She is also venerated at Llangwicke (Llangiwa) near Swansea.

There is a beautiful Norman doorway inside the porch that is dated probably between 1125 - 1150, and various Norman stones show that there was once a church before the building of the Norman Church of St Paul. The main north doorway, the two lower windows west of the pulpit, the east window and the arch into the chapel indicate a decorated Period church, others are of a Perpendicular Period. The clerestory (a rather unusual feature in Mendip Churches), pulpit, chancel and tower arches, the rood loft staircase and the tower and various buttresses are proof of a Perpendicular Period restoration in the 15th century. The pulpit, octagonal in design, is a beautiful example of 15th century stonework. It is believed that the stone originated from Caen in Normandy. The design and handiwork are very like the others in several local churches. It is believed to have been the work of a travelling band of masons.

Roderick Sleep   The Church of St Paul in Kewstoke

The list of Priests together with their dates, as far as is known, is John Manne (1322), Bartholomew de Mora (1326), John Price (1336), Michael de Graynton (1348), Abraham Hoper (1430), Henry Hoggys (1463), William Crosse (1477), John Towker (1479), Olybns. Smyth (1485), John Cherbury (1486), Richard Spryng (1491), Christopher Hamilton (1500), John Chaplayn (1500), Richard Carter (1520), and then this church ceased to be used for Catholic worship, and became Anglican, and is still in use today.

During repairs in 1849 a reliquary was discovered in the north wall of the nave. A stone with an effigy carved on it was found to have a hollow cavity behind it containing the remains of a wooden vessel, which had traces of a dark substance in it. It is believed to be one of the cups sold by the monks of Canterbury Cathedral claiming they contained a mixture of blood and water, the blood of St Thomas à Becket.

This cup originated from Worspring Abbey; the Canons spirited it away just before the Dissolution of the Monasteries to protect this most treasured relic of the Priory from profanation, the Canons foreseeing a possible desecration of their conventual church. The relic is preserved in the Taunton Museum.

The Church of St Augustine at Locking

Roderick Sleep

The Church of St Augustine at Locking

Not far away from Worle is the village of Locking with its Church of St Augustine. This village is not mentioned in the Doomsday Book as it was a part of the great Manor of Banwell. The Patent Rolls of King Edward II (1307 - 27) has a list of landowners who gave gifts of land to Prior John and his Canons of Worspring Priory: William de Courtenay, who was probably the first Lord of the Manor; Henry de Pendenay and Richard de Hordwell. In 1214, Prior John of Worspring Abbey and Convent of Dodlinch obtained from Geoffrey Gibwinne the Manor of Locking (otherwise Lockingheved). Geoffrey Gibwinne had it from William de Courtenay previously, except for four freemen, with their tenements, which he kept for himself. The name of Lockyng (Locking) did not appear until the 13th century. The above information was gleaned from a charter of Edward II dated 1325. The Church of St Augustine ceased to be used for Catholic worship, and became Anglican, and is still in use today.

The known vicars of St Augustine's are Richard de Lincumb (1319), Henry de Cary (1325), Walter de Sanford (1333), Walter Aleyn (1337), John Wylton (1440), Henry Crakul (1445), John Baker (1445), John Gefferey (1455), William Grendham (1459), John Feyland (1475), Odo Odellan (1477), David ap Griffith (1478), Christopher Gomulton (1498), Robert Paunton (1500), Thomas Lewys (1501), John Batturyl (1505), Thomas Dey (1524) and then the Reformation.

The Church of St Bridget at Brean

The history of the south side of Brean Down is quite different from that of the bay of Uppepull. A cemetery on the south side of Brean Down was carbon dated to 410AD, the year the Romans left Britain. The position of the village is unknown and perhaps was washed away by the sea, which is still steadily removing the soft cliffs.

In the 7th and 8th century, Irish monks came to this part of the Somerset coast, building their churches dedicated to their Irish saints such as St Mary, and St Bridget, the Abbess of Kildare from 451 – 525 AD. The Irish preferred the sea and did not venture far inland. The churches of Brean and Berrow are close to the sea or by a navigable river. There has been a church on the site of St Bridget's since the 6th century, although the present church is dated as 13th century. At the time of the Doomsday Book, the Manor belonged to Walter de Douai.

> "Walter de Douai holds Brien. In the time of King Edward Merlesuain held it, and paid Danegold for two hides. There is land for eight plough-teams. In the demesne there are three plough-teams, with one serf, and nine villeins, and seven boors and eight cotters, with three plough-teams and a half. There are thirty acres of pasture. It is worth a hundred shillings."

Roderick Sleep   The Church of St Bridget in Brean

The short tower was built in 1729 after the previous tower had been struck by lightning. There is a bell tower housing 5 bells, which are occasionally used for services and weddings. The interior includes a 17th century pulpit and a 14th or 15th octagonal stone font.

St Bridget's is part of a benefice with St Mary's of Berrow in the Anglican Archdeaconry of Wells in the Diocese of Bath and Wells.

The Church of St Mary at Berrow

The penultimate church and the last to go to Worspring Abbey was the church at Berrow. Brithius, Abbot of Glastonbury (1017 - 27) built a church at Berrow, St Mary's Church, but this is unlikely to have been the first built there. It was built from Mendip limestone with Hamstone for decoration. The south aisle is from the 15th century. The two-stage tower, which dates from 15th century, contains a bell dating from 1801, with four other bells. The interior contains 14th and 15th century fonts. It can be seen from the sea and at one time was painted white to act as a lighthouse. It stands among the sand dunes in the middle of Burnham and Berrow Golf Course.

In 1189, a new Bishop of Glastonbury had an inventory of all the manors owned by the Abbey. The one at Berrow refers to a chaplain who owned land near the church and paid 2 shillings a year instead of doing manual work. It is a Norman church, but the Manor of Berrow does not appear in the Doomsday Book being regarded as a small part of the Manor of Langford. The Bishop of Bath and Wells, in 1193, confirmed the right of the infirmary at Glastonbury to receive ½ a mark yearly (6s. 8d).

In 1203, there was a quarrel between the Abbot of Glastonbury and the Bishop of Bath and Wells over the patronage, the right to appoint the clergy of certain churches. Pope Innocent III set up a court to investigate the matter, which judged that the Bishop of the Isle of Meare and the rest of the Isle of Glastonbury belonged to Glastonbury Abbey. Outside the isle, the Bishop of Bath was awarded 10 manors, two of which, East Brent and Berrow, the Bishop granted to Glastonbury Abbey in exchange for two manors in Wiltshire. This quarrel continued until 1248, when Pope Innocent IV had to grant the request of the Abbot and Convent of Glastonbury by confirming that the Church of St Mary at Berrow was under the patronage of Glastonbury.

Between 1288 and 1291, Pope Nicholas IV assessed the value of all the churches in a kind of ecclesiastical Doomsday Book: St Mary's Church was valued at £16, with a yearly grant to Glastonbury Infirmary of 2 marks, double of what it had been in 1191; Burnham and East Brent the same as Berrow; whilst Lympsham was worth £12 but St Bridget's Church at Brean was valued at only £2. During this period, almost all the churches in the area were being rebuilt in the fashionable Early English style.

The first Rector of Berrow that we know about was Andrew Springhouse. Shortly after his appointment, he was given permission to spend a year of study at Oxford. In 1328, he moved from Berrow to be Vicar of West Monkton (near Taunton). His successor was Rector John de Worth, but shortly after his appointment, the Archdeacon of Wells became Patron of the Parish, receiving an acre of glebe in Berrow. When the Archdeacon was appointed he also became the Rector, so that de Worth agreed to move to another vacancy.

Chapter 1

In the same year, John de Hampton was instituted as vicar and the Manor of Berrow was transferred from Glastonbury Abbey to the Archdeacon, who in return gave the Abbey of Middleton Abbas near Ilchester. Not long after Glastonbury lost the Manor of Berrow it regained it, but not for long. Later that year, the Manor of Berrow ceased to be the property of Glastonbury Abbey going to Worspring Priory, although Glastonbury still held extensive lands in the parish.

In 1413, Knight Leonard Hakluyt bequeathed 5 marks to the Parish of Berrow for one pair of vestments on condition that prayers for his and his wife's soul were made.

From 1503 - 9, Richard Spryng, who had been the Vicar of St Paul's in Kewstoke from 1491 - 1500, became Vicar of Berrow and Worle as well as holding the Priorship of Worspring Abbey. The addition of St Mary's church would provide him with an increased income and he could appoint a curate to deal with local church matters. After the Dissolution of the Monasteries the Church of St Mary ceased to be used for Catholic worship, and became Anglican, and is still in use today.

In the time of King Edward, the Confessor, prior to the Norman Conquest, the village of Mideltone (a Town [ton] in the middle, i.e. between Ashcombe and Worle) was one of the Saxon Royal Manors held by one Alwaker (father of Aelfric) and was part of the ancient parish of Kewstoke.

> "Anschitil himself holds Mideltone. Osward held it in the time of King Edward, and paid Danegold for one hide. There is land for one plough-team, which is there, with one villein and two serfs. There are six acres of meadow and two acres of copsewood, and twenty acres of pasture. Formerly and still worth fifteen shillings."

Roderick Sleep   The Church of St Mary in Berrow

Our historic first mention is from the Doomsday Book, when the holding had passed to one Richard. Milton is described as a small and probably scattered agricultural settlement having land for two plough-teams for 3 villagers. The actual geographical location of Milton appears to have been mainly on the hill to the north of our present church. It was then in the Ecclesiastical Parish of Kewstoke. Our forebears would therefore have had to travel to the Church of St Paul, Kewstoke to attend Mass, receive Baptism, Holy Matrimony and Christian Burial. What are called the "Monks Steps" going down the hill to Kewstoke Church seem to have been the old church way from Milton.

It was not until the 19th century that there appears to have been any significant development in Milton. In 1886, to serve the obviously burgeoning village of small farms, market gardens, lime-stone quarries, kilns, and cottages (many of which still exist) the pretty little Victorian Anglican Church of St Jude was built. This became St Andrew's Greek Orthodox Church.

The Old Parish Church of St John the Baptist of Weston-super-Mare

Although this church is not associated with Worspring and yet is probably one of the closest churches too it, it was the Parish Church of Weston-super-Mare, the Church of St John the Baptist. Weston was not mentioned in the Doomsday Book (it was regarded as a part of Ashcombe). There is evidence that the original church was Norman. When the Church of St John the Baptist was pulled down (except for the chancel) in 1824 to be rebuilt in 1837, a very small Norman window was found. This was decorated by two rows of rather shallow carving, the inner row showing a tooth pattern with a zigzag outer row. At the time of discovery, this was removed to Weston Museum. The font also revealed Norman characteristics despite having been reworked and ravaged by neglect.

This Norman church was probably built on the foundations of an earlier Saxon church. A cluster of Romano-British finds around the area of Grove Park and the present St John the Baptist's Church backed up by a document of 1226 (in the reign of Henry III 1216 – 1272), and subsequent ones, suggest to the archaeologists that there was a continuum of Saxon, Romano-British and Celtic occupation. This document confirms that there was a stable community associated with this Norman Parish Church.

The date of the original stone foundation is unknown, but in the Dean and Chapter of Wells records it is stated, that in 1221 the Advowson of the Church of Weston (right of benefit from) was granted to Bishop Jocelin, the Bishop of Bath and Wells. Another entry in 1234, records an Ordinance of this Bishop, out of the income of the Church of Weston propre Worle, 100 pounds of wax should be paid annually to Wells Cathedral Treasury – 50 pounds at the Passion of St Andrew and 50 pounds at the Translation of St Andrew – with the wax to be burnt close to the altar of the glorious Virgin at all houses in which the divine office is celebrated by day and by night. Again in 1226, we discover a mention of the Church of St John in the village of Weston from documents referring to this same payment to Wells Cathedral Treasury.

In 1256, the Church of Weston was appropriated to the Convent of Bath, followed by a later record showing that the Abbey confirmed the grant of appropriation.

In 1246, the payment of 100 pounds of wax was included among the assets of the Church of Wells in the list of church property made out by Bishop Roger, the successor to

Bishop Jocelin. The amount of 100 pounds of wax was a considerable burden, bearing in mind that a single hive would generate about a pound of wax per annum, so that 100 hives would be necessary to produce the required payment, which would mean the taking of perhaps a ton of honey. The Wells records show that the payments were not kept up without duress. In 1277, the Rector of Weston, Guido de Schevyngdon, was sued before the official of the Bishop by the treasurer for arrears of wax, and was ordered to pay up 30 pounds before the Feast of St Gregory, thirty pounds in Lent, and 40 pounds before the Translation of St Andrew; furthermore, he was directed to continue the half-yearly payments of 50 pounds on the appointed days. A later entry testifies to the difficulty in collecting wax lasted at least into the next century.

In 1349, John the Rector was sued by the treasurer for arrears, and ordered, under threat of sequestration, to pay up 50 pounds of wax within 15 days. The Dean of Axbridge, the Rector of Uphill and the Vicars of Kewstoke and Worle were given a commission to carry out the order.

In a document of 1375, the Rector of Weston, Sir (here meaning Reverend) John Horn, was admonished for non-payment. He went to Wookey to promise on oath, laying his hand in the hand of the Bishop of Bath and Wells, in the presence of the Precentor, the Chancellor and a Canon of Wells, that in future he would faithfully pay the 100 lbs of wax that was admittedly due from his parish.

In 1333, Bishop Ralph of Bath and Wells sent notification of his intention to visit St John's Parish, and in 1353 he issued his mandate to the Rural Dean of Axbridge that within the parish churches of Uphill, Kewstoke, Weston and other places, the Dean was to proclaim that certain evil despoilers of the Church, disturbers, evil-doers and usurpers were to be warned that they were liable to the sentence of greater excommunication. In this way, Weston was treated in the same fashion as all the other local parishes.

The Old Parish Church of St John the Baptist at Weston-super-Mare

The list of vicars extends from 1277 to the present day: Guido de Schevyngdon 1277, John --- 1297, Roger de Pykeslegh 1311, John de Oterhampton 1340, John Powey 1348, Philip de Oterhampton 1349, John Horn 1375, John Cator 1425, Richard Mayhow 14 ---, Henry Aleyn 1471, Thomas Onesteby 1474, the Reformation. Note the effect of the Black Death in 1438/9.

The Church was very small, and from woodcuts appearing in the Gentleman's Magazine of 1805 drawn by Mr Bennett, a solicitor of Banwell, was like nearly all the other Somerset churches, being built in the Perpendicular style. It was about 84 ft. in length and 20 ft. in breadth. There was one step up into the chancel and at the west end a proportionately short tower in which hung three bells. It was situated on a hill commanding a panoramic view of the bay.

Weston was growing by the 19th century such that the Church was getting too small to accommodate the parishioners. The Lord of the Manor, the Reverend Wadham-Pigott of Brockley, donated a £1000 to the Church to remedy its insufficiency. It is typical for the poorer villages that they were unable to develop and maintain their churches. The old church was pulled down and destroyed, except for the chancel, in 1824. A new church was built in the same year to replace the old.

The Priories

St Michael's Priory at Steep Holm

St Michael's Priory of Stepholm (Steep Holm) was probably built in the early 12th century. Documentary evidence linking Uppilla with the Priory was from an undated charter by Robert son of Richard, who gave the Church of St Nicholas of Uppilla as alms to St Michael's of Stepholm and the Augustinian Canons serving there. In return, he requested the brothers to pray for his soul and those of his parents, antecedents, and successors in perpetuity. This charter is slightly earlier than the first of the Stepholm charters. A subsequent one is not extant. In all, five charters appertaining to this period were discovered in Berkeley Castle.

In the Augustinian tradition, it was customary for the Canons to arrive after the lay brothers and artisans had built the priory ready for the Canons to concentrate on their religious duties. For such a small priory built in an inaccessible place, there probably being fewer than a dozen Canons, occasionally the Prior and several lay brothers would have to leave their prayers to assist in practical duties. The inaccessibility of Stepholm was magnified by the facts that the estuary had the highest rise and fall of the maximum tide combined with a maximum flowrate of 4 knots in the known world. This was on tranquil days. Life under such conditions must have been exceedingly difficult, with a resulting neglect of religious obligations. Certainly, the priory was up and running before Robert son of Richard wrote his charter. Robert son of Richard was possibly related to one of the knights who each worked a quarter of the land in Uppilla and Christon that Serlo de Burci had given to them.

When Robert died, his daughter and heiress, Agacia, was married to John of Ken (Kenn) near Clevedon), who took over the lands of Uppilla and Stepholm. From 1150 onwards, the family adopted the name of the village, which means that John of Ken's charter confirming the charters of Robert son of Richard must have been post 1150. John's charter confirms Richard's charters and continues the patronage with St Michael's, giving the Church of St Nicholas, 15 acres of land, free use of the mill and four cows and twenty sheep with pasture – a very valuable gift. This charter was written during the reign of King John (1199 -1216). From the handwriting and the style of presentation Robert's charters were produced during the reign of Richard Coeur de Lion (1189 - 99).

Many of Serlo de Burci's original land holdings eventually came into the hands of the Fitzmartins of Blagdon. William Fitzmartin son of Robert son of Martin drew up a charter confirming another lost document of Robert son of Richard. This document was written before 1209, the date of his death. This confirmation was of great importance to the Priory because, at the death of a benefactor, the Prior and his Canons would lose income should the patronage be discontinued (albeit intended in perpetuity). Evidently perpetuity always has a date.

Early in the reign of King Henry III (1216 – 72), Thomas de Muncketon, a witness to John of Ken's earlier charters, added his own gift to the brothers living on Stepholm. At the same time, to protect them he handed over earlier charters as proof of ownership. In 1236, Henry son of Richard gave half a virgate of land (a virgate is used for tax purposes rather than an area and is a quarter of a hide or about 30 acres) in Kercheston (Christon) to the Priory. In return Prior William received Henry and his heirs into all benefits and orisons in St Michael's Priory for ever. In 1256, Robert de Sparkford, another witness to previous charters, disclaimed his right to the Church of St Nicholas in favour of Reginald de Long and others. The brothers of St Michael's lost some of their land in this deal; they had already lost two vital grants previously.

Returning briefly to 1243, the Prior had to deal with a different problem, when two lay-brothers, evidently sent on an errand to the mainland, were accused of larceny. Brother Gregory of la Houme (Stepholm) with Robert, his brother, quickly absented themselves. The court left it to the Prior to punish them. It is not known what happened to them or even whether they were innocent or guilty.

The owner and patron of Stepholm in 1260 was Lord Robert de Tregoz. Apparently, he had obtained his property through the dowry of his wife, Julia. Exactly how this came about is uncertain because her father, grandfather and great-grandfather were all called William. The first of these Williams was William de Cantelupe who died in 1238. He had endowed a small priory in Studley, Warwickshire, giving the Canons of Studley lands for a hospital at the Priory gates for the poor and infirm. Her father endowed Studley with lands in Locking, Worle, Kewstoke and Norton. With St Michael's Priory failing, Lord de Tregoz favoured giving it to Studley. The final Stepholm charter dated 1260 was by William de Button (Bitton) I, Bishop of Bath and Wells, consenting to the transfer of Canons from Stepholm to Studley provided that at least two Canons from Studley shall remain on Stepholm, and that one, who ought to be in charge, shall be called Prior of Stepholm. It had been felt that in the past the Canons' discipline had been lax, that they had spent insufficient time in prayer, making an excuse for the transfer to be effected smoothly.

What happened next was hardly the fault of the Canons of Stepholm: King Henry III (1216 – 72) was at odds with his barons, leading to the decisive Battle of Evesham (1265). Both the baron's leader, Simon de Montfort, Earl of Leicester, and Lord Robert de Tregoz were killed. The de Tregoz lands immediately defaulted to the Crown.

Maurice the third of Berkeley restored the Priory about the end of the 13th century or the beginning of the 14th as recorded in the Berkeley archives:

> "This Lord Maurice (1281 - 1326), new built the friery for the fryers and the brethren in the Holmes, an Iland in Seavern and not far from his manor of Portbury."

The last mention of St Michael's Priory of Stepholm in the Berkeley Manuscripts is in the life of Thomas the fourth of Berkeley:

> "In the 13th of Richard the Second [1399], the Lady Elizabeth his mother dying, this lord entered upon the lands which shee held in Joynture and dower… And upon the Isle of Stepholmes, in the County of Somerset."

Studley Priory, after losing the Priory of St Michael, continued with reasonable prosperity until 1536, when the Dissolution of the Monasteries was enacted. Long before that the Priory of St Michael had foundered: its walls dismantled bit by bit for use in other buildings until only the foundations mark where it had once stood against the fierce storms on Stepholm.

Woodspring Priory

The Doomsday Book records that Worspring (Woodspring) was the property of William de Falaise, passing with his daughter to Baldwin de Bullers, whose daughter married William Fitz Urse, the father of Reginald Fitz Urse, who inherited his father's lands. The property eventually passed to Robert de Courtenay (Courtenai) by marriage to Matilda Fitz Urse.

> "William [de Faleise] himself holds Worspring. By consent of King William Serlo de Burci gave it to him with his daughter. Euroac held it in the time of King Edward, and paid Danegold for six hides and one virgate of land. There is land for twelve plough-teams. In the demesne (hiatus). There thirteen villeins and six boors have six plough-teams. There are ten acres of pasture and ten acres of copsewood. Always worth a hundred shillings.

Roger de Pont Leveque, the Archbishop of York, Gilbert Foliot, the Bishop of London, and Josceline de Bohon, the Bishop of Salisbury, crowned the heir apparent, Henry the Young King, at York in June 1170 on King Henry II's orders (1154 - 1189). This was in breach of Canterbury's privilege of coronation. In the following November, Thomas à Becket, returning from exile to Canterbury, excommunicated all three of them. He followed this by excommunicating his other opponents in the Church. The first three fled to France to visit King Henry II

"Who will rid me of this troublesome priest?" These are the words King Henry II uttered - although the historian Simon Schama believes that the sentence used was less terse - but was it cried out of a fit of pique or as a Royal command? Four knights, Sir Reginald Fitz Urse, Sir Richard le Breton (Richard Brett or Breto), Sir Hugh de Morville and Sir William de Traci, took him at his word, as a Royal Command. In 1170 Thomas à Becket was murdered by these four assassins, who approached him while the monks were chanting vespers, and sliced him to death within the Cathedral of Canterbury, when he refused to be arrested by them. The monks of Canterbury scooped up the blood of the martyred archbishop in wooden cups. In later centuries water put in these bloodstained cups called "Canterbury Water" was held as a precious relic.

Chapter 1

One story told of the miracles associated with Canterbury Water is of a man on his way home after visiting Thomas à Becket's shrine was stranded late at night at Rochester. In vain he sought shelter, but at door after door he was refused admittance. At last, "for the sake of the Blessed Martyr" he was taken in. The town caught fire in the night. When the citizens were fleeing, panic-stricken, "the pilgrim, whose faith was more fervent than fear of the flames, remaining boldly on the roof called for a spear or something long. A fork – a pitch fork – was handed up to him; then taking from his neck the Reliquary containing the Canterbury Water, he fastened it to the fork, held it outwards towards the fire," thus keeping the flames at bay. For "the fire, as if fearing a contrary element, turned aside." Finally, the whole town was burnt, with the single exception of its one hospitable house.

The assassins fled north to Knaresborough Castle, which was held by Hugh de Morville, where they stayed for about a year. De Morville had property in Cumbria that, if necessary, could be used as a bolt hole in the separate Kingdom of Scotland. In part-reparation, Hugh de Morville, Richard le Breton and William de Traci built a church at Alkborough near Scunthorpe in North Lincolnshire. Until 1690 there was a commemorative stone on the chancel recording the event.

Pope Alexander III excommunicated them in 1171, and in August of that year, they sought King Henry's advice, but he did not help them, although he did not confiscate their lands or arrest them for such a despicable crime.

After the excommunication of the four errant knights, William de Traci went to Rome alone to seek the Pope's forgiveness, but before he left, which was between the end of September and King Henry's expedition to Ireland in October 1171, he settled some business matters: he made appearances in the Shire Court at Oxford, certifying a renunciation of a claim relating to land of Winchcombe Abbey at Gagingwell, near Enstone, north of Oxford, and was still present there when the charter recording the transaction was offered up on the High Altar at Winchcombe Abbey. Some time, later he granted the Canons of Torre in Devon all his lands at North Chillingford. After 1170, he rebuilt the Church of St Peter, Paul and Thomas in Bovey Tracey as part-atonement for his crime. The name of the town is a combination of the River Bovey and the de Traci family. He rebuilt the chancel and porch, adding a tower, to the Church in Lapford, Devon, which was then rededicated to St Thomas.

Richard le Breton delayed in joining him because he was waiting for Reginald Fitz Urse and Hugh de Morville who were now fighting against the King in the Rebellion of 1173/4. Then the three of them joined Reginald de Traci in Rome to ask for the Pope's forgiveness, which was granted, conditional that they spent fourteen years at the crusades. They left Rome for the crusades.

Did these four complete their penance and fight in the crusades for the full fourteen years? Sir William de Traci's journey east was confirmed by Romwald, Archbishop of Salerno, and Roger of Hoveden. Traci died in 1189 and could have fulfilled his penance. Sir Reginald Fitz Urse (born 1145 - 1173) was the first to die and could not fulfil his penance. Legend has it that he fled to Ireland where he fathered the McMahon clan. Sir Richard le Breton later retired to the Island of Jersey. He may have completed his 14-year penance, but this is unknown. He left his daughter and heiress, Grace, to marry John de Sudely. Sir Hugh de Morville died in Knaresborough in 1202. It is believed he went to the Holy Land. The Lordship of Westmorland passed to de Morville's sister (some say niece),

Maud, in 1174. He must have been confirmed dead by 1202/3, when his English lands were given to co-heiresses.

For his part, King Henry II was forced to carry out penance during the revolt of 1173/4. He humbled himself with public penance at Thomas à Becket's tomb as well as at the Church of St Dunstan. Thomas à Becket was canonized in 1173.

All four murders had association with Worspring or the surrounding districts: Reginald Fitz Urse was born in Williton (near Minehead); Richard le Breton (Richard Brett or Breto) held the Manor of Sampford Brett, a mile away; Hugh de Morville and William de Traci came from Devon. Richard le Breton's daughter and grand-daughter bequeathed lands to Worspring.

By 1210 there was a chapel in Worspring dedicated to St Thomas the Martyr of Canterbury. When Robert de Courtenay died, his son William buried him in the Chapel to hasten his father's salvation, that of his mother, himself, his wife and his ancestors and successors. In an undated letter that William wrote to Jocelin Bishop of Bath he proposed to give all his land at Worspring and to convert the chapel into a "Conventual House of the Order of Augustinian Canons of Bristol", to God and the Blessed Mary and the Blessed Martyr Thomas. Bishop Jocelin approved this in 1210. In Dugdale's Monasticon there is a copy of the letter to Bishop Jocelin written in the year 1210, which was in the Cottonian Library in the British Museum. There is great uncertainty on which branch of the de Courtenay tree this Robert and his son, William, may be found.

A 13th century seal for the Worspring Priory shows the martyrdom of St Thomas à Becket beneath the tower of Canterbury Cathedral. There is a cup pictured beside the head of the martyr, with a sword levelled at his forehead.

The situation of the little chapel at the northernmost tip of the parish, close to the muddy waters of the Bristol Channel, was advantageous to mariners, soldiers, merchants and pilgrims, forming a northern alternative to the busy port of Opopille. The position of the chapel is isolated and rural, close to Middle Hope at the eastern end of Sand Point, and not far from a convenient, sheltered landing-place known as Worspring Pill, in the lea of St Thomas's Head. Welsh pilgrims from the north on their way to Glastonbury Abbey would have found Worspring Pill an excellent place for taking on provisions for the journey ahead. Connections existed to other religious sites, St Nicholas's, at Opopille, St Michael's Priory on Stepholm and Worspring Priory itself. Drovers' lanes across the lowland from Worspring gave access to the village of Norton, leading on towards Kewstoke Village and the Church of St Paul and from up Monk's Steps to the top of Worlebury Hill and the interior.

In 1217 Bishop Jocelin drew up a charter instructing the Canons of Dodlinch (Dodelyng) to transfer to Worspring, which they did sometime before 1226. The house of Dodlinch was in existence in 1214 when Geoffrey Gibwinne (Gilberyn or Gilbewyn) gave it to the manor of Locking. Gibwinne was a lawyer who had previously served the Courtenays. Four years later the Bishop confirmed the previous charter and confirmed to the Canons a gift from William de Courtenay of the Church of St Martin at Worle and a gift from Master Geoffrey Gibwinne of the Church of St Augustine at Locking, which he had previously obtained from William de Courtenay. This must have been a relief for the Prior, who had the same arrangement with Master Geoffrey Gibwinne that he had previously with William de Courtenay. No revenue was lost. The Bath Cartulary has an inspeximus by Walter the

Prior of a charter of William de Button (Bitton) I, Bishop of Bath and Wells, dated 1262 confirming a charter of Bishop Jocelin to the Canons of Dodlinch in 1230 and the charter of 1217 to the same Canons.

In 1243, during a vacancy at Worspring Priory, 26 Canons were present at the election of the new prior. The successful candidate was Richard of Keynsham. Now the main possessions of the Priory were the manors of Locking and Worle, a variety of other local properties as gifts, including land from the Offre family, descendants of Richard le Breton. In addition, the Priory owned land in Devon, Dorset and Wiltshire, but this realised insufficient income to fund the most modest of building programmes, with rumours of the first debts as early as 1277. William de Button II, Bishop of Bath and Wells, fortunately came to the rescue with a legacy of 210 marks (a mark was not a coin but a unit of account), which was repeated in 1279, on condition that the Prior and the convent agreed to support the memorial service of the Bishop of Wells and a chaplaincy for his soul. In 1281, the Prior was a conservator acting on behalf of Pope Martin IV during the investigation of a bogus rector at Burnham.

The construction of the Priory church, which had been long delayed, had no roof to its chancel until 1291. Until then the Canons were probably still using the old Chapel of St Thomas with a dormitory range and additional wooden buildings. The chancel and Lady Chapel were completed by 1317. Bishop Drokensford recorded a fine of 20 shillings imposed on the Prior for failing to have the church and altars consecrated. It seems that the gatehouse was completed next with the construction of the cloister following, but little is known about the building work carried out in the 14th century.

Another problem for the Prior in 1317, when an appropriately ill-named brother, Thomas le Taverner, was found wandering outside the precincts, using foul language and misbehaving during service in the choir. The Bishop ruled that Thomas was to be confined to the Priory where he was to occupy the lowest place, to follow severe rules of fasting, devotion, silence and scourging that were to be ceased when he was penitent. Unfortunately, these severe remedies seemed to have little effect for soon afterwards Thomas and Brother Lundrias, another wayward Canon, were removed to Bruton to be kept at the cost of Worspring until penitent. A similar case was recorded much later in 1458, when Worspring and Keynsham exchanged Canons who were not to return until both had atoned for their offences.

In an *inspeximus* of 1325 of King Edward II (`1307- 1327) is a confirmation of earlier endowments to the Priory stating that the Canons owned all the land belonging to William de Courtenay and Robert de Newton. Half of the manor of Worle was granted by Henry Engayne together with the homage and dues of his tenants of Worle, Worspring, Kewstoke, Milton, Ebdon and Locking. The same year Alicia Offre gave half an acre of meadow in Estredolmore and another half an acre of meadow in Westredolmore. In 1331, Henry Carey, Vicar of Locking, obtained a licence to give to the Priory his lands in Sandford Marsh. Much later, in 1410, licence was granted to Robert Pobelow and John Venables to alienate to the Priory 174 acres of land in Worle, Winscombe, Rolstone and Poke Rolstone.

This good fortune did not last long. In 1438, the Priory lost land and the Prior and Canons were recorded three times within a month of appointing consecutive vicars at Worle, with new appointments at Locking and Kewstoke. The Black Death had struck the area. Locally the Dean and Chapter of Wells wrote off the arrears of Worspring, but insisted that future debts would have to be met in full.

The Black Death proved to be one of the most devastating pandemics in Britain, killing 40% to 60% of the population between June 1348 and December 1349. Before the coming of the Pestilence, the average number of annual appointments of clergy made by the King was about 100. Between June 1349 and the middle of September of the same year, there were 440, compared with 46 in the corresponding period the year before. The country did not suffer the extreme reactions seen in Europe such as the persecution of minority religious and foreign groups together with lepers and those with other skin diseases such as psoriasis. The immediate effect in England was to halt the campaigns of the Hundred Years War. Over a longer period, the decrease in population caused a shortage of labour, with a concomitant rise in wages fiercely resisted by the landowners. This gave rise to a deep resentment among the lower classes, which boiled over in the Peasants' Revolt of 1381. This gradually ended serfdom in England.

The 15th century seems to have been much more prosperous. Worspring commenced an ambitious building programme for the construction of a barn, an infirmary and a new Priory church built in the Perpendicular style. The source of this income is unknown. Dame Margaret Chocke mentions the building work in her will of 1484. The choir stalls of the new church appear to have been installed by Prior Richard Spryng (Sprynt) (1491 – 1525). The north aisle was added to the church shortly afterwards but the final embellishments were cut short by the Dissolution of the Monasteries.

Roderick Sleep　　　　Woodspring (Worspring) Priory

Chapter 1

Priors of Worspring

Reginald	Died 1243
Richard of Keynsham	Elected 1243
John	Mentioned in 1266 and 1276
Reginald	Mentioned 1317
Henry	Mentioned 1325
Thomas de Banwell	Mentioned 1383 and died 1414
Peter Loviare	Elected 1414
William Lustre (Lusshe)	Died 1458
John Gurman	Elected 1458
Henry Benet	Mentioned 1485
Richard Spryng (Sprynt)	Elected 1491 and resigned 1525
Roger Tormenton (Tormynton)	Elected 1525 and surrendered the Priory 1536

In Bishop Fox's Register a Papal letter (dated 1505) is recorded concerning Prior Richard Spryng (1491 – 1525). The contents describe the enlargement of his duties and explain his powers. It permitted his appointment as Vicar of Berrow with licence to hold simultaneously Berrow and Worle with the Priorship of Worspring.

Despite all this enlarging of Worspring Priory the community remained small, much smaller than in earlier days: there were seven persons including the Prior, the Sub-prior and the retired Richard Spryng, who was permitted to stay within the Priory. A visit recorded tells that morale was low: the Canons were resentful and suspicious of the new prior, Roger Tormenton (Tormynton).

Little remains of the Priory as built by William de Courtenay. There is one stone, a Norman capital, built into the wall at the entrance gate, which is believed to be a relic of the even older chantry, which was standing before de Courtenay's time. A greater part of the rest is probably not earlier than the 14th century. Some authorities say that the lower part of the tower, the cloister walls, and the walls of the outer enclosure are most likely 14th century. The upper part of the tower and the now detached building called the Refectory or the Friars' Hall date from early 15th century. The nave, the north aisle and the monastic barn at some little distance to the north-west, were probably late 15th or early 16th century.

Excavations in the autumn of 1885, in the east side of the tower, revealed the heavy foundations of the choir, showing that part of the building must have been more than 40 feet long and only slightly less than the width of the nave. A quantity of 14th century pavement was discovered on the site of the altar consisting of ornamental tiles bearing the arms of England, France and the Isle of Man. Many fragments of carved stonework, parts of the choir windows, were discovered, together with leaden coffins and parts of skeletons. Pieces of burnt stone and wood suggested that that end of the church was destroyed by fire.

The most striking feature of the Priory, the Woodspring Tower, was in the centre of the church; and around the chamber at its base, whose vaulted roof is of beautiful fan tracery carved in Caen stone, can be seen four arches, though all but one are built up, and the only way into it now is by the ancient entrance of the choir. It has been said that the tower was at first rectangular in its plan, and that the original 13th century work still remains encased in the square and symmetrical masonry of two hundred years later. Around the belfry are four tall, graceful Perpendicular windows, with open carved stonework in the centre.

The Reformation

The Acknowledgement of the King's Supremacy was drawn up in 1534 finalising the break with Rome. In a letter from the opportunist Richard Byschoppe, the ambitious Sub-prior of Bruton, to Lady Lisle, he suggested rumours existed that Prior Tormenton would refuse to sign the Acknowledgement. Should he refuse to sign he would be dismissed, putting Byschoppe as the potential King's man, but he greatly underestimated the wisdom of the Prior.

On 21st August 1534, the Canons resident were Roger Tormynton, Prior; John Serche, Sub-Prior; Brother Robert Coke, Brother Thomas Glastunbery, Brother Rychard Adams, Brother John Axbryge, Brother William Brynt and Brother Robert Evans.

When the document arrived, Tormynton and seven other brothers dutifully signed. Meanwhile the wily Prior had already sold some of the Priory's lands to Thomas Horner of Mells for £50. The Crown Survey of Monastic Wealth was drawn up and presented in the Valor Ecclesiasticus of 1535. From this document, it seems that Prior Tormenton had already dispersed the proceeds of his sale and the remaining assets, comprising land in Worle, Ebdon, Locking and Sandford Marsh, a farm known as Willett's Place at Butcombe, the site of the Manor of Worle, the tithe of Kewstoke and the rectorial farm at Locking to a total of £87.2.11d.

The community was suppressed on 27th September 1536, but Roger Tormenton was permitted to stay in the priory with a pension of £12 per annum until he was instituted to the Rectory of Enborne, near Donnington. Most of his remaining lands were leased to his business partner, Thomas Horner. The leases were valid for 21 years, when they went to Sir John St Loe, an influential member of the King's court. The Dissolution of the Monasteries closed Worspring Priory. The chancel of the Priory Church was destroyed but that was all.

Within a week of the closure of the Priory, Edward Fetyplace of Donnington, Berkshire, obtained a lease of the Priory and the adjoining meadows. In 1546, a letter from Humphry Stafford said the house was regarded as a desirable private residence. The Priory was never used again for religious purposes while all its associated churches became Protestant.

In 1566, the St Loe family sold the priory to William Carre, a Bristol merchant and MP. Later the property passed by marriage to William Younge of Ogbourne St George (in Wiltshire) in 1605. Throughout this time, the nave appears to have been used as a family residence and the chancel and much of the claustral buildings had been demolished for building material.

The Priory was acquired towards the end of the 17th century by the Smythe-Pigot family, who seemed to have built the farmhouse range erected between the north side and the gatehouse in 1701. The name Worspring by common usage had become Woodspring by this time. A fire is recorded at the Priory in 1876 when the original nave roof of the Priory may have been destroyed.

Woodspring was used as a golf club during the closing years of the 19th century. In 1918, the Smythe-Piggots sold the Priory, which remained as a farm until, in 1968, the National Trust purchased the coastline and the estate and subsequently passed everything on to the Landmark Trust in 1972.

The fate of Cuthbert Mayne

Cuthbert Mayne was born at Youlston, near Barnstable in Devon and baptised on 20th March 1543/4, St Cuthbert's day. He was the son of William Mayne. His uncle was an Anglican Vicar so that Cuthbert's family expected that the good natured, rather shallow, Cuthbert would follow his uncle's religious convictions. This uncle financed his nephew's education at Barnstable Grammar School, which led Cuthbert to be ordained a minister at the tender age of seventeen to become an Anglican Rector of the village of Huntshaw. After this, he attended university first at St Alban Hall, followed by St John's College, Oxford, where he became Chaplain. He gained a BA on 6th April 1570.

At Oxford, Mayne met Edmund Campion, Gregory Martin, Humphrey Ely, Henry Shaw, Thomas Bramston, Henry Holland, Jonas Meredith and Roland Russell, all Catholics. Cuthbert followed suit and he too became a Catholic. Late in 1570 Gregory Martin wrote to Cuthbert urging him to come to Douai to train as a Catholic priest. This letter fell into the hands of the Bishop of London who immediately issued a warrant to a pursuivant (an officer of the Crown) to arrest Mayne and others mentioned in the letter. Thomas Ford warned Cuthbert, who evaded arrest by travelling to Cornwall, thence in 1573 to the English College at Douai.

Cuthbert Mayne was ordained a priest at Douai in 1575 and on 7th February the following year he obtained a degree of Bachelor of Theology of Douai University. On 24th April, the same year, he left for the English mission with another priest, John Payne.

Missionaries from Douai were regarded as papal agents intent on overthrowing the Queen, causing the authorities to begin an intensive search in June 1576, when the Bishop of Exeter, William Broadbridge, came to Cornwall. High Sherriff Sir Richard Grenville, a noted anti-Catholic, raided Tregian's House, Golden, on 8th June 1577. He and his Crown Officers beat on the door of Mayne's chamber. On gaining entry, they intercepted a Catholic devotional article, an Agnus Dei around Mayne's neck, and took him into custody together with his books and papers.

He was imprisoned in Launceston Gaol chained to his bedposts awaiting trial. Despite having frail evidence, the authorities sought the death sentence for treason. At the opening of the trial on 23rd September 1577 there were five counts against him: first, that he had obtained from the Roman See a "faculty" containing absolution of the Queen Elizabeth's subjects; second, that he had published the same at Golden; third, that he had taught the ecclesiastical authority of the Pope and denied the Queen's ecclesiastical supremacy while in prison; fourth, that he had brought into the Kingdom an Agnus Dei – a Lamb of God sealed upon a piece of wax from a Paschal candle blessed by the Pope – and delivered it to Francis Tregian; and fifth, that he had celebrated Mass.

Chapter 1

Mayne answered all counts. The trial judge, Justice Sir Roger Manwood, directed the jury to return a verdict of guilty, stating that "where plain proofs were wanting, strong assumptions ought to take place". He also argued that it was illegal to bring any Papal letter into the country. The jury found Mayne guilty on all counts. He was sentenced to be hanged, drawn and quartered. Mayne replied, "Deo Gratias".

Francis Tregian and eight other laymen were sentenced to seizure of their goods and life imprisonment. Tregian was sentenced for harbouring a Catholic priest, suffering imprisonment and loss of possessions.

One Judge disagreed with the proceedings, referring the matter to the Privy Council. The Council submitted the case to the whole bench of judges, which was inclined to leniency on the grounds of insufficient evidence. Nevertheless, the Council ordered the execution to take place.

Mayne admitted to serving Mass during the examination after the trial. The Records Office also recorded that among his papers were notes that brought him under suspicion of the charge that Catholics were bound, with right opportunity to rise against the Queen. It was also recorded that he admitted to this during the trial. On the night of 27th November, Mayne's fellow prisoners reported that his cell had become full of a great light.

Before being taken to the place of execution, Mayne was offered his life for a renunciation of his religion together with an acknowledgement of the supremacy of the Queen as Head of the Church. He rebuffed both these conditions and kissed a copy of the Bible, declaring that, "the Queen neither was, nor is, nor ever shall be the Head of the Church of England".

An especially high gibbet was erected in the market place in Launceston. Mayne was executed there on 29th November 1577. He was permitted to say his prayers quietly but not to address the crowd. Just as he was about to be hanged, he refused to implicate his fellow accused Catholics. It is unclear whether he died on the gibbet. One source claims he was still alive when he was cut down, but in falling struck his head against the scaffold. Whatever the truth, mercifully he was unconscious when he was drawn and quartered.

Relics of Mayne's body survive in various locations, one being our own church in Milton; hence his relevance to our story. He was the first "seminary priest to be martyred", a group of priests who trained in houses of study on the Continent. He was also one of the group later known as the "Forty Martyrs of England and Wales". In 1921, an annual June pilgrimage was initiated in Launceston to commemorate Blessed Cuthbert Mayne. In 1977, the name of the Catholic Church on St Stephen's Hill in Launceston was changed from the Church of the English Martyrs to the Church of St Cuthbert Mayne: it is the site of his National Shrine. Pope Leo XIII beatified him on 29th December 1886 and canonised with others by Pope Paul VI on 25th October 1970. His name could not be used on a church until he had become a saint.

Stories like this forced the Catholic Church underground, but Cuthbert Mayne was not the only brave priest who was prepared to suffer death rather than to compromise their conscience. Blessed Richard Whiting and two companions were put to death on Glastonbury Tor overlooking the Abbey Church (1539), while Venerable John Hambley and Blessed William Lampley were hanged at Salisbury (1587) and Gloucester (1588) respectively.

Chapter 1

One last martyr very much associated with the West Country not far from Weston was Blessed Edward Powell, who suffered his fate a little before those above, just after the Reformation. He was born in Wales about 1478. He was an M.A of the University of Oxford, and became a Fellow of Oriel College in 1495. On 26th June 1506, he received the degree of Doctor of Divinity and styled perdoctus vir by the University. He was Rector of Bleadon (Somerset), and prebendary (honorary canon) of Sentum Solidorum of Lincoln, which he exchanged for Carlton-cum-Thurlby in 1505, and twenty years later exchanged this for Sutton-in-Marisco. He also held the prebends of Lyme Regis, Calstock, Bedminster in Bristol, St Mary Redcliff in Bristol, and the income of St Edmund's, Salisbury. King Henry VIII held him in high regard as a preacher, and ordered him to publish a reply to Martin Luther, which was published in London in 1523 and comprised three books in the popular form of an imaginary dialogue between Powell and Luther. The University of Oxford commended his work in a letter to King Henry, calling him "the glory of the University". Powell was one of four theologians selected to defend the legality of the King's marriage to Catherine of Aragon, in which he published a very rare treatise.

In March 1533, Powell was selected to answer Latimer in Bristol, where he was alleged to have criticised his moral character. Latimer complained to Thomas Cromwell. Powell followed this up by denouncing Henry's marriage to Anne Boleyn. He was discharged from the proctorship of Salisbury in January 1534, and in November he and Blessed John Fisher were charged with high treason for refusing to take the oath of succession. Powell was deprived of his benefices and imprisoned in the Tower of London. Sentence was not carried out until 30th July 1540, when three Catholics (Powell, Abel and Richard Featherstone) and three Protestants were dragged on hurdles from the Tower to Smithfield, a Catholic and a Protestant on each hurdle. Powell's companion was Robert Barnes, the Protestant Divine. The three Catholics were hanged, drawn and quartered as traitors; the Protestants were burnt at the stake. Blessed Edward Powell was beatified in 1886 by Pope Leo XIII but has not yet been Canonised.

Catholic families such as the Stourtons and the Arundells persevered despite threats of fines or the offer of temporal inducements. Ralph Buckland of West Harptree, Edward and Henry Mayhew of Dinton, Wiltshire, and other young men travelled abroad to study for the priesthood, while the daughters of some of the wealthier families made their way to the continent to study – some entered the religious life.

When Mary Tudor became Queen, she and her husband, King Philip of Spain reintroduced the Catholic faith to England and persecuted the Church of England. Memories of this did not help the Catholic cause. Catholic bishops and priests were ordained. This reign lasted a very short time (1553 – 1558), and, when Mary died, Elizabeth I became Queen, and the persecution of Catholics began again with increased vigour.

There were several plots involving Catholics to kill Queen Elizabeth I, some involving individuals, such as John Somerville of Warwickshire, who had been stirred up by anti-Queen Elizabeth I propaganda circulated by the Jesuits, who wanted, "her head on a pole for she was a serpent and a viper"; and Dr William Parry, who was a Welsh MP, who hid in the Queen's garden at Richmond Palace to carry out his intention. Another occurred while the Queen was travelling in a barge along the River Thames, when a shot rang out and one of the bargemen fell. As the Queen passed him a handkerchief to staunch the bleeding she said, "Be of good cheer, for you will never want. For the bullet was meant for me." No one was caught for this attempt.

The more well-known plots were the Ridolfi Plot in 1571, whose aim was to replace Queen Elizabeth with the Catholic Mary Queen of Scots, the natural successor; the Throgmorton Plot of 1583 with the same objective; and the Babington Plot of 1586, again with the same aim. The major reason for these plots to assassinate the Queen was removed by the beheading of Mary Queen of Scots at Fotheringay Castle on 8th February 1587 as the direct result of the failed Babington Plot.

The plot that most people remember is the famous Gunpowder Treason Plot or Jesuit Plot to kill King James I of England/James VI of Scotland in 1605 by a group of English provincial Catholics led by Robert Catesby. The plan was to blow up the House of Lords during the State Opening of the English Parliament on November 5th. Guy Fawkes, the gunpowder expert, was the person in charge of the 36 barrels of gunpowder. He was caught in the act. His notoriety is still celebrated every year on Bonfire Night, when the Guy is placed at the top of the bonfire to be burnt. A penny for the Guy anyone? In a fight with the pursuing Sherriff of Worcester and his men, Catesby was killed. Eight of the surviving conspirators were hanged, drawn and quartered.

These plots did not help the Catholic cause in any way, and it took a long time for people to become more sympathetic towards Catholicism and Catholics in general.

In 1623, Pope Gregory XI appointed a Vicar Apostolic, William Bishop, who did not have the powers of a diocesan bishop, but who was responsible for organising the missionaries in England. England for the next 225 years was to be regarded as missionary territory, and as such remained under the care of the Vicars Apostolic.

All the Stuart Queens were Catholic, and when the Catholic King James II came to the throne in 1685, Catholic hopes were raised for better times ahead. This lasted for three years only when Protestant William III took the throne.

In 1700, an act was passed (the Popery Act of 1698 which was enacted in 1700) that rewarded £100 to any informer who brought about the conviction of a priest. Such a priest would be sentenced to life imprisonment. Such informers were not popular with anyone, Catholic or Anglican, and there were few prosecutions. No one liked those who betrayed for money. How could the Catholic faith survive under the Popery Act forbidding worship and church building? Gradually tolerance towards Catholicism grew – but would this continue?

Chapter 1

The Main Villages Mentioned in the Text that are Recorded in the Doomsday Book

	Ashcombe	Brean	Butcombe	Kewstoke	Milton	Norton Malreward	Uphill	Woodspring	Worle
Total Households	18 medium	25 quite large	17 medium	4 very small	6 quite small	19 medium	12 medium	34 quite large	30 quite large
Total Tax Value (Geld Units)	3.5 medium	2 quite small	3 medium	1.5 quite small	1.5 quite small	5 quite large	6.5 quite large	6 and 1 virgate of land very large	6.5 quite large
Value to Lord (£) 1066	5	8	4	1	1.3	5	6	5	10
Value to Lord (£) 1086	5	5	4	1.5	1.3	3	6	5	7
Households									
Villagers	6	9	11		3	5	7	13	22
Small holders	5	7	4	2		11	4	6	3
Slaves	7	1	2	2		3	1		5
Cottagers		8							
Land for Ploughland (Plough-teams)	5	8	3	2	2	8	10	12	15
Lord's	2	3	1	2		1	4		4
Men's	3	3.5	5		1	3	3	6	9
Other resources									
Lords (Plough lands)	2.25	1	0.25			4	5.75		3.37
Pasture (acre)	100	30					100	10	13 × 2 furlongs
Woodland (acre)	3		30	10		6		10	

Chapter 1

	Ashcombe	Brean	Butcombe	Kewstoke	Milton	Norton Malreward	Uphill	Woodspring	Worle
Meadow (acre)	40		10	20		34	70		50
Miscellaneous			1 mill val. 0.08			1×1 league mixed measures and 1 mill value 0.16			
Livestock									
Cobs - short, stout horses			1			1			1
Cattle	30	10	6	18		9	8	16	24
Pigs	18	4	2	30		18	25	2	18
Sheep	136	53	124	18		147	100	92	60
Goats	60			15					
Lord in 1066	Brictric	Merleswein (The Sheriff)	Alward	Edric	Alwaker (Father of Aelfric)	Alwold	Alwaker (Father of Aelfric)	Alwaker (Father of Aelfric): Alward: Cola	Esger (the Constable)
Lord in 1086	Herlewin of Shelwell	Walter de Douai	Fulcran of Butcombe	Osbern	Richard	Wulfeva of Norton	Four men-at-arms	William de Falaise	Walter de Douai
Tenant in Chief	Bishop Geoffrey of Coutances	Walter de Douai	Bishop Geoffrey of Coutances	Gilbert (son of Turold)	Walter de Douai	Bishop Geoffrey of Coutances	Serlo de Burci	William de Falaise	Walter de Douai

Berrow, Ebdon, Locking, Sandford Marsh, Wick St Lawrence and Weston are not mentioned in the Doomsday Book because they were parts of larger manors.

Chapter 1

CHRONOLOGY

314 AD	Three British Bishops attended the Council of Arles in France.
410	A cemetery on the south side of Brean Down was carbon dated to this date.
451 - 525	St Bridget was the Abbes of Kildare.
476	St Gildas was born.
497	St Cadoc was born in Monmouthshire.
506	St Gildas fled from Wales.
507	St Gildas' wife died.
516	Gildas mentioned a visit by Joseph of Arimathaea with Jesus.
520	St Gildas opened a monastery on the Islet of Rhuis.
6th Century	St Kew
	There has been a church on the site of St Bridget's in Brean since this date.
527 - 529	St Gildas stayed at Llancarfan Monastery in South Wales with his friend St Cadoc, who was the Abbot there.
570	St Gildas died at Rhuis on 29th January,
580	St Cadoc died on 21st September.
597	The arrival of St Augustine.
673	At the Council of Hertford Theodore, Archbishop of Canterbury, began an era of ecclesiastical reorganisation throughout Britain.
909	The Diocese of Wells was formed,
1017 - 27	The Church of St Mary at Berrow was built.
1066	The Battle of Hastings.
1080	The Church of St Nicholas was built.
1086	The Doomsday Book was published.
	It recorded that the land at Worspring (Woodspring) was the property of William de Falaise, passing with his daughter to Baldwin de Bullers, whose daughter married William Fitz Urse, the father of Reginald Fitz Urse, who inherited his father's lands. The property eventually passed to Robert de Courtenay (Courtenai) by marriage to Matilda Fitz Urse.
1088	The Diocese of Wells became the Diocese of Bath.
1125 - 50	The Church of St Martin at Worle was built.
12th Century	The Church of St Paul at Kewstoke was built.
1150	John of Kenn takes up the name of the village just time after this date. He had already married Agacia, the late Robert's (Robert son of Richard) daughter. John's Charter confirms all of those of Robert son of Richard.
1170	Thomas à Becket was murdered by Four knights, Reginald Fitz Urse, Richard le Breton (Richard Brett or Breto), Hugh de Morville and William de Traci.
1171	Pope Alexander III excommunicated the four murderers.
1173	Thomas à Becket was canonised.
1173 - 4	King Henry II was forced to carry out penance during the revolt. He humbled himself with public penance at Thomas à Becket's tomb as well as at the Church of St Dunstan.
1189	The new Bishop of Glastonbury had an inventory of all the manors

Chapter 1

	owned by the Abbey.
1192	The Diocese of Bath became the Diocese of Bath and Glastonbury.
1193	The Bishop of Bath and Wells, confirmed the right of the infirmary at Glastonbury to receive ½ a mark yearly (6s. 8d) from St Mary's in Berrow.
1197	The dispute between the rectors of Banwell and Uppepull (Uphill).
1189 - 1199	St Michael's Priory on Steep Holm (1189 - 99). The Church of St Bridget at Brean was built in the 13th century.
1203	There was a quarrel between the Abbot of Glastonbury and the Bishop of Bath and Wells over the patronage, the right to appoint the clergy of certain churches. The quarrel ended in 1248.
Pre 1209	William Fitzmartin son of Robert son of Martin drew up a charter confirming another lost document of Robert son of Richard. This document was written before 1209, the date of his death.
1210	Already there was a chapel in Worspring dedicated to St Thomas the Martyr of Canterbury. When Robert de Courtenay died, his son William buried him in the Chapel to hasten his father's salvation, that of his mother, himself, his wife and his ancestors and successors. In an undated letter that William wrote to Jocelin, Bishop of Bath proposing to give all his land at Worspring and to convert the chapel into a "Conventual House of the Order of Augustinian Canons of Bristol", to God and the Blessed Mary and the Blessed Martyr Thomas (possibly 1210).
1214	Prior John of Worspring Abbey and the Convent of Dodlinch obtained from Geoffrey Gibwinne the Manor of Locking, including St Augustine's Church.
1217	Bishop Jocelin drew up a charter instructing the canons of Dodlinch (Dodelyng) to transfer to Worspring.
1218	The Bishop confirmed the previous charter and confirmed to the canons of Dodlinch a gift from William de Courtenay of the Church of St Martin at Worle and a gift from Master Geoffrey Gibwinne of the Church of St Augustine at Locking.
1219	The Diocese of Bath and Glastonbury became the Diocese of Bath and Wells.
Before 1226 1226 Post 1216	The canons of Dodlinch (Dodelyng) transferred to Worspring. The Parish Church of Weston, St John the Baptist was built. Thomas de Muncketon, a witness to John of Ken's earlier charters, added his own gift to the brothers living on Stepholm.
1236	Henry son of Richard gave half a virgate of land in Kercheston (Christon) to St Michael's Priory.
1238	William de Cantelupe died. He had endowed a small priory in Studley, Warwickshire, giving the canons of Studley lands for a hospital at the Priory gates for the poor and infirm.
1243	The Prior had to deal with a different problem, when two lay-brothers, evidently sent on an errand to the mainland, were accused of larceny. During a vacancy at Worspring Priory, 26 canons were present at the election of the new prior. The successful candidate was Richard of Keynsham.

Chapter 1

1256	Robert de Sparkford, another witness to previous charters, disclaimed his right to the Church of St Nicholas in favour of Reginald de Long and others. The brothers of St Michael's lost some of their land in this deal.
1260	Lord Robert de Tregoz became the owner and patron of Stepholm. The final Stepholm charter was by William de Button (Bitton) I, Bishop of Bath and Wells, consenting to the transfer of canons from Stepholm to Studley provided that at least two canons from Studley shall remain on Stepholm,
1262	The Bath Cartulary has an inspeximus by Walter the Prior of a charter of William de Button (Bitton) I, Bishop of Bath and Wells, dated confirming a charter of Bishop Jocelin to the canons of Dodlinch in 1230 and the charter of 1217 to the same canons. The Church of St Augustine at Locking was first mentioned.
1265	During the Battle of Evesham, both the baron's leader, Simon de Montfort, Earl of Leicester, and Lord Robert Tregoz were killed. The de Tregoz lands immediately defaulted to the Crown.
1277	There were rumours of the first debts. William de Button II, Bishop of Bath and Wells, came to the rescue with a legacy of 210 marks.
1279	Another 210 marks was given to alleviate debt.
1281	The Prior was a conservator acting on behalf of Pope Martin IV during the investigation of a bogus rector at Burnham.
1291	A roof was put on the chancel of Worspring Abbey.
1288 - 1291	Pope Nicholas IV assessed the value of all the churches in a kind of ecclesiastical Doomsday Book.
1317	The chancel was completed and a Lady Chapel was built. Bishop Drokensford recorded a fine of 20 shillings imposed on the Prior for failing to have the church and altars consecrated. Another problem for the Prior occurred Thomas le Taverner, was found wandering outside the precincts, using foul language and misbehaving during service in the choir.
1318	The earliest known Rector of St Nicholas' Church was John de Gidding.
1322	The first known Vicar of St Paul's at Kewstoke known was John Manne.
1328	The first Rector of Berrow that we know about was Andrew Springhouse. John de Hampton was instituted as vicar and the Manor of Berrow was transferred from Glastonbury Abbey to the Archdeacon, who in return gave the Abbey of Middleton Abbas near Ilchester.
1318 – 1498	The patrons of St Nicholas' Church included the Longet family, Philip de Lung (1318), Thomas Cheddre Esquire, who was associated with Cheddar, (1441) and King Henry VII (1498).
1319	The first known vicar of St Augustine's in Locking was Richard de Lincumb.
1325	The first recorded vicar of St Martin's in Worle was Alias of Coleshull. In an inspeximus is a confirmation of earlier endowments to Worspring Priory stating that the canons owned all the land belonging

Chapter 1

	to William de Courtenay and Robert de Newton. Half of the manor of Worle was granted by Henry Engayne together with the homage and dues of his tenants of Worle, Worspring, Kewstoke, Milton, Ebdon and Locking.
1331	In 1331, Henry Carey, Vicar of Locking, obtained a licence to give to Worspring Priory his lands in Sandford Marsh.
1347	The Vicar of Worle, John de Stodelegh, died.
1348	The Black Death proved to be one of the most devastating pandemics in Britain, killing 40% to 60% of the population between June 1438 and December 1439. The Black death struck Worle and claimed John le Hayward, Robert Geffray, and William Hareforde – the three of them within a month. The Black death struck Uppepull. Worspring Priory lost land and fortune such that the Dean and Chapter of Wells wrote off its arrears, but insisted that future debts would have to be met in full.
1381	The Peasants' Revolt.
1410	A licence was granted to Robert Pobelow and John Venables to alienate to the Priory 174 acres of land in Worle, Winscombe, Rolstone and Poke Rolstone.
1413	Knight Leonard Hakluyt bequeathed 5 marks to the Parish of Berrow for one pair of vestments on condition that prayers for his and his wife's soul were made.
1458	Worspring and Keynsham exchanged canons who were not to return until both had atoned for their offences.
1484	Worspring commenced an ambitious building programme for the construction of a barn, an infirmary and a new Priory Church. The source of this income is unknown. Dame Margaret Chocke mentions the building work in her will.
1491 - 1500	Richard Spryng was the Vicar of St Paul's in Kewstoke. At Worspring the choir stalls of the new church appear to have been installed by Prior Richard Spryng (Sprynt) (1491 – 1525).
1496	There are records of two wills: one was the record of a gift to the Parish Church of Uppepull; the other by Sir Richard West.
1503 - 9	Richard Spryng, Prior of Worspring Abbey, became Vicar of Berrow as well.
1505	In Bishop Fox's Register a Papal letter is recoded concerning Prior Richard Spryng. The contents describe the enlargement of his duties and explain his powers.
1534	The Acknowledgement of the King's Supremacy was drawn up. In a letter from the opportunist Richard Byschoppe, the ambitious Sub-prior of Bruton, to Lady Lisle, he suggested rumours existed that Prior Tormenton of Worspring would refuse to sign the Acknowledgement.
1535	The Crown Survey of Monastic Wealth was drawn up and presented in the Valor Ecclesiasticus. Prior Tormenton had already sold some of the Priory's lands to Thomas Horner of Mells for £50.

1536	The Dissolution of the Monasteries.	
	When the document arrived, Prior Tormenton of Worspring and seven other brothers dutifully signed. Roger Tormenton was permitted to stay in the priory with a pension of £12 per annum until he was instituted to the Rectory of Enborne, near Donnington. Within a week of the closure of the Priory, Edward Fetyplace of Donnington, Berkshire, obtained a lease of the Priory and the adjoining meadows. Studley Priory, after losing the Priory of St Michael, continued with reasonable prosperity until 1536, when the Dissolution of the Monasteries was enacted. Long before that the Priory of St Michael had foundered.	
1539	Blessed Richard Whiting was put to death on Glastonbury Tor overlooking the Abbey Church,	
1543/4	Cuthbert Mayne was born at Youlston, near Barnstable in Devon and baptised on 20th March.	
1546	In 1546, a letter from Humphry Stafford said the house was regarded as a desirable private residence. The Priory was never used again for religious purposes while all its associated churches became Protestant, which they are today.	
1556	Missionaries from Douai were regarded as papal agents intent on overthrowing the Queen, causing the authorities to begin an intensive search in June, when the Bishop of Exeter, William Broadbridge, came to Cornwall.	
1566	The St Loe family sold the priory to William Carre, a Bristol merchant and MP.	
1570	He gained a BA on 6th April. Gregory Martin wrote to Cuthbert urging him to come to Douai to train as a Catholic priest.	
1571	The Ridolfi Plot	
1573	He travelled to the English College at Douai.	
1575	Cuthbert Mayne was ordained a priest at Douai.	
1576	On 7th February, he obtained a degree of Bachelor of Theology of Douai University.	
1577	High Sherriff Sir Richard Grenville, a noted anti-Catholic, raided Tregian's House, Golden, on 8th June. Cuthbert Mayne's trial opened on 23rd September. On the night of 27th November, Mayne's fellow prisoners reported that his cell had become full of a great light. Mayne was executed there on 29th November.	
1583	The Throgmorton Plot	
1586	The Babington Plot	
1587	Venerable John Hambley was hanged at Salisbury. Mary Queen of Scots was beheaded at Fotheringay Castle on 8th February.	
1588	Blessed William Lampley was hanged at Gloucester.	
End of the 16th Century	The Smythe-Pigot family acquired Worspring.	

1605	The property passed by marriage to William Younge of Ogbourne St George (in Wiltshire). Gunpowder Treason Plot or Jesuit Plot to kill King James I of England and James VI of Scotland on November 5th by a group of English provincial Catholics led by Robert Catesby.
1623	Pope Gregory XI appointed a Vicar Apostolic, William Bishop, whose job it was to organise missionaries to England.
1698 - 1700	The Popery Act of 1698, which was enacted in 1700, that rewarded £100 to any informer who brought about the conviction of a priest.
1701	The Smythe-Pigot family built the farmhouse range erected between the north side and the gatehouse. The name Worspring by common usage had become Woodspring by this time.
1729	The short tower of St Bridget's in Brean was built.
1844	The new Church of St Nicholas was consecrated.
1849	During repairs a reliquary in St Paul's Church Kewstoke was discovered in the north wall of the nave containing a cup – a relic of St Thomas à Becket.
1870	There was a major restoration and extension to St Martin's in Worle.
1876	A fire is recorded at Woodspring Priory when the original nave roof of the Priory may have been destroyed.
1886	Pope Leo XIII beatified him on 29th December.
End of the 19th Century	Woodspring was used as a golf club.
1918	The Smythe-Piggots sold the Priory land, which was a farm.
1921	An annual June pilgrimage was initiated in Launceston to commemorate Cuthbert Mayne.
1968	The coastline and the estate of Woodspring were purchased by the National Trust.
1970	Pope Paul VI canonised Blessed Cuthbert Mayne on 25th October.
1972	They subsequently passed Woodspring Priory on to the Landmark Trust.
1977	The name of the Catholic Church on St Stephen's Hill in Launceston was changed from the Church of the English Martyrs to the Church of St Cuthbert Mayne: it is the site of his National Shrine.

CHAPTER 2 - THE RETURN OF THE CATHOLIC CHURCH TO THIS AREA

The early history of Weston

Whereas Weston is not mentioned in the Doomsday Book, the villages of Ashcombe, Brean, Butcombe, Kewstoke, Milton, Norton, Uphill, Woodspring and Worle are. Uphill, for instance, had a population of 209 in 39 dwellings in 1821; growing to 518 in 109 dwellings (1901); 1200 inhabitants in 400 dwellings (1953); and 6511 inhabitants in 2400 dwellings (1971). Precise figures are difficult because it depends very much on which source you use and what area it includes.

When the Romans left in 410 AD, Weston was a very small village in a low-lying moor, and centre of village life was the church, typical of most villages. The cottages were thatched and situated along what is now the High Street, bounded by a stream with river beds, reeds and bull rushes, similar countryside to the Somerset Levels today.

Everything changed during Tudor times, when in 1568, the mineral calamine (crucial in the production of brass) was discovered in Worlebury Hill, then the only place in Britain where it had been found. Another important mineral, galena (a lead ore), was also mined from Worlebury Hill. Mining in these regions continued well into the 19th century. This made significant changes to village life: the population expanded dramatically with the attendant increase in activity. By 1600, Weston had its own Manor held by William Arthur of Clapton, eventually passing on by marriage to the Winter family. They held it until 1696 when the estate was sold to John Pigott of Brockley. The Pigotts built a summer holiday cottage in The Grove. This wooded copse, which is now Grove Park, was situated next to the old rectory and the Parish Church of St John the Baptist on the slope above the marshy lowland. In 1791, the Reverend Leeves of Wrington followed their example, building his own seaside cottage on the dunes, a fragment of which survives as "The Old Thatched Cottage Restaurant 1774". The Piggots (slight change of spelling) held the manor until 1914 when the estate was sold. The title "Lord of the Manor" was sold in the 1970s and nothing remains of that estate now. Glebe House, once the Rectory, together with "The Old Thatched Cottage Restaurant 1774" are all that remains of the 18th century village of Weston.

During the great storm about the year 1810, a ship called the Rebecca foundered near Steep Holm. Casks of rum were washed ashore on the beach at Weston, and in the face of a weak force of Preventative men on the scene, the casks were seized and taken away by the villagers and tapped. Farmers from the surrounding countryside rushed to the spot with carts and took away milk pails full of spirit.

The population of Weston was still only a 100 in 1810, and much smaller than the former busy port of Uphill. At this period, Weston had been described as a place without history. In 1815, the Weston Enclosure Award was completed. This award finalised the layout of the roads and ownership of the land. Weston's future looked rosy because of the plentiful local supplies of building materials and the increasing popularity of the Sea Cure.

This dramatic change occurred in the middle of the 18th century, when doctors began to praise the virtues of drinking and bathing in the seawater (the former is not recommended today). This was known as the Sea Cure. When King George III (1760 – 1820) followed this suggestion in 1789 in Weymouth, he set up a fashion for the upper classes to follow avidly. Weston was the nearest coastal village for the inhabitants of Bath and Bristol within easy access to a road. It also offered a gorgeous setting of a romanticised gently windswept rural village in an idyllic seaside setting.

During the 18th century, it was customary for people to bathe naked. The secluded and sheltered cove at Anchor Head was chosen as Weston's premier bathing place for ladies, whilst gentlemen merely stripped off on the sands and quickly ran down to the water. The horse-drawn bathing machine was invented for the use of those who preferred to maintain their modesty. The bathers would undress in it, while the horse would pull it so that the bather could slip directly down the steps and neatly into the sea without even the merest glimpse of an ankle.

In summer the population of Weston grew dramatically with these first holidaymakers, necessitating the building of hotels and guest houses, with slowly increased numbers of permanent residents to run the facilities and infrastructure. The locals were used to having no Post Office, no delivery of letters; when not only beer but bread had to be brought from Worle. Idyllic setting had its drawbacks. The first hotel was built in 1810, which is part of what is now the Royal Hotel. This proved such a momentous occasion that when the foundation-stone was laid, a company of the West Mendip Militia fired volleys from their flintlock muskets to celebrate. In the past visitors rented rooms or a whole house from the locals. Weston's first guidebook for holidaymakers was published soon after, in 1822. It proclaimed Weston as a vivid portrait of village life, the population being 735. One hotel, two inns, several lodging houses and a Post Office catered for the visitors, while the Parish Church and a Methodist Chapel supplied for spiritual needs. However, there was no Catholic church. Weston was described as a "penny post from Bristol".

What really drove Weston to its popularity occurred when, in June 1841, Brunel's Bristol and Exeter Railway finally reached the terminus in Regent Street, where the floral clock now stands. The single-tracked branch line lay between the small terminus in Regent Street and Weston Junction Station on the main line, and comprised two or three carriages hauled by a team of three horses. If a headwind were blowing, it was quicker for the passengers to disembark and walk. By 1850, some trains were pulled by steam locomotives, although the residents were not keen on having the arrival of a smoky steam train in the middle of their lovely town. Horses continued to be used to pull certain trains from Weston Junction until 31st March 1851. When future changes were made, the terminus area became disused and was gifted to the town. Trees were planted and a floral clock was constructed, which is now a flower bed. In the 2nd World War the track was replaced by Winterstoke Road, which was extended over the main line with a bridge to reach Oldmixon and its aircraft works.

The improvements provided new goods facilities at Locking Road in 1862; then on 22nd July 1866 a large passenger station was opened adjacent to the goods yard. The branch line was given a second track at the same time. The new station featured a train shed that covered the platforms. This was designed by Francis Fox, the Railway's Chief Engineer and successor to Isambard Kingdom Brunel. An excursion platform next to the goods depot supplemented the two platforms. Until now the branch line was a part of Brunel's broad gauge, but on 1st July 1875 a third rail was introduced to each line so that standard gauge trains could reach the station as well. From 1879, no broad gauge trains were used on the branch. In 1875, the Bristol and Exeter Railway obtained an Act of Parliament to construct a new loop line through the town, which would enable the trains to serve the town and then continue along to the main line.

Chapter 2

In the meantime, the Bristol and Exeter Railway amalgamated into the Great Western Railway. No action was taken for many years to build the proposed loop line through the town. This led to a planning blight along the proposed route. An 1880 court case forced the Great Western Railway Company to pay 5% interest to the affected property owners, which nudged the Railway Company into action.

The new line and station were opened on 1st March 1884. However, this was not the end of the old branch line, as for several years a trolley was taken along the old tracks to collect mail from a postal train at the old Junction Station each night. There was also a need to serve the town's gasworks until 1972. This was achieved along a short section of the old branch line including the level crossing over Devonshire Road, which had a roundabout built on it after the remainder of the branch became Winterstoke Road.

The new station consisted of three platforms – two through platforms with an east-facing terminal bay. It was given hipped glass and iron canopies to protect the passengers from the weather. A carriage siding was provided between the two main platforms and some more were built on land to the south of the station. Even more sidings and an engine shed were constructed on the North side of the line near the 1886 station, which was recalled into service for goods traffic until they were finally closed on 30th June 1966.

A new terminal station was opened in 1914 called Locking Road Station to deal with excursion traffic, while the main station was called Weston-super-Mare General. Locking Road closed on 6th September 1964. The area once used by the 1866 and Locking Road Stations, together with the sidings, have been replaced by a Tesco store and a large car and coach park. The sole surviving railway building is the old signal box originally controlling the 1866 station. It shows signs of a later extension to allow for extra signal levers for the larger station.

The loop line was turned into single line on 31st January 1972 and most of the sidings were removed at the time. The bay platform (Platform 3) was downgraded to the status of a siding. Two signal boxes, one at each end of the station were closed, with new colour light signals replacing them. A Panel Signal Box at Bristol Temple Meads control these signals, with an emergency panel situated in the Station Supervisor's Office, which can be used to control the line from the Puxton Signal Box to Uphill Junction along both the loop line and avoiding line when there are problems with the normal signalling system.

The Improvement and Market Act was granted on 13th May 1842, in which eighteen local townsmen became the first Commissioners, the posts being subsequently elected. The act gave them wide-ranging powers for the improvement of the town. From this moment, no new property could have a thatched roof, front doors had to open inwards and gutters and down pipes became obligatory so that passing persons would not get drenched from rain water off a roof. Byelaws were introduced to control and license hackney cabs, the market, welfare, and control of animals, or causing a public nuisance - for instance bathing in the sea without using a bathing machine – could be subject to a £2 fine.

Birnbeck Pier was completed in 1867, affording the visitors more room to walk and take in the salubrious air. The town grew with villas, estates and boulevards. In addition, there were drives and walks on the hill to the North, through Weston Woods, which were planted by the Lord of the Manor in the 1820s and intended as a private game reserve. From the top of the hill one could enjoy the grand vistas as far as Exmoor and Wales.

Chapter 2

The train service, and the Sea Front Improvement Scheme of the 1880s were the most important developments of Weston-super-Mare as a holiday resort. The project has left us with the sea walls and a two-mile stretch of promenade. It was also now that Weston gained a through railway station when the present station and loop line opened into the town in 1884. Weston became a focus for thousands of visitors, day-trippers on Bank Holidays and works outings. Resulting from this, new and improved facilities grew up, with more permanent residents to provide them. Irish navvies, who had probably left Ireland during the potato famines, looking for employment carried out much of the construction work. Private schools were set up in Weston-super-Mare throughout the 18th and early 19th centuries for the children of wealthy families, as it became fashionable to send their children to seaside boarding schools. Many of these schools made it a prerogative to mention in their prospectuses the efficacy of the healthy air, particularly for delicate children. Roald Dahl was sent to St Peter's Boarding School between 1925 and 1929, but was homesick for his family life in Cardiff. Many of these Boarding Schools have now closed because of the expensive nature of private education.

Local traders were unhappy about the fact that there were so many amusements on Birnbeck Pier that the day trippers arriving by steamer from Wales never reached the town centre. For this reason, it was decided to build a second pier closer to the centre of town. In 1904, the Grand pier was opened, which had a large theatre offering all the top music hall stars of the day, instead of the amusements available on the Birnbeck Pier.

Weston played an active part in the First World War (1914 - 1918). Eighty per cent of the trees in Weston Woods were felled for military use. The loss of horses and men in the battlefronts gave unexpected opportunities for women to take over many jobs normally done by men: Weston had the first female tram drivers in the country. The beach also played its part in the war effort when large numbers of soldiers were billeted here for training exercises in digging trenches while awaiting a posting. This war left many grieving widows and many disappointed spinsters.

After war was over, Weston developed a lot further, capitalising on its holiday industry. Marine Lake was built, providing a safe shallow beach where the tide was always in. The Winter Gardens and Pavilion were opened in 1927, followed in the 1930s by the Open-air Pool, Odeon Cinema and an airport. Weston Airfield was officially opened in June 1936, just in time to provide an airstrip for the war yet to come. The first to use the airport facilities were the South Wales miners in travelling from Cardiff airport to Weston on their days off. Over the 1937 Whitsun Holiday 2555 passengers travelled on Western Airways from Weston Airport, a world record at the time. It was now that the first amusement arcades opened mainly in Regent Street. Prior to this, the amusement machines were placed on street corners as well as along the piers. Much later a third pier was added in 1995 in the form of the SeaQuarium. In 1937, the town was granted Borough Status. Henry Butt, a local entrepreneur, became the first mayor. The town's motto "Ever forward" was adopted.

The name "Weston" is constructed from two old English or Saxon words meaning the West tun or settlement. The name Weston being very popular throughout Somerset and the country as a whole, the super-Mare was added to avoid confusion with other Westons. These two words are from medieval Latin, with super with a small s meaning on or above, and mare being Latin for sea.

Chapter 2

It is not known when Weston-super-Mare took on its name. The first mention of Weston without its sophisticated Latin addition is in the Dean and Chapter of Wells registers of 1226, which give an ordinance of Bishop Jocelin setting out the many dues to be given to the Treasurer of Wells. By 1234 Weston was referred to as Weston-propre-Worle meaning Weston near Worle. In 1311, it was Weston-juxta-Worle, which means the same as the former. From this it is referred to as Weston-juxta-Mare, Weston-upon-More, Weston-on-the-Moor, Weston-supra-Mare, Weston-by-Worle and so on. The earliest known reference to Weston-super-Mare is in the register of another Bishop of Bath and Wells, Ralph of Shrewsbury in 1348.

Milton

One of the places in whose direction Weston was expanding, after filling along the promenade towards Uphill, was Milton. A picture taken from across the lake in Ashcombe Park towards Milton Road shows that around the two large stone houses facing the park there is open land on either side. The park had just received the bowling green ahead. The date is about 1912. One advantage that Milton had at this time was the amount of open land it had into which Weston expanded along the Locking and Milton Roads. These roads were separated by the Weston, Clevedon and Portishead Light Railway, which ran from the junction of Milton Road and Ashcombe Road between Locking Road and Milton Road to Milton Road Halt, across Baytree Road and through the gates of what is now Baytree Road Recreation Ground and out to Bristol Road Halt and Worle Town Station in Station Road, Worle, before it wended its way out to Clevedon and Portishead. Rhynes, where children used to fish, ran alongside the line in several places. The railway was opened in 1897 and closed in 1940. The Station Master's house was built at the terminus of the railway probably at the same time. The housing around the terminus was built around 1900 and just after, for instance the housing at the top of Elmhyrst Road, nearby, was erected in 1903.

Local stone was used with a yellow sandstone facing. Milton grew largely by infilling, sandwiched as it is between Weston and then the larger Worle, with some stone buildings at Ashcombe, at Milton Rise and Milton. Later houses, such as those nearer Westbrook Road and Seabrook Road, are brick built, and there is a greater proportion of bungalows than in other places nearer town, but more of that in the next chapter.

By courtesy of Betty Terrell and digitally mastered by John Such

A view over the lake in Ashcombe Park to the new bowling green and towards Milton Road showing the available land for development. The postcard was posted in 1912.

Chapter 2

The rapid growth of Worle

While Weston was barely a hamlet, Worle was a well-established village. The Worle and Tickenham Enclosure Act was passed in 1803 for dividing, allotting, and enclosing certain Moors, Commons, or Wastelands lying or being within the Manor or Parish of Worle, in the County of Somerset. This enabled the village of Worle to be put into some order and planning, but at the same time it confiscated the common land in favour of more efficient farming.

George Bradshaw in his Railway Handbook of 1863 recommended Worle over Weston for its old streets and quaint buildings, without the marring bank of mud left when the tide receded. One person noted that it was not so much the tide rolling out as the mud sloshing in. The people of Weston, however, maintained that the unattractive mud was efficacious, especially when combined with the bracing summer breezes and the beautiful blue sea, as shown on the postcards, until somebody complained.

Meanwhile, Weston changed drastically in the 19th century, especially after the arrival of the railway in the 1840s, and the Sea Front Improvement Scheme was completed in the 1880s, when the population explosion really got into gear, leaving the village Worle far behind. Worle might have settled down to being a mere suburb of Weston, but it did not.

In the 1960s and 70s, the population of Worle exploded into life, with the completion of the M5 motorway (1968 - 73). Worle's position made easy access to the motorway from Junction 21 for those who worked in Bristol but preferred not to live in the city. In the early expansion of Worle the number of dwellings built was at a much faster rate than the available community facilities could cope with. In 1981, Worle was the fastest growing suburb in Britain, with a population of no less than 15,000 people. Nevertheless, Worle managed to retain much of its old village atmosphere: some of its "olde worlde" charm was retained. The top of the Scaurs area, where it meets Church Road, used to be the centre of the village, and is typical of what old Worle used to look like. By 1984, when the rate of new building in Worle had lessened, because there was little room for expansion, development focussed on Locking Castle, with plans to build on the airport.

From what has been introduced, we can appreciate how Weston in the 19th century completely outgrew the surrounding villages due to the arrival of the railway, while it was not until the 20th century, with the arrival of the M5 motorway that a similar burgeoning of the population in Worle swallowed up the smaller villages in a similar manner: Milton, however remained small, by comparison, even today.

Some of the statistics are misleading because of different ways of presenting the data, partly because the boundaries have changed and the rest due to lumping different numbers of districts together. Weston's population doubled between 1851 and 1861, a change not noted in the population statistics for Worle or Uphill. A similar change in the population of Worle occurred between 1961 and 1971.

Catholic Emancipation

The Western District, established in 1688, consisted of the whole of Wales and the present dioceses of Plymouth and Clifton. It was by far the poorest of the four districts into which the whole country was divided. The Papist Act of 1778, the Catholic Relief Act of 1791 and the Catholic Emancipation Act of 1829 showed there was more tolerance of the Catholic Faith, although that was not sufficient to prevent some friction. In 1830, Bishop Peter Baines, the Vicar Apostolic, bought the Prior Park Estate near Bath, establishing a school and a seminary there to provide a good supply of priests for the district.

The change in population with time for three areas of Weston-super-Mare

Date	Weston-super-Mare	Worle	Uphill
1801	108	422	144
1811	160* in 1812	467	209
1821		673	270
1831	1310	770	306
1841		885	400
1851	4033	960	422
1861	8033	980	429
1881	12,872	965	645
1891	15,864	1018	835
1901	19,846	1299	888
1911	23,235	1497	648
1921	34,039 W-s-M Municipal Borough	1490	749
1931	31,706	4449	839
1939-45			
1951	40,396	6168*	
1953			1200
1961	43,938	4710*	5374*****
1971	50,894	8515*	6511*****
1981	58,206		7480*****
1991	64,253**		7587*****
2001		28,410***	8988*****
2011	76,143	28,446****	8997*****

Data obtained by Philippa Taylor of the Free Library Enquiry Centre in Taunton.

* Milton and Worle Ward.
** Weston-super-Mare including all the surrounding villages.
*** 3 wards Milton and Old Worle (9936), North Worle (9933) and South Worle (9081).
**** 3 wards Milton and Old Worle (8947), North Worle (9599) and South Worle (9900).
***** The whole ward.

At present, there are three Catholic churches in Weston-super-Mare. Why then was the first church, St Joseph's, built away from the town centre higher up, near to the Encampment, on Worlebury Hill?

Before a church may be constructed the Diocesan Bishop must approve the site. The considerations that a bishop needs to make are that the site should be chosen in a prominent position to attract attention, yet it should be away from the commotion and haste of the market place or the vulgarities of everyday life. The House of God should be a haven of peace to which people may flee from the turmoil of life. In the Middle Ages, in country places, it was always possible to have a cemetery surrounding the church, so that both could be separated from the rest of the world by a wall or fence. This is rarely possible today and many churches do not have accompanying cemeteries.

Just as Muslims are directional in their prayer, turning towards Mecca, so too Christians down the centuries have been directional. Vesuvius erupted in 79AD, which buried Herculaneum. There, we can see preserved the house of the Christians who had placed a cross on the wall of their home to indicate East as the direction of prayer. Tertullian, the Christian author from Carthage, (ca. 155 – 240 AD) in 200AD describes Christians "praying in the direction of the rising sun". The East was, for the Romans, a lucky point of the compass, although they faced South when divining or consulting their Gods.

St John Damascene in De Fide Orthodoxa IV.12 said:

> "When ascending into heaven, He rose towards the East, and that is how the Apostles adored Him, and He will return just as they saw Him ascend into heaven … waiting for Him we adore Him facing East. This is the unrecorded tradition passed down to us from the Apostles".

Origen in 231AD wrote in De Oratione 32:

> "We must add a few points on the direction which we should face while praying. There are four cardinal points – North, South, East and West. It should be immediately clear that the direction of the rising sun obviously indicates that we ought to pray inclining to that direction; an act which symbolises the soul looking toward where the true light rises".

Therefore, the catechumens turned to the West when making their public renunciation of Satan, and then at once to the East (St Jerome, In Amos, 6).

The Gospel was read facing North from ancient times until 1970 (and still is in the Latin Mass). This is because the direction North is associated with pagans and barbarians. It was one of the first things that distinguished Christians from Jews in the earliest days of the Church, that the Christians faced East in the hope of the resurrection (from the East), whereas Jews turned to face Jerusalem.

When Mass is celebrated, the important object of worship is God. In the Latin Mass both the congregation and the priest face the altar, attention is focussed on God. We come to Mass to give God glory by offering Him a fitting sacrifice. He is the one we all face. At the Mass the priest and the people are addressing God so that all face the same way, with the priest having his back to the congregation. This had changed after Vatican II, but this did not mean that either the priest or the congregation were meant to change their focus on the worship of God.

Chapter 2

Before erecting a church, the bishop must make a decision based not merely on utilitarian grounds, but also, if possible, with due consideration to Christian tradition and long term observance and the law of the Country. Under the restoration of the Church's hierarchy, Catholics were under various prohibitions introduced by the Popery Act of 1698 and enacted in 1700. At last the First Catholic Relief Act, the Papists Act, (1778) gave permission for Catholics to build chapels and churches on the proviso that they should not be free-standing, i.e. they should be a part of something else. Most of these restrictions (apart from Catholics and the Royal Family) have now been lifted. However, when our first churches were built, we were not permitted to build them on a main road. So that the vast majority of pre-war Catholic churches are away from the main road. In the 19th century this suited Catholics because there was concern about being attacked, especially after the Gordon Riots, which began in 1780 as an anti-Catholic response in London to the Papists Act of 1778, whereby some of the restrictions imposed on Catholics by earlier acts (namely the Popery Act) were repealed. Disorder spread across London until the army was ordered to shoot at assemblies greater than three. About 285 people were shot dead, with another 200 wounded; around 450 rioters were arrested of which 20 or 30 were tried and executed.

At first it seems a rather extreme reaction to Catholicism, but it is against a background of wars with France, Spain and the Dutch Republic while the American War of Independence was still at its height. There were great fears that France and Spain were trying to destabilise Britain before an imminent invasion like the Armada of 1779. It should be recalled that two hundred years previously there had been treacherous Catholic plots to murder both Queen Elizabeth I and King James I. People have long memories for some incidents.

From 1779, Lord George Gordon was the President of the Protestant Association of London, which had the backing of leading Calvinist figures whose aim was to repeal the Papist Act. He used his position and gift of oratory to inflame passions and fears that, given the opportunity, Catholics in the Armed Forces would rebel and join forces with their co-religionists on the Continent.

Despite his efforts, the Papist Act was not repealed, but even with this increased freedom, there were the above-mentioned restrictions on the positioning of churches, even on bells. When choosing a church site, it could not be prominent, and, in practice in some places, land had to be bought secretly because of the anti-Catholic prejudice. In London, some priests wore lay clothes to buy land for the church incognito. In other places land was donated, so that Catholics used what they were given.

It is rare for a Catholic church to have a cemetery. Cemeteries are regulated by the Local Authority, and burials additionally come under the watchful eye of the Home Office. If there were any restrictions preventing Catholic churches having cemeteries, they do not apply now, and in recent years some Catholic churches have begun burying ashes.

When the church site has been approved, a cross is planted as near as possible to where the principal altar will be placed. First, the Diocesan Bishop sprinkles Holy water on the spot where the cross has been erected, while a psalm is sung. The antiphon of the psalm explains the symbolism of the cross. The Bishop turns his attention to the stone that is to be the first in the walls of the new church. Two prayers are recited and at the conclusion, the Bishop sprinkles the stone with the Holy water, and with a mason's trowel, or some other sharp object, he cuts a cross on each face of the stone, while giving the blessing. The prayer that follows mentions the reward to the church builder, followed by the singing of the Litany of all the Saints. The Bishop places the stone in position, which is permanently set by the mason. The Bishop then sprinkles the whole of the foundations with Holy water, if they are uncovered, or, the place, where they are, is traced out. For this purpose, he walks around the entire site while the choir sings three psalms. When this is completed, the Bishop returns to the place where he has laid the first stone, there he prays once more for the success of the undertaking. This is followed by an invocation to the Holy Spirit in the hymn, "Veni Creator".

In conclusion, the Bishop prays that the Holy Spirit will come down into the building that is about to rise from the ground, that He would find acceptable the offerings of the clergy and the people, and by His indwelling purify the hearts of the people. The final petition is that the building will last forever as an unfailing source of Heavenly blessings. The ceremony ends with the Pontiff's blessing.

Ideally, the ceremony should be followed by a Mass celebrated by the Prelate, or some other priest, on the site of which God has now taken possession. If a Mass is celebrated that day on the new site, it must be that of a saint, or a mystery, in whose honour the new church is to be erected. Moreover, it should take place on a date when a good congregation is likely to be assembled. For St Joseph's ceremony, for reasons to follow, this service was a very secretive affair.

The Church of St Joseph

Attitudes towards the Catholic Church had ameliorated, although there was still a great deal of animosity and suspicion such that it was considered unwise to be too conspicuous. Catholic churches were beginning to be built again, but sites were usually in side streets and in the quieter districts of towns. Weston was no exception. There were many churches here but none were Catholic. The nearest one was in Bridgwater, 18 miles away.

Franciscan fathers came on a mission to Weston-super-Mare in 1806, when Pastor Pascal O'Farrell from St Mary's on the Quay, Bristol, preached at Greenway Cottage, a building in High Street, the first to preach in Weston since the Reformation. During the summer season priests came from Bristol to say Mass at Weston. Around that time the winter population was only 160 in 1812, but many visitors over 20 to 30 years came to Weston in the summer. Perhaps that is the reason the Franciscans only came in summertime. By 1850 things altered, when Pastor Pascal O'Farrell secured Greenfield Cottage at Knightstone as a presbytery and the Weston mission commenced.

This was the same year that Blessed John Henry Newman preached his sermon entitled, "The Second Spring". He drew a beautiful picture of the ancient Catholic Church in England, going on to recount its tragic destruction at the hands of the Reformation. He followed by speaking of the happy resurrection to life that was beginning to take place. He spoke of the time-honoured church of Augustine and St Thomas and the poor residue left to their children at the advent of the 19th century. It was a miracle to have pulled down such lordly power; but there was an even greater and truer one in store. No one could have foretold its fall; still less could anyone have ventured to foretell its rise again.

The Catholic faith in Weston received a big fillip in 1851 when, with the approval of Bishop Hendren, the Jesuit Fathers from Bristol rented the Old Assembly Rooms, in Regent Street - not far from the railway terminus, which served as a chapel during the summer holiday season. This later became the Railway Hotel, which, after various names, is now The Tavern Inn the Town Public House (in this case Inn is correct). These Jesuit

Chapter 2

fathers had started this mission for 30 Catholics in 1858. It was handed over to Fr John Bouvier twenty years later. At the time, there were some plans to build a Catholic Church in Weston, but feelings against Catholics flared up again because of Pope Pius IX's establishment of a diocesan hierarchy, so that when the time approached to lay the foundation stone, it would be necessary to be discreet.

The Poole family were noted for their philanthropy. Joseph Ruscombe Poole lived with his family in an imposing mansion in Cannington (near Bridgwater), but to obtain land for the purpose for siting a church, he bought a house and garden in Weston called Westgate House, Prince Albert Terrace, at the foot of Worlebury Hill. A corner of the garden was allotted to a putative church, St Joseph's, and cordoned off later by a white rose hedge. The nearby quarry was owned by John Hugh Smyth-Pigott, who gave the stone from which the Church of St Joseph was built.

In a letter of June 1858 to his brother, William, Joseph described the credentials of his chosen architect, who was Charles Hansom, a younger brother of the famous JA. Hansom, the designer of the Hansom cab. This was a minor commission for Hansom whose designs for Bristol's Pro-Cathedral had been accepted and whose Clifton College is a great testament to his style and work. He was engaged to design a simple chapel in an Early Gothic Style such that the nave would remain should other parts be demolished to make way for an extension later. The builder employed was said to have been Samuel Morgan, and it was to be erected, furnished and ready for use by the following Christmas, i.e. within six months, at a cost of £300 including the benches. The church was to be large enough to hold a congregation of 100 and have room for a sanctuary and vestry. The builder completed the work on time. It was a phenomenal rate of building.

From a painting by an unknown Artist. Photographed by Sandys, Ltd
St. Joseph's Church before the building of the Presbytery and the addition of the side aisles.

Taken from "How the Second Spring came to Weston-super-Mare".

Digitally mastered by John Sach.

The photograph was taken before 1893, when the planned extensions of side chapels, a sacristy and an organ loft to designs by Canon A J C Scholes were carried out. The Smyth-Pigott family donated the side chapels. Fr Bouvier was the Parish Priest.

Only a few witnesses were present at the laying of the church's foundation stone on Thursday 8th July 1858. A sovereign and a shilling were buried in the foundations. The local newspaper stated that "a gentleman in attendance" blessed the stone, and Charles Joseph Ruscombe Poole aged eight, the oldest of the four children, placed it in position. The news of the foundation of the first Catholic Church in Weston was given in a few insignificant lines in the Weston Mercury. Their readers were assured that afterwards the locality "resumed its retired aspect". It was much later that Mgr Lyons identified the stranger as Bishop William Clifford, Bishop of Clifton, who was incognito.

The first resident priest was Fr Van de Voorde, who arrived in 1854 but regrettably there is no record of his work in the district. The first priest-in-charge was both the patron and inspiration for Joseph Ruscombe Poole, the gentle, modest and ascetic Fr William Pippett. He was scrupulously anxious to live within his slender means. His presbytery was the same Greenfield Cottage at Knightstone used on a temporary basis since 1850. Initially, he hired a daily servant, but after a while, based on financial grounds, he managed alone.

As a pastor, he was expected to be shepherd to his little flock, but not the invasive woolly flock from next door. His next-door-neighbour was John Hugh Wadham Smyth-Pigott, who gave the stone for the church together with a stipend of £15 p.a., as such he had a near-proprietary interest in the church.

The Lordship of the Manor did not include advowson of St Joseph's Church, nevertheless John Hugh Wadham Smyth Pigott endowed the church as explained, whereas a stained-glass window in St Joseph's is a memorial to the Ruscombe Poole family, the donors of the land on which the church was built. These two benefactors caused Fr Pippett some anxious moments, probably by accident. Fr Pippett, through his patience, managed to ward off a difficult situation when J H W Smyth-Pigott wanted the pews situated facing the Ruscombe Poole family rather than all the pews facing the altar, but in such a small church it just was not practical. In the end, John Hugh and Joseph Ruscombe agreed to face the altar, with rest of the congregation, satisfying their needs by having brass name-plates on the pews to reserve their seats. The original altar was broken and kept in the garage, and the altar paintings are by Dundry (note in the Diocesan Archives probably from Helen Halloway).

*

In the Catholic Church, blessing is a rite consisting of a ceremony and prayers performed in the name and with the authority of the Church by a suitably qualified minister so that persons or objects are sanctified as dedicated to Divine service, or by which certain marks of Divine favour are invoked upon them. The notion of blessing has been with us for millennia. The Old Testament demonstrates that, in the patriarchal ages, heads of a tribe and family were privileged to confer blessings, and priests when directed by God administered blessings to the people. The Catholic Church states that every baptised person is called to be a "blessing" and to bless, although the more a blessing concerns ecclesiastical and sacramental life, then it is reserved only to the ordained ministry, such as deacons, priests or bishops in ascending order of qualification.

Chapter 2

The Catholic Church teaches that things used in daily life, particularly in the service of religion, should be rescued from evil influences and endowed with a power for good. Hence the blessing of chapels intended as a temporary provision for services, or for churches before they have been consecrated, which is not allowed to take place until the church is discharged of debt. Very few Churches are consecrated immediately they are opened because of mortgage repayments.

Before the first service given in a new church, the Bishop, or some designated person such as the Parish Priest must give a solemn blessing to the church, which is quite often the day before the chosen day for the Pontifical High Mass on a Sunday. This consists of sprinkling the outside walls with Holy water watched by the assembled congregation. The Bishop then enters the church and for the first time the congregation follows. They watch the Bishop as he gives his solemn blessing to the inside walls of the church, sprinkling them with Holy water, after which he sprinkles water along the centre of the church and then from side to side signifying the Sign of the Cross. A Pontifical Low Mass follows this blessing.

*

In a letter to Bishop William Clifford dated 21st December, 1858, Fr Pippett wrote that he gave the Benedictus loci as instructed by the Bishop (for the chapel had not been consecrated), at the first Mass, which was on a Tuesday. In the afternoon, there was Benediction which, he assumed, would be attended only by his own parishioners. To his alarm, a noisy set of boys and young men entered the church and behaved very badly. Father Pippett temporarily stopped the service in the hope that their curiosity would subside. Benediction is a mystery to people brought up in the Protestant tradition: Holy Communion for them is the Lords Supper, simply a meal with bread and wine. God within the species is just not possible. Therefore, to adore the Eucharist is idolatry, but not for Catholics: it is the worship of Almighty God within the Consecrated Host. Fr Pippett attributed the unruly intervention as curiosity, but perhaps his judgement was too generous.

In a letter from Greenfield Cottage, Knightstone Road, to the Bishop he reported the disturbance, adding that he had decided to hold nothing on Christmas afternoon, and that it would be unwise, in the near future, to hold Benediction. Mr Poole was of the same opinion. After a while the curiosity might subside.

Fr Pippett reported the disturbances to the authorities: Services were being interrupted on the Sabbath day by parties who behaved in a most unseemly manner. The Chairman asked the police to look well to their duty, and the parties were cautioned that anyone disturbing the congregation of any denomination would receive the full severity of the law.

Fr William Pippett's income was £100 p.a., with his expenses of £78: he lived most frugally, ensuring that he did not overspend. He emulated the Patron of Parish Priests, St John-Baptiste-Marie Vianney, the Curé of Ars, who insisted that a magnificent chasuble went well with a shabby soutane.

The little church had been designed to hold 100 worshippers, but in 1862 the parish could claim only five families, Bradbury, Poole, Piazzi, Sheppard and Smyth-Pigott, with a congregation at Easter time of 24. The Parish was very dependent on the summer visitors to Weston. Fortunately, the number of parishioners had increased to 59 by 1865. The town was beginning to grow rapidly and had nearly doubled by 1891. Some of this was due to the Catholic Irish, who, driven by the Potato Famines of 1845 and 47, had come to

England, notably to the great ports of Liverpool and Bristol and their hinterlands, looking for work and to escape starvation. It was estimated that the famine had caused the death of a million Irish with another million leaving for the USA. There was certainly work for the increasing building of Weston.

Fr Pippett was transferred to Arno's Vale as Chaplain to the Convent, with Canon Maurice J Power the newly-appointed Parish Priest. He resided in post for 16 years. Sadly, very little is recorded in the archives about events during his tenure, which ended with his death in 1878.

In contrast, Fr John Peter Bouvier is mentioned as having a kindly disposition and a charming simplicity: his nature won for him and his religion much respect throughout the town. During his twenty years at St Joseph's, the congregation outgrowing the church, he had the church lengthened, and the Smyth-Piggots [now with two gs] added the two side chapels in the manner foreseen in the original planning.

Sometime after 1880, Fr Bouvier reported to Bishop William Clifford that an old maid had £60 in store, which will be given to him on the express condition that a sacristy shall be built almost at once. Fr Bouvier also stated that he had a good few pounds that he had collected and some more were promised in small sums from another quarter. He was willing to take on the building of the sacristy behind the altar in perfect harmony with the Church, and would pay for it, should it be judged unsatisfactory. Fr Bouvier said it was a splendid job and the sacristy was built in accord with the body of the Church.

By courtesy of St Joseph's Parish, W-s-M

Church of St Joseph, Weston-super-Mare

This building and planning work was just what he liked. He had foreseen that eventually a much bigger church would be needed to cope with the increased population. He had champagne tastes on scarcely more than a beer income, but he was utterly charming and well-liked. He was Mgr Bouvier by the time he retired, a weary old man, to his native Normandy in 1898.

The next Parish Priest, Canon Eustace Barron, arrived in 1898. He was born in 1847 in Ireland and ordained at the Pro-Cathedral, Clifton, in 1876. He was trained in law and had been at the Irish Bar before studying at Prior Park for the priesthood, a late vocation. He was apparently an amazing kind of man with ambitious schemes and an original imagination. He had already proved his exceptional drive and ability in his previous parishes, including his work as Administrator at the Pro-Cathedral, and thence to St Joseph's four years later to improve the growing parish. He was very artistic and had exhibited two paintings at the West of England Royal Academy.

Moreover, he was musical as well: in 1883, he conducted the music for Bishop Clifford's funeral at Prior Park and three years later he conducted the orchestral accompaniment while the choir sang Stehle's Mass in D, when Bishop Dr George Burton opened St Peter's after refurbishment in 1886.

He was an ecclesiastical entrepreneur with a knowledge of Irish law, who did not mind bending the rules a bit. One such scheme, which caused him a great deal of trouble, was for making leather out of seaweed. It was not his original idea, but, somehow, while he was fully occupied as the Parish Priest of St Joseph's, he became involved in it, but more of that later.

In 1901 Canon Barron borrowed money from Bishop William Brownlow's Fund to build the present presbytery West of the Church, which connects to it by way of a lobby. Scant expense was spared to erect a luxurious building with a large bathroom and lavatory in every bedroom, with mahogany seats, patterned pans and patent quick-flush cisterns. Bishop William Clifford was displeased with Canon Barron's reckless endeavours because his unbounded enthusiasm outpaced his resources, and thereafter he was obliged to apply to the Bishop for future funds. The Bishop wrote sharply to him that he did not even want the presbytery in the first place.

As time went by St Joseph's became too small to accommodate the growing Catholic Community in Weston: there would have to be another church. Canon Barron conceived the idea of a second Catholic church for the town, although he was not able to bring it about. He hoped to buy a Non-conformist chapel that had become available, claiming that he had the money to buy it. Miss Georgina Barham of Weston had promised him £3000, but instead, she gave the money for the purchase of the Bishop's House, St Ambrose, Leigh Woods, after Bishop George Burton came to see her on Holy Saturday in 1904.

La Retraite

Prompted by the rapidly increasing numbers of catholic residents in Weston, Canon Barron recognised the urgent need of an educational establishment. In June 1898, he wrote to the Mother Superior at Burnham-on-Sea to ask her to send nuns to Weston to open an elementary school and a day school. Mère St Césaire, the Superior General, was interested in forming a third foundation in England, so that she and some of her Sisters came to Weston on 1st July 1898 to meet Canon Barron at his request.

> "The weather was magnificent, and the journey from the station to the house chosen by Canon Barron as a rendezvous, was most agreeable. The open cab allowed us to admire the wonderful panorama: the sea, the sands on our left, before us a wooded hill."
>
> Extract from La Retraite: Origins and Growth by Sr Catherine Appleby by courtesy of the © Congregation of La Retraite in England and Ireland.

The sisters admired the grey stone buildings, which they compared favourably with the red brick houses of London and Burnham. Unfortunately, Canon Barron had not returned from Bristol in time to meet them: their journey was in vain. All they could do was to question the housekeeper about the Parish and send Canon Barron a telegram. The housekeeper's responses were not very encouraging: there were scarcely half a dozen of very poor families; the town was very Protestant; the house they had hoped for, in Atlantic Terrace, had very poor drainage. Abbé Bouvier had never wanted them to come to Weston, and soon we may see why.

Mère St Césaire and her companions waited for a telegram reply from Canon Barron, which they never received, and so they returned to the station. Nothing happened for almost a year, but Mère Pérot desired this foundation: she believed that it would strengthen Burnham's apostolate if there were another convent on this coast, in a very Protestant area. She persuaded the Assistant-General to return to Weston to look at property, resulting in Rossmore in Atlantic Road being rented in June 1899. In September, the Community was selected: Mère St Ignace was to be Superior (of the Société de Marie) with four sisters to accompany her – the first two were from (Quimper) Burnham; Mothers Mary-Angela and St Ethelburga and the other two were from (Angers) London, Sisters St Zita and M. Francis, both French. Interestingly, after less than twenty years in England, the two communities could send four English sisters for this new joint foundation. On 15th September, Mère. St Ignace was summoned from London to go immediately to Weston to meet Canon Barron. She arrived at Rossmore during the afternoon, and waited for Canon Barron to come to bless the house. This meeting was very short: the Canon glanced round the rooms, did not even sit down as he was in such a hurry, for he was off next day on his holidays. Sadly, this set the pattern for their relationship.

Not only was there likely to be friction between the Canon and the Sister, but unfortunately, the anti-Catholic prejudice had not completely faded. Soon, hostile notices "Beware of the Nuns" appeared on defaced hoardings all over the town to intimidate the Sisters, coupled with cries after them of "Beware the nuns!" or "Roman candles." Sometimes the Sisters were pelted with mud, and some shopkeepers even refused to serve them. Some members of the Community were openly stoned in the main streets. With all this hostility towards the Catholic Religion, it was hardly surprising that 'the little church on the hill above the Old Pier' found itself still unconsecrated one hundred years later.

Two converts to the Faith, Thomas Shaw and R. N. Green-Armytage, were skilful defenders of the Community, taking up their pens and championing the Nuns in an effort to reduce the hostility.

It is difficult to believe now that this could ever have happened. Such was the anger, fear and distrust caused by events that had occurred centuries before. The spiritual life and good works of the Community as the Nuns proceeded quietly and steadily with dignity and determination about their business was their best response to such atrocious behaviour.

The new community began in a very insignificant way. Burnham paid the rent because there was hardly any income: there was one boarder at Rossmore [at the top of Paragon Road] and 4 day-pupils in the day school. Within ten days of arrival they opened an elementary school in Florence Villa, Quarry Road, about twenty minutes-walk from Rossmore. The elementary school was divided into two parts: a free school was set up in the basement, while the upper rooms were for fee payers, which it was hoped would finance the free school. It opened on Oct. 2nd with one pupil. He was proud enough to introduce a friend a few days later, and gradually a few other children joined. Burnham also sent one lady boarder. The sisters took in lady boarders and summer visitors in their home in Rossmore – a Spanish countess stayed with them for a while. The Community was dreadfully poor, with Sister St Zita having to sleep in her tin trunk for the first few weeks. They were sometimes grateful to their landlady for the remains of her pudding for supper.

By courtesy of the © Congregation of La Retraite in England and Ireland

La Retraite Convent South Road in the early 20th century

Canon Barron was ill frequently or simply away, so that they were often deprived of Mass on weekdays, and when they did have Mass, they frequently had to wait outside the church in the rain because the Canon had not thought to give them a key. During this hardship and poverty Mère St Ignace reduced the fees for two of the day-girls and sent an offering to one of the French houses in need. Her generosity was eventually rewarded: she must have had great faith in those days when everything seemed to conspire against them. Why did the Canon invite them here in the first place, when the way he behaved towards them was so inconsiderate? Besides, the Sisters of Mercy would have done a better job, because they were trained for parish visiting and for work with the poor and infirm.

They were still seeking a larger house, but met hostility from owners of available property, crying "Get out! We won't have Catholics here!" Bishop Brownlow was afraid to let them take in boarders for fear of drawing away pupils from Burnham and Taunton. Canon Barron wanted them to start a boys' school, but they objected because they had never traditionally taken on boys in France. In 1901, the Bishop allowed them to take in up to a dozen pupils as boarders, on condition that they needed sea-air for their health. As mentioned earlier Weston was a favourite place for this.

In the meantime, Canon Barron was in discussion with another congregation, La Sainte Union at Bath, inviting them to Weston to open a boys' boarding school. During the Easter holidays of 1903, nine girls were seen at Mass under the care of these sisters. Would this undermine the Bishop's restriction on numbers? Their efforts failed because of the shortage of Catholic families in the area: the first Catholics attending school in Burnham were nearly all from Ireland.

By 1903, the nuns felt sufficiently confident to open a Secondary School in South Road, which developed into the main Convent buildings. The Infant's School was at the top of the main site and was known as Pen Maria La Retraite. The pupils were initially supplied from Ireland and France. The school was very slow in growing because what Catholics there were in Weston lived far from the church and were mainly lapsed. By 1904 the day school had closed and there were only three boarders at Rossmore. The new Superior, Reverend Mother St Pacome helped to make extra money by giving lessons in French and in painting. It was not until Fr Lyons came, and, in all weathers, untiringly push-biked all over the town that the numbers began to grow, converts were made, and the school began to receive local pupils in any numbers.

When Mother Imelda arrived from London in 1905, the elementary school was still very small. She had the gift of giving a great impetus to anything she took on: her energy and perseverance with parents as well as children paid dividends. At last the school began to grow!

In 1907, the elementary school was transferred to a better house, as by then the numbers had risen from four or five to thirty, although the day school was still closed.

In those early days, when student numbers were small, there was, fortunately, one postulant. On Christmas Eve 1907, a young woman arrived, in floods of tears, and asked for Mother St Alban (assistant). The young woman had come all the way from Bath. She just had to confess to her mother that she no longer felt able to receive Communion in the Anglican Church at Christmas. The shock was so terrible to her mother that the young woman had to leave home. On the advice from her Catholic Uncle she came straight to La Retraite, Weston, to ask for a room during the catastrophe. At first, Mother St Alban hesitated, but, fortunately, one of the lay boarders knew her family, and would vouch for her. In this way, the young woman stayed at La Retraite, and asked for instruction, receiving Baptism a month later. She must already have contemplated a religious life.

Chapter 2

Accompanied by her faithful Uncle, she left for Angers on 26th September 1908. On November 3rd, she was given the religious name of Mother St Cuthbert. It was her destiny to carry a heavy cross, the loss of her sight. By the time that she made her final profession in 1917, she was blind.

In January 1908, they could extend the property in South Road, by buying Fortfield from which a tenant, at last, had moved. Next door was a boys' boarding school kept by Mr Ibbs, under the powerful protection of Canon Barron. His school was in two large houses, Woodlands and Holywell; theirs was in Fortfield. There seemed, therefore, no hope of extending in that direction, nor of reopening the day school, which had closed in 1904.

In 1909, two more postulates left for Angers (London). They had been lay-boarders for some months in Weston. One, who had been in a temporary profession, transferred to the Sisters of Charity, while the other returned more than once to Weston during her long career.

The Convent's grounds were adjacent to St Joseph's Church, which encouraged a strong and lasting association between the two religious communities. Although primarily a girls' school, boys were later accepted into the kindergarten classes. Much later, with changes in attitude to the education of girls, day girls and boarders alike were encouraged to study for 'A' Level Examinations before seeking a university education.

In September 1910, something unexpected happened, when Mr Ibbs left very suddenly and the sisters hoped and prayed for his house for a boarding school.

A month later, Bishop George Burton asked them to open a secondary school for girls in Weston. Reverent Mother St Pacome replied that they would do so by Christmas. By October, the negotiations had not even begun for a property. The contract was signed on 22nd December and the new building was blessed in January 1911. Mr Ibbs' school became La Retraite. In April five children from the best families in Weston came as day pupils. The boarding school with French girls began to develop too, and the lady-boarders rose to over 30. The biggest problem was the scant facilities for Mass, aggravated by the poor health of Canon Barron, during which time the nuns had no Mass for three days at the beginning of Lent. In the summer of 1911, he spent time in hospital with pneumonia. It became imperative that they get a chaplain to cater for the growing number of pupils as well as lady-boarders. Besides, the sisters were getting a little frustrated with Canon Barron's absences on business as well as his illnesses - not that he could help that - and many weeks went by without a weekday Mass. Canon Barron, for some reason, was against the proposal. The sisters committed the affair to the prayers of the Curé of Ars, the Patron Saint of priests.

> "After difficult and protracted negotiations, Fr Palmer, who was well acquainted with the Community, was appointed as Chaplain on 5th January 1912. In February, he had a cold for a few days. His first sermon had not been very promising according to the sisters, and during his bad cold he did not give them Mass or Benediction. It was left to him, on 1st March, to break the news to R. M. St Pacome that she was dying. She received the news peacefully and summoned the Community: 'I have made the sacrifice of my life; so, when you hear that I am dead, don't worry about me, but think that I have gone to God'."

Extract from La Retraite: Origins and Growth by Sr Catherine Appleby by courtesy of the © Congregation of La Retraite in England and Ireland.

This was the highlight of R.M. St Pacome's career but at the cost of her health: she fell ill on 15th January and died on 26th March at the age of 59. Her dynamism had completely overwhelmed her strength.

In 1912, J S Campbell of London patented a process for making a material called seagumite, which was derived from seaweed, with similar properties to India-rubber, vulcanite and leather. It was, therefore, a very promising material derived from a cheap and widespread source.

Reverend W J Potter (1872 – 1939), a Baptist Minister, aeronautical pioneer and inventor from Essex served only two pastoral appointments, both ending in bad grace. Evidently, he had temperamental issues. He began his entrepreneurial exploits in 1908, when, while in his second post as a minister, he applied for a patent for Improvements in Motor Road Vehicles. He set up the Aerial Manufacturing Company of Great Britain and Ireland Ltd. in 1909. The company's illustrated catalogue made such outrageous claims that he came to the notice of the airship pioneer, Ernest Willows. Not astonishingly, this business venture ended in a disastrous lawsuit in 1911. Potter's company went into official receivership with debts of over £3000 later that year.

While he was still a part-time preacher, he acquired another company within a year of his failed one. By some means he had obtained the rights to the wonder material seagumite, starting the British Seagumite Company. What had happened before, probably repeated itself, resulting in a host of short-lived Company Directors and shareholders. By 1914 there were only two directors, Potter - with the casting vote - and Barron – more irascible than ever because of illness with lumbago and rheumatism. The previous year the doctor had suggested to Canon Barron that he go to Aix-les-Bains in France to try the cure. Many of the letters between the Canon and his Bishop were concerning his health and that they needed more priests.

How Barron and Potter came together is a mystery, but Barron with his knowledge of law and skill in financial matters could justify becoming a businessman while he was a priest. This forbidden combination was made clearer three years later, when Canon Law was codified: canon 142 of the new code was tightened such that no interpretation could be made that would allow a priest to engage in trade or business.

The inevitable clashes between Potter and Barron eventually led to Barron refusing to have anything to do with Potter; until Potter refused Barron's request for a company meeting. As a shareholder, Barron called for one himself, to take place in London on 24th February 1914. Barron's aim was to dislodge Potter by appointing additional directors. Potter beat him to it. Potter met Barron from the train at Paddington the day before the meeting. Barron refused to speak to him. Potter later claimed that he had put forward three additional directors; that he still had the casting vote; that the encounter on the railway platform indeed constituted a board meeting; and that the directors were duly elected. Barron countered by saying that only one name had been proposed and that the background noise at the station had prevented him from hearing it. The board meeting of the 24th took place as arranged. The vote went against Potter, who rejected the directors appointed at the meeting.

Claims and counter-claims ensued until the case was heard in the Chancery Division before Mr Justice (Sir Thomas) Warrington. The Judge was later reported to have claimed that the whole thing was a comic opera.

On 12th February 1915, Barron brought an action of fraudulent misrepresentation by Potter regarding the shares and financial position of the Company. This action failed, with a comment from the Judge indicating that he thought Barron had been dealing with matters with which he was not so familiar as a businessman would be. A little knowledge can be a dangerous thing.

The British Seagumite Company went under and the seagumite itself was consigned back to the sea, both now forgotten. The case itself, however, is still very much remembered as a classic case in Company Law, in legal textbooks the oft-quoted, *Barron v Potter*.

Meanwhile Canon Barron had been running a parish. Mother St Alban of La Retraite wrote to the Bishop on 8th February, a few days before the last action was brought, to the effect that the Diocese would fare well if the Seagumite Company be secure... [that] Canon Barron had gone off to London again as his business matters had not been concluded the week before. No doubt these business troubles had taken him away from the Parish on several other occasions.

During these difficult years for the sisters and the Canon, there was a long sequence of misunderstandings between them. They just did not understand him, he was an enigma. His letters to Bishop Brownlow and to Bishop George Burton are enlightening. His main problem, probably unsuspected by the nuns, was his acute poverty. The parish was too poor to support him and his requirements, and the demands of the sisters, as he saw them, were an added burden. His health was undoubtedly bad; and he complained, not of the sisters individually, but of their entire dependence on France. It is probably true that Révérende Mère Ste Hildegarde could have had little knowledge of the very special difficulties of a priest in a town like Weston in that era. Nor did he, probably, know how great was the displeasure of those French sisters in adapting to English life.

When he died in 1917, he had amassed £800 towards the foundation of a second church for Weston. He had never given up his dream, but it was left to his successor, Fr John Joseph Lyons, to realise it for him.

The continuing history of St Joseph's

Bishop Dr George Burton appointed Fr John Lyons as a suitable replacement. Fr John Lyons a priest to gain the gratitude of all, a priest in gift and virtue, had charm and goodness that endeared him to everyone he met. He took up the parish at a tough time in 1917, towards the end of the First World War. He continued the difficult job of spreading the Faith throughout Weston. It is known that through his humble and untiring work he made many firm friends amongst all denominations in the town.

In 1919 Fr Lyons made temporary arrangements for Sunday Mass to be said in one of the bigger rooms of the Catholic School at St Helier's, 25 Beach Road, far more central than St Joseph's. Soon the chance came to buy an adjoining property in Carlton Street, a large disused stable and coach houses, which were soon replaced by the new Chapel-of-Ease on the old foundations. This was opened in 1921, and called Corpus Christi (the Body of Christ). These moves to open a church farther towards the centre of town meant that the pressure to extend St Joseph's was suddenly relieved and it probably would never happen.

Chapter 2

Local people appreciated the chapel as well as the Catholics:

> "We do love your little chapel down here" a lady commented. "It is a pretty place. It has tidied up our street and made it look so nice. But all the same, I do think it is hard that the landlord has raised my rent just because your chapel has made our street more respectable."

Fr Lyons was an imaginative money-raiser: a teddy bear begged for funds outside St Joseph's long before the advent of appealing to adults through their demanding children. He was instrumental in the building of Corpus Christi at Ellenborough Park South, and of Our Lady of Lourdes at Milton, thus realising the dream of Canon Barron, who had become too old and infirm to achieve it.

Until Corpus Christi was completed, only one priest was responsible for the whole of Weston, but then in 1935 the parishes divided. Canon Lyons, as he became in 1924, went to Corpus Christi after his 18 years' sojourn at St Joseph's, and Fr Joseph T Judge replaced him.

He was born in Ireland but the family came to England when he was seven, and he was one of the first pupils when the Christian Brothers opened the school in Bristol that became St Brendan's College. He studied in Paris for the priesthood and was ordained at the Clifton Pro-Cathedral 1909.

Fr Judge was an outstanding character and will be remembered particularly for his faith. He was a little odd, affirming with evidence that Our Lady never let him down. He would walk through Worlebury Woods scattering medals, while invoking the assistance of the Holy Queen. His faith was well matched by his bravery. If a fine day were required for an event, then it would be fine. The County Council supported his centenary celebrations on the beach lawns with unexpected enthusiasm. He disregarded gloomy predictions for weather. He was a dedicated, warm and generous man, who performed his ministry in a tranquil and caring manner that commended him to all. He had a dog that seemed quite accessible to learning: when he said to the dog, "Pray for the Pope", it put two front paws together, and when he said, "Fight for the King," it would bark fiercely.

During the latter part of Canon Judge's tenure, the question of the Consecration of the Church was well overdue. It was nearly 100 years since St Joseph's had been built. Perhaps the 100th anniversary could be celebrated at the same time?

It was while he was removing some of the trappings of the church, including the paintings, to prepare for its redecoration, that he took notice of one that had been hanging in the Lady Chapel for possibly 80 or 100 years. The three central images could be seen on it but the rest was dirty and ill-defined. None of the older parishioners could say when it had been put there. The first mention of it was in 1931 but there was no reference to it in the archives.

There are three theories for the provenance of this painting: first, it may have been bought by or given to Canon Barron, who had an interest in and was a practitioner of art, who hung it in the Lady Chapel; second, someone may have bequeathed it to the church; and third, another former priest may have been given it or have bought it.

The Canon then decided to start an appeal of £1000 to pay for the redecoration of the church. Since St Joseph's was linked to the growth of Weston, he directed the appeal to all Catholics and to townsfolk generally. He would not have dared do that a century ago.

Chapter 2

1 Bishop Joseph Rudderham decided that the year of St Joseph's Centennial Anniversary was a suitable time in which to consecrate the church, but this could not happen until certain conditions had been satisfied, which, in this case, that all church debts be honoured. A wonderfully enthusiastic response from the parishioners allowed the cost of repairs and refurbishment of the church as well as outstanding debts to be cleared.

*

Before continuing with the story, a few words about the history and tradition of the consecration of a church. Why is it necessary? How is it done?

Consecration or Dedication is an act by which an object is separated from a common and profane usage to a sacred use. This can be applied to an object or to a person or persons. Consecration involves prayers, rites and ceremonies, and is mentioned among many cultures over many millennia. Among the Semitic tribes, it consisted of the threefold act of separating, sanctifying or purifying, and devoting or offering to the Deity.

The Church distinguishes between consecration and blessing regarding persons and objects. In a consecration, Holy oils are used, whereas at a blessing Holy water is used. The consecration is altogether a more solemn and elaborate ceremony than a blessing. The new state to which consecration elevates a person or an object is permanent and cannot be repeated; a blessing is temporary and may be repeated many times. By a decree of the Council of Trent (1545 AD – 1563 AD) Mass should not be celebrated in any place except a consecrated or blessed church, and thereafter the church cannot be used for common or profane purposes. The Diocesan Bishop normally carries out a consecration, but, under special conditions, another bishop may perform the consecration if so delegated by the Diocesan Bishop. A priest may perform a blessing.

Churches may only be consecrated if they are debt-free. It would be contradictory to consecrate to the service of God a mortgage-ridden building. Although it is permitted to bless such a building.

The custom of consecrating churches is as old as Christianity itself. It is probably of Jewish origin, and may be regarded as a continuation of the Jewish rite instituted by Solomon. Reasons for believing this are: the consecration or dedication of Solomon's Temple (1 King's 8); the Second Temple of Zerubbabel (Ezra 6); its rededication by Judas Maccabaeus; the dedication of the Temple of Herod the Great; and Jesus' attendance at the Feast of Dedication (John 10: 22 -23).

Some historians attribute the origin of consecration to Pope St Evaristus (ca 105 AD), but he possibly spread it as a law, which previously had been only a custom before his time, or decreed that a church cannot be consecrated without the celebration of the Holy Sacrifice. St Cecilia prayed for a cessation of war against the Christians so that her home could be consecrated as a church by St Urban I (222 - 230 AD). St Marcellus (308 - 309 AD) appears to have consecrated a church in the home of St Lucina.

Before the time of Constantine (308 – 337), the consecration of churches was, because of persecution, kept private until after the conversion of that emperor, when it became a solemn public rite, as appears from Eusebius of Caesarea, who reported the consecration of churches rebuilt after the Diocletian (284 – 305 AD) persecution, including the church at Tyre in 314 AD.

The consecrations of the Church of the Holy Sepulchre at Jerusalem in 335 AD, which had been built by Constantine I, and other churches after he died, are described by Eusebius and other ecclesiastical historians. From them we understand that every consecration was accompanied by a celebration of the Holy Eucharist and a sermon, together with special prayers of a dedicatory character, but without a trace of the elaborate ritual of the medieval pontifical, dating from the 8th century onward.

The separate consecration of altars is provided for by Canon 14 of the Council of Agde in 506 AD, and by Canon 26 of the Council of Epaone (in Gaul) in 517 AD, the latter containing the first mention of the use of anointing of the altar with chrism. The use of both Holy water and of unction is attributed to St Columbanus (513 - 615 AD).

There was an annual commemoration of the original consecration of a church introduced by Pope St Gregory I the Great (590 – 604 AD), which was a feast with its octave extending over eight days, accompanied by the erection of booths and general feasting on the part of the parishioners to compensate them for the abolished pagan festivities.

At an early stage, the right to consecrate churches was reserved to bishops, as by a canon of the First Council of Bracara in 563 AD, and by the 23rd of the Irish collections of Canons, once attributed to St Patrick, but hardly to be put earlier than the 8th century.

The rite of consecration changed throughout time and location. At some times and in some places, a vigil was kept before the consecration, sometimes a translation of the relics, and of the tracing of the Greek and Latin alphabets on the pavement of the church. Some ancient forms of consecration suggest that the Host consecrated by the bishop be deposited.

The earliest Christian altars were made of wood, but around 324AD the Pope decreed that in future they should be made of stone. The first legislation against wooden altars is dated 517AD, when the Council of Epaone, forbade the consecration of any but stone altars. This applied to only a small part of Europe, but gradually stone altars were used universally in the West. The custom of using stone altars is derived from celebrating the anniversaries and other feasts in honour of those who had died for the Faith. Probably, the custom itself was suggested by the message in the Apocalypse (6: 9): "I saw under the altar the souls of them that were slain for the word of God." With the age of peace under Pope Damasus (366 -384 AD), basilicas and chapels were built in Rome and other places in honour of the most famous martyrs, and, where possible, the altars were positioned directly above their tombs. The "Liber Pontificalis" attributes a decree from Pope Felix I (269 – 274 AD) to the effect that Mass should be celebrated on the tombs of the martyrs. This custom was mentioned at the beginning of the 6th century as very ancient. The altars of the basilicas of St Peter and St Paul built by Constantine were directly above the Apostles' tombs. The translation of the bodies of the martyrs St Gervasius and St Protasius by St Ambrose (339 – 397 AD) to the Ambrosian basilica in Milan testifies that the practice of offering the Holy Sacrifice on the tombs of martyrs was long established.

The stone slab enclosing the martyr's grave suggested the stone altar, and the presence of the martyr's relics beneath it was responsible for the adoption of the stone altar with an under-structure known as the confessio, where the last resting place of a martyr or usually relics of a martyr reside. Martyrs were Confessors of the Faith, i.e. Christians who confessed before men at the cost of their lives. Hence the name confessio or confession.

The consecration may take place on any day of the year, but a Sunday or feast day is preferred. The consecrator and those who ask for consecration are obliged to observe the day before consecration as a day of fasting and abstinence. If the day be a Monday, the fasting and abstinence must take place on the preceding Saturday. On the evening preceding the consecration, the consecrating Bishop replaces in a reliquary the relics of the martyrs that are to be placed in the altar, three grains of incense and an attestation written on parchment. The reliquary is then placed in an urn, or in a tabernacle of an altar in a nearby church, oratory, or in an adjacent room or a sacristy. At least two candles are kept burning before these relics during the night. Matins and Lauds, or of the proper Office of the martyrs whose relics have been placed in the reliquary, are sung or recited. At the beginning of the consecration on the next day the candles under the crosses on the walls of the church are lighted. After this the Bishop and the clergy go to the place in which the relics of the martyrs were deposited the previous evening, meanwhile the church being left in the charge of a deacon.

The Bishop is to vest in a tent or covered place outside the church. He then proceeds alone to the door of the church, where a single deacon is locked inside. Outside the church the Bishop blesses the water, with him are 12 lighted candles; there are another twelve candles on the inside of the church with the deacon. The Bishop sprinkles the walls all around the outside with Holy water, the first time sprinkling the upper part of the walls, the second time the lower part, and the third time, level with his face, and knocks on the door with the base of his crosier after each circuit. This triple sprinkling and circuit of the walls symbolises the triple immersion at Holy Baptism. He may then enter the church with his attendants, leaving the clergy and the rest of the congregation outside, and the door is firmly shut.

The Bishop traces with the point of his crosier in ashes previously spread over the floor, first, the Greek alphabet, beginning on the left side of the church door and proceeding to the Epistle corner of the church near the altar, then the Latin alphabet beginning at the right side of the church door and proceeding to the Gospel corner of the church near the altar. The "Liber Sacramentorum" and the Pontifical of Egbert, Archbishop of York, attest to the antiquity of this ceremony, which symbolises the instruction given to the newly baptised in the elements of faith and piety. The crossing of the two lines points to the cross, that is Christ crucified, as the principal dogma of the Christian religion. The Greek and Latin languages represent the Jews and the Gentiles respectively. The Greek alphabet is written first because the Jews were first called to the Christian Faith.

This ritual is known as the abecedarium, which can be traced back to the 8th century, but may be even older. Its origin and meaning are unknown. One explanation was suggested by Rossi and adopted by the Bishop of Salisbury, which interprets the St Andrew's cross as the initial Greek letter of Christus, and the whole act as significant of taking possession of the site to be consecrated in the name of Christ, who is the Alpha and Omega, the word of God, combining in Himself all letters that lie in between, every element of human speech.

The Bishop then genuflects before the altar or cross, blesses water mixed with salt, ashes and wine, as prescribed by Gregory I, to be used at the consecration of the church. After this the Bishop goes to the main door of the church, and with the point of his crosier traces a cross on the upper part and another on the lower part of the inside of the door. The ingredients of this water are to recall to our mind the legal purifications and the sacrifices of the Jewish people, the wine taking the place of the blood. The cross traced on the door is to be a guard lest the work of redemption in the church be thwarted by malignant influences from outside.

The altar is consecrated next: the Bishop traces, with Gregorian water, five crosses on the altar, and sprinkles the support and tables of the altar seven times, passing around it seven times, whilst the chanters sing or recite the Psalm "Miserere". The altar table is washed, censed and wiped with a linen cloth. Next, the centre of the altar is anointed with oil of the Catechumens in the form of a cross. After the altar-stone has been anointed with chrism, the whole altar is rubbed with oil of the Catechumens and with chrism. Incense is next blessed, and the altar censed, five grains of incense being placed crosswise in the centre and at the four corners. On the five grains, slender candle crosses are placed and lit. Afterwards, the altar is scraped and cleansed. The altar cloths and ornaments are sprinkled with Holy water and placed on the altar, which is then censed.

He then sprinkles the walls on the inside of the church three times, beginning at the altar. First on the lower part, then level with his face and last the upper part. He next sprinkles with one swing each time the centre of the church lengthwise and crosswise on the floor of the church. He goes outside the church and sprinkles the walls three times as previously, before re-entering, whereupon he sprinkles Holy water to the four points of the compass, and up towards the roof. Finally, he walks around the church three times censing it outside, and returns to prepare some cement at the altar.

He then goes to the place where the relics have been kept overnight, and starts a solemn procession of the clergy and the laity with the relics around the outside of the church. There a sermon is preached and two decrees of the Council of Trent are read together with the founder's deed of gift or endowment. Then the Bishop anoints the pillar on each side of the door with chrism three times, enters the church with the procession of the clergy, laity and with the relics, and deposits them in the cavity or confessio (confession) in the altar. Having been enclosed they are censed and covered in and cemented; then the cover is anointed. Next, he anoints the 12 internal and 12 external wall-crosses with chrism before walking around the inside of the church three times censing it. Then begins the celebration of Mass.

Hopefully this abridged explanation will be enlightening because so much is conducted out of sight of the congregation (see http://www.newadvent.org/cathen/04276a.htm). The story now picks up with the consecration of St Joseph's, and from this it should be noted that, according to the newspaper report, the Bishop carried out the consecration in a slightly different order from that above, which gave the congregation the chance of seeing a little bit more of the ceremony, but they had to clear the church to do so.

*

Bishop Joseph Rudderham brought the relics of two 3rd century martyred Roman saints, St Reparatus and St Eutropius, from Rome. On the day before the consecration, they were sealed in the reliquary kept in a private chapel. These were to be placed on the main altar and on the altar of the Lady Chapel the following day.

Chapter 2

To make room for the impressive and elaborate ceremonies all the seating had to be removed from the little church for the four-hour service. Even then there would scarcely be sufficient space. The original church was only designed for 100 occupants, and, even with the two side chapels added later, it is still a very small church. The church was locked overnight.

Next day, the Bishop blessed the exterior of the building with Holy water. Then the Bishop, assisting clergy, servers and the choir carried the relics in procession into the church. The Bishop blessed the interior of the church and the Holy relics were placed on the two altars. He traced the Greek and Latin alphabets in ashes scattered over the church floor, followed by the blessing of the altars with oil of chrism. Quietly, with only the soft plainchant of the choir and the light footfalls of the clergy and servers as they pattered about the sanctuary, the ceremony began.

Then, quite dramatically the fires were lighted on their tables. The Consecration Crosses on the walls of the church were anointed with chrism.

Fifteen clergy were present from all parts of the diocese assisting the Bishop in the ceremonies. Those present included Canon J T Judge, Canon P Long of the Clifton Pro-Cathedral, the Diocesan Chancellor, Dr Joseph Buckley, and the Reverend T J Hughes of St Joseph's, Fishponds.

There were no seats in the church for the public, allowing parishioners to wander in and out to glimpse at these theatrical rituals. The rear and entrance of the church were crowded. There were television cameramen in the sanctuary, and in the organ loft nuns were photographing the exciting scene with cine-cameras. It was an impressive scene as the Bishop carried out rites and ceremonies dating back over many centuries to the cantors softly singing Gregorian chant. The Consecration ended with a High Mass of dedication celebrated by Canon Long in the presence of the Bishop.

After the Consecration ceremony, the Bishop and Clergy with invited guests from St Joseph's and Corpus Christi Churches attended a dinner at the Crosby Hall Hotel in Royal Crescent. The Winston family, who attended Mass at St Joseph's and whose girls went to the Convent, managed the hotel.

Many dignitaries, including the Mayor and Mayoress of Weston Council, Councillor and Mrs Leonard Holtby, joined by robed Aldermen and members of the Borough Council were invited to the High Mass of thanksgiving the following Sunday.

The Bishop with at least ten clergy took part in this Mass, which was celebrated by a former parishioner's son, Fr Raphael Appleby (a Benedictine monk). The Sub-Deacon was Fr Martin Griffin (another Benedictine), who had also spent his early years at St Joseph's. Fr Bertrand Ahearn (a Franciscan friar who had been baptised fifty years earlier at St Joseph's) gave the sermon, while Canon J T Judge acted as one of the Deacons-at-the-Throne.

Before going on, there are a couple of terms that require explanation. The throne refers to the local Bishop's special chair, the Cathedra, the great symbol of his teaching authority. When he is at the throne he has two additional deacons at his side. They are the Deacons-at-the-Throne.

It was astonishing that the eighteen clergy and altar servers fitted on to the sanctuary without constantly colliding with each other. Following the Mass, a sherry party and reception were held for the Bishop and honoured guests hosted by Canon Judge and the Church Committee. It took place in the Church Hall where many parishioners could attend.

The Consecration Celebration was a great occasion. The town dignitaries joined in whole-heartedly. The crosses with candles mark the Church's Consecration. What a change had taken place! Just under 60 years earlier, mud had been thrown at the nuns and some shopkeepers had refused to serve them.

Sadly, Canon J T Judge died in February of the following year at the age of 74. The new Parish Priest was Fr Henry John Carter. He took over St Joseph's as his first parish. Previously, he had been a curate for many years at the Pro-Cathedral in Clifton. His background was that he was born in 1919 in Wallington, Surrey, and educated at Downside School. He studied for the priesthood at St Edmund's, Ware, Hertfordshire, and was ordained a priest at Downside Abbey in 1944.

Bishop Joseph Rudderham celebrated the ceremony of his induction. The church was filled as the procession of clergy entered for the induction service, in which the Bishop was assisted by the Rt Rev Mgr Canon P Long, Vicar General of the Clifton Diocese; Fr William O'Callaghan, the Bishop's Secretary; Fr Daniel of Portishead, Fr Michael Roche of Corpus Christi. The other clergy present were Fr P Leahy of Corpus Christi, Fr F P Rynn (Christ the King, Bristol). The choir was under the direction of Mr H. G. Watjen, assisted by Pat Maxwell.

At the beginning of the service the new priest knelt before the Blessed Sacrament to make the formal declaration of his faith and his loyalty to the church, and the mandate of induction was read bestowing on him "the rights, privileges, emoluments and obligations" of his office. Fr Carter then knelt before the Bishop as his Lordship ceremonially appointed and inducted him into "all that belongs to the Church and Parish of St. Joseph's". The newly-inducted priest then received from the Bishop the symbols of his office – the keys and Missal.

The new Parish Priest, Fr Henry John Carter, thought it would be a good idea to keep the restored painting *The Adoration of the Shepherds in the Stable at Bethlehem* as a tribute to his predecessor by hanging it back in the Lady Chapel, where it had resided for so many years. This decision was irrespective of the result of its valuation. The central three figures could be seen through the dirt but the rest of the painting was too murky. He approached Messrs. Frost and Reed, Bristol, who said the work would cost £160 and take a few months to value (they had the painting from April to December 1959). He immediately started a collection for the work.

When the restoration of the painting had been completed, Frost and Reed, Bristol, judged the painting to be a genuine Pittoni altarpiece. Giovanni Battista Pittoni was a famous 18th century Venetian artist (1687 – 1767). One other of his paintings, *"The Nativity, with God the Father and the Holy Ghost"*, another altarpiece, was bought some time before on behalf of the National Gallery for £7200. The painting in the Lady Chapel is called, *"The Adoration of the Shepherds in the Stable at Bethlehem"* and is about 8 ft. x 6 ft. There was later some disappointment, because, after a second examination, the painting is now regarded as a Florentine work carried out by painters in a school as identified by the variation of the painting style across the artwork. The master had painted the central figures and left various students in his class to paint the remaining outer figures and background.

In 2017 two of the editors of this book travelled out of curiosity to see if this painting had been fairly treated at Chipping Campden, a fine town at the north end of the Cotswolds, where the Catholic Church, built with a large endowment from a noble house, is a splendid setting for weddings, and at least two families from our congregation at St. Josephs have made use of it in recent years. We met the Parish Priest who was rushing about preparing for another ceremony of that kind, so made ourselves useful by staying to welcome people for the funeral of a villager who had died in a London hospital. You can see a fragment of the amazing building in the photos below.

The picture *The Adoration of the Shepherds in the Stable at Bethlehem* believed at first to be by Giovanni Battista Pittoni.

On looking through the archives of St Joseph's (2017), the Diocesan Assistant Archivist, Gill Hogarth, happened upon a single sheet of unsigned typescript in an exercise book with sheets of typescript glued in, comprising a history of St Joseph's. The note reported:

> *"Adoration of the Shepherds is not Pittoni's work: thought to be of [a] School of Florence. It has been over-restored (1959) and worth about £3000."*

Chris May

Here we see the painting hanging in the chancel of Saint Catharine's Church, Chipping Campden.

Chris May

Fr John Brennan, the Parish Priest of St Catharine's Church in Chipping Campden, used to be the Diocesan Archivist for Art and Architecture, when he was not out riding to hounds. In the summer of 1964, he visited St Joseph's Church to look at other paintings that were there. To his utter astonishment they had all disappeared. At that time an unofficial opinion had formed that all such unnecessary finery should be removed from churches to revert to a basic simplicity. Some parishes complied, getting rid of all unwanted artwork in its various forms. In 1987, the altarpiece was hanging in the choir loft at Corpus Christi, but when Fr John Brennan found it, it was hidden in the choir loft behind the organ for safekeeping, because, according to him, no-one wanted it. As a connoisseur of art and architecture, Fr Brennan was very disappointed at what had happened.

A handwritten note on the typescript found by Gill Hogarth is dated 19/3/87. This could be from Helen Halloway, who wrote the history of St Joseph's up to Fr. McManus' retirement in 1986. This acted as the main source for our story of St. Joseph's. Others have reported that the painting was the work of a Flemish art school. Recent enquiries to the National Gallery showed that they have no recollection of dealing with this painting.

Fr Carter sustained his interest in theology and history when he took over after the death of Canon Judge. Some parishioners said he was a very "English" sort of man with an active interest in Catholic tradition and literature. He encouraged lectures and meetings to discuss different aspects of Catholicism. He had the former stables (where the Ruscombe Poole children sought sanctuary from the bombing during the war) refurbished and refurnished to make a parish room suitable in which to hold lectures. The Catholic Women's League had flourished during Canon Judge's tenure, with visiting speakers such as Hollis and Hyde and Fr Gordon Albion. Fr Carter ably supported this work. He became a prominent member of the local Debating Society, eventually serving on its Council. He had a genius for organisation together with old-fashioned charm and courtesy. He was very good with people, being a great spiritual help to many of them.

He was the first curate in the Diocese to have permission to own a car so that he could be the official driver for the Vicar General. He loved large motorbikes and fast cars; he liked tinkering with them. The older girls thought he was really cool on his motor bike in his leather gear.

There was a slot machine on the Grand Pier that identified one's occupation from the strength of one's grip: Fr Carter was adjudged to be a plumber. As it happened he was very good at plumbing as well as a motor-mechanic. He arranged the Parish treasure hunts as well such that many of the clues ended up at Public Houses. His departure was a great loss to his parishioners.

Canon Rea exchanged parishes with Fr Carter in 1967, so that the latter could go to the large Parish of St Mary's, Bath, while Canon Rea came to St Joseph's. He was a scholarly priest who had taught in the seminary at the time when lectures were given in Latin. For two years, he had been secretary to the Bishop of Clifton. The Second Vatican Council occurred during his incumbency. He instituted a Parish Council to follow diocesan directives and vocal progressive parishioners. The idea of open confession captured the imagination of certain penitents. These progressive members of the parish asked for the enlargement or replacement of the one existing confessional box. They suggested extending the church for an 8ft alcove incorporating a more modern confessional and a new font, at a cost of £700 - £800. Despite a donation, the work was never taken on. St Joseph's was blessed for the suggested architectural changes were never carried out, so that the church remained as it was in 1890.

Canon Rea was a powerfully built and sportsman-like person, and would challenge anyone to a swimming race in the breast stroke. He was a very keen walker and, on one occasion, he persuaded another priest to walk with him all through the night from Bristol to Gloucester. Despite his powerful bearing, he died comparatively young. He used to tell his students that the best sermon they would ever give is the way they said Mass.

During Canon Rea's last illness, several priests celebrated Mass at St Joseph's, including Fr Moriarty, Fr Tranter, Fr Norbury SJ, Fr McDonald and Canon William Ryan. St Joseph's was popular as a last posting for sick or ageing pastors. In a similar way, Fr Mathias McManus arrived at St Joseph's in 1971 after serving several parishes within the diocese. This was to be his last. His health was not good, but, despite having back trouble, he was still very active in making his parish visits. No one slept during his sermons because he liked to prowl up and down the central aisle and look people straight in the eye. He was a strenuous upholder of the Truth and Holiness of the Catholic Church, and as such was not always popular. He liked classical music, but, being somewhat hard of hearing, he turned up the volume so much that the housekeeper complained. He was quite a big man and by some magic managed to fit himself into the tiny Fiat. He was a very keen golfer, concentrating so intently that his games were conducted in complete silence – not very sociable. He had many friends, who appreciated his sense of humour and his patience with his health problems. Towards the end of his career he was more of an invalid: then he had to give his sermons seated, emphasising his point by gesticulating with a penny catechism. After he had completed his celebration of Masses, he like to retire to the Pier Hotel nearby for a little whisky and some relaxation. It was during his tenure that the Stations of the Cross were installed in 1969.

He retired to a flat in the Boulevard in Weston in 1986 and died the same year. He held that the Parish Priest is the Bishop's representative. He believed a priest has a very special relationship with his own parishioners; he is bound by links of charity to all, but to those of his own parish he has a further tie of justice, so that he has an obligation to work for them even to laying down his own life should it be necessary.

The next experienced pastor, Fr James Stirrat, had spent short periods of time in several parishes, not really settling in any. The parishioners of St Joseph's may have been concerned about this. We shall see that they need not have worried, for when he arrived, he settled in very well and the parishioners were glad to have him.

He was an excellent pianist who could play all kinds of music; he also enjoyed playing the organ, having two of them. He was very good with children and young people and enjoyed playing for them. He had an excellent sense of humour: when he walked towards the altar to begin the Mass he would often give a little twirl in his vestments to amuse the children. On the contrary, when he instructed those preparing to join the church he did so very thoroughly.

During his tenure, the presbytery was renovated; the church roof was retiled in 1996 at a total cost of £20913.10 to be shared equally between St Joseph's, Corpus Christi and Our Lady of Lourdes (£6971.03 each); the organ pipes were reconditioned; the children's liturgy was introduced (amongst the first in the diocese); in the late 1990s the site of the former parish hall was redeveloped with housing; and in February 1999 he had the current church hall built to the East of the Church, which proved a great asset to the parish. The construction of the hall created difficulties for access to the priest's garage: it was a great problem to get his large car in and out of the garage without scraping it against the walls. Nevertheless, he was quite philosophical about it. He faithfully visited the sick and was very welcoming to visitors and newcomers to the parish. He achieved a great deal while in the parish, but his health was not good: sometimes, towards the end of his career, he was too ill to celebrate Mass. On one occasion, he turned up on time at the Crematorium, but one of the pall bearers there said that his Service was not even on the list for that day, and suggested he should be somewhere else. After double checking, they discovered he should be at the cemetery in Milton Road, and, as he had no means of transport, this obliging attendant drove him there, where everyone was patiently waiting for him. This kindly "Good Samaritan" had met him several times at the Crematorium and was quite fond of him, saying he was a lovely old chap who was just "beginning to lose it".

In the latter part of his tenure, Fr Stirrat always became a bit anxious during weddings because he was afraid that he may might some fatal mistake. He would rather have a visit from the Bishop, or so he told one of the Registrars who usually attended his weddings. The photographers used to like to enter by the back door of the church so that they could get a frontal shot of the couple while they exchanged rings. This annoyed Fr James, who locked the door to deny them access, giving instructions to the lady Registrar for Weddings not to let them in. After the ceremonies were over he used to make her a cup of tea and give her a chocolate biscuit, while he complained bitterly about his bad feet. She found him very pleasant company. He retired from his parish work in 2000, living for a while in a house in Weston before moving back to Ireland to be with his sister and brother.

Deacon Tom Moffatt was closely involved in any significant activity in the parish even before his ordination to the Diaconate (13th July 2002). This was crucial because so many of the later priests were infirm or elderly, and certainly did not have his energy. Since ordination, he exercised his ministry at Mass giving excellent homilies that were greatly appreciated. He brought a new perspective regarding marriage and family life. As a Deacon, he could officiate at baptisms, weddings and funerals. He also did a great deal in fostering ecumenical relationships. St Joseph's had no Parish Priest for about six months, leaving the parishioners wondering if they would ever get one, with the shortage becoming worrying. Tom Moffatt ministered Eucharistic Services on Saturdays, and continued to participate in the prayer group and numerous other church services. When he was not available, priests from the two neighbouring parishes of Corpus Christi (Mgr Gabriel Leyden and Canon Timothy Barry) and Our Lady of Lourdes (Fr Michael O'Sullivan) said Mass on Sundays and Holy Days.

The parish was delighted when the retiring Bishop Mervyn Alexander took up the post of Parish Priest. The humble Emeritus Bishop took up his duties as Fr Mervyn, working very hard. Fr Mervyn had no intention of coming back to Weston to retire and quickly became immersed in parish work. He directed the renovation of the Lady Chapel and St Joseph's Chapel. The parishioners cleaned and repainted the font, the statues and the walls of the chapels, and both the altars were renovated and cleaned. The present wooden altar in St Joseph's chapel was supplied by the Dorville Hotel while it was being altered. The original altar rails in from St Joseph's chapel and the Lady Chapel were stored in the garage and finally thrown out in 1989. The gate of the Lady Chapel rails was repainted and given to Weston Museum (19/3/1987). Carpets were provided, which were laid by a member of the church.

He introduced several spiritual developments, such as a weekly Rosary Group for World peace, special prayers for the sick and housebound during Mass, a monthly Holy Hour, a quarterly Healing Service after Mass, with anointing of the sick and an annual day of Retreat.

He was an excellent and sympathetic listener who made people feel that what they were saying was very important to him. He was wise and comforting: his humility endeared him to all. During his long service as an Ordained Priest, he made very good friends. He would think nothing of travelling as far as Kent to minister at a Wedding or a Christening. He enjoyed all the parish functions, staying right to the end, whether it be bingo or a knockout croquet tournament.

Eventually in 2007 Fr Mervyn could not carry out his duties anymore, moving to St Angela's Nursing Home in Clifton, Bristol, operated by The Sisters of the Temple, but now closed, which is where many of the retired priests from the diocese used to go when they were no longer well enough to stay in their respective presbyteries with the working priests. He died on 14t h August 2010 aged 85. May we give thanks to the Lord that he lived and worked in our diocese – a dearly loved man!

The Parish Priests from Corpus Christi (Mgr Gabriel Leyden and later when he left, Mgr Richard Dwyer, and when he left Fr Kevin Hennessy) and Our Lady of Lourdes (Fr Martin Queenan and when he left, Fr Alexander Redman) shared the responsibility for the running of the parish, ably assisted by the reliable and experienced Deacon Tom Moffatt. During this period, the Church of St Joseph was repaired or maintained, with no major building work or projects.

From this, one may have believed that the parish of St Joseph was going into slumber, forgotten, but not so. The congregation was keen with good numbers attending the Masses. In addition, with so many young Europeans and foreigners from outside Europe coming to Britain to find work, with some setting up permanent residence here, the numbers at Mass were increasing all over the country, and Weston was no exception. There were two significant introductions that affected St Joseph's in a positive way.

The Ordinariate

An Ordinariate, often referred to as a "a personal Ordinariate" for former Anglicans is a religious structure within the Catholic Church designed for Anglicans to have full communion within the Catholic church. The Ordinariates integrate the former Anglicans into the Catholic Church, while maintaining the liturgical, spiritual and pastoral traditions of the Anglican Patrimony within the Catholic Church, as a precious gift nourishing the faith of the members of the Ordinariate and as a treasure to be shared in part of the Latin rite, within the full communion of the Catholic Church, and professes all the Church's doctrine on faith and morals. The Holy See has authorised an Ordinariate Mass to include some of the best-known prayers from the Eucharist Anglican Prayer Book of Common Prayer.

The Ordinariate is equivalent to a diocese, a diocese of former Anglicans. Ordinariates would overarch the existing Catholic dioceses, yet members of the Ordinariate may attend any Catholic church, being in full communion with the local Catholic members. Three Ordinariates exist: the Personal Ordinariate of the Chair of St Peter (United States and Canada); the Personal Ordinariate of Our Lady of the Southern Cross (Australia and Japan); and the Personal Ordinariate of Our Lady of Walsingham (England, Wales and Scotland). Despite the definition of the Ordinariate, it is not just restricted to Anglicans, but is open to most non-Catholic Christians. The idea of an Ordinariate is intended as a bridge to Christian unity and a force for true ecumenism.

Chapter 2

The Ordinariate is a response by the Holy See of Pope Benedict XVI to requests coming from Continuing Anglican churches, particularly the Anglo-Catholic sections of the Traditional Anglican Communion, such as those involved with Forward in Faith. It is in these sections of Anglicanism whose congregations were unhappy with the modern changes evolving in the Anglican Church and the direction in which it was going.

In October 2007, the Traditional Anglican Communion presented to the Holy See a petition for the full union with the Catholic Church. In July 2008, Cardinal Levada responded to their formal request, assuring that the Congregation for the Doctrine of the Faith would give the request serious consideration. On 20th October 2009, Cardinal Levada announced the institution of the Personal Ordinariate at a press conference in Rome, and by the Archbishop of Canterbury, Rowan Williams, and the Archbishop of Westminster, Vincent Nichols, at a press conference in London.

The Apostolic Constitution enacting the introduction of personal Ordinariates for former Anglicans was released on 9th November 2009. Provision was made for the ordination of Catholic priests of married former Anglican clergy, but married men could not be ordained as bishops. If a married Ordinariate Priest becomes a widower, he cannot remarry. There is an "Ordinary" appointed by the Pope, Mgr Keith Newton, who is married and cannot therefore be a bishop in the Catholic sense. However, he has the same powers and is a member of the Bishops' Conference in this country.

In December 2009, Cardinal Levada responded to each of the bishops of the Traditional Anglican Communion who had signed the October 2007 petition. The Traditional Anglican Communion arranged some discussions, planning to give formal response after a meeting of bishops at Eastertide 2010. Several Anglican groups soon petitioned the Congregation for the Doctrine of Faith for acceptance into Ordinariates.

As a result of the very long-term history of pilgrimage to the Shrine at Walsingham, Pope Francis raised the sanctuary of Our Lady of Walsingham to the status of a minor basilica on 27th December 2015 through an apostolic decree from the Congregation for Divine Worship and the Discipline of the Sacraments. Before going on with our history an introduction to the story of Our Lady of Walsingham is necessary to understand its significance as a place of pilgrimage. There are two shrines at Walsingham: one is the Anglican Shrine and the other is a Catholic Shrine – the Slipper Chapel. Many of the early English Kings went on pilgrimage to the Slipper Chapel, but it was not until the reign of Henry III (1216 -72) that the pilgrimages to Walsingham really became popular. Henry visited Walsingham in 1229, 1232, 1235 and 1242.

The Rev Hope Patten was the Anglican Vicar of Walsingham who, in 1922, started an Anglican Shrine of Our Lady of Walsingham, and a new statue of Our Lady from the seal of the Priory and accounts culled from the British Museum and elsewhere, was placed in the south porch of the Anglican Parish Church by a procession formed from village inhabitants who carried the image. In 1931, a shrine church on the site of the Shrine Church destroyed by Henry VIII was built and has continued its mission and evangelism in the Church of England. A monthly Mass on the 2nd Sunday is celebrated for the Bristol Ordinariate Group using the Ordinariate Mass.

The history of Our Lady of Walsingham (1061, in the reign of Edward the Confessor, 1042 - 1066) is taken from the Pynson Ballad, which was printed by Richard Pynson in

Chapter 2

1493, but perhaps dates to about 1465, not so many decades before the Dissolution of the Monasteries.

A noble widow, Richeldis, sometime lady of the Manor, well-known for her virtuous life, asked Our Lady if she could honour her in a special way. The Blessed Virgin asked Richeldis to build a special chapel. In spirit Our Lady led Richeldis to Nazareth, to the house where the Angel Gabriel had greeted her with the knowledge that she would conceive a son owing to her humility, and conceive God's son in virginity. Our Lady told her to take measurements of this place and build another like it in Walsingham for my praise and special honour. Everyone who visits me there shall find help. Richeldis received this vision three times. Full of gladness she thanked Our Lady and immediately called the best architects to design the chapel to the exact measurements given to her.

That night the meadow was soaked with Heavenly dew sent down by Mary, except in two places, which were completely dry. Richeldis was in a quandary as to which of the two places the chapel should be built, for both areas were of the same size and shape.

The widow thought the best place was where the chapel of St Lawrence now stands, because it was close by two wells. The carpenters immediately started the work, but nothing seemed to fit together properly. They were completely dumbfounded. They were experts in their trade and this failure could not be explained. In frustration, they left their tools aside and Richeldis sent them home to rest.

Richeldis remained in prayer all night wondering what she should do to put things right. Meanwhile, by the hands of angels, Our Lady not only raised the house, but set it two hundred feet or more farther away.

When the carpenters returned next morning, they found every part faultlessly joined together, far better than they could have done it themselves. Each man returned home perplexed, and the good widow thanked Our Lady for the great favour she had shown.

Since that time, many miraculous cures by Our Lady's power have been recorded, the dead revived, the lame made whole, the blind had their sight restored. Mariners had been brought home safely to port through tempest and storm. Deaf-mutes, lunatics and lepers have all been cured through Our Lady's intercession. People troubled by evil spirits have been delivered from them. All souls suffering spiritual temptation have been comforted. Every tribulation, bodily or spiritual, found a remedy there by devoutly calling upon Our Lady.

The feast day of Our Lady of Walsingham is 24th September for RCs and 15th October for Anglicans. Blessed John Henry Newman is the Patron of the Ordinariate in this country because he started his career as an Anglican Vicar and later converted to Catholicism at a lot of personal grief.

No more need be said and the history continues with two stories on the next page.

Fr Peter Clarke of the Ordinariate has run occasional services at St Joseph's, for a congregation of around 35. Fr Peter lives at West Carmel near Yeovilton, so his rosters are now changing in favour of Somerset locations.

Chapter 2

"Remembering my days as a Westonian

In 1941 and 1942 living in Hastings on the Sussex coast proved dangerous for families and children. A threatened invasion by German troops was feared along that coastline. As a direct result a government directive was passed that all children of a certain age should be evacuated to different parts of the country considered safer. A young boy of four-and-a-half was evacuated and left home along with several of his classmates accompanied only by a teacher.

Their designation – Weston-super-Mare! After a long and tedious journey via London, accommodation had been found for all of them in a large house (St Margaret's), which had been a Children's Home in All Saints Road at its junction with St Joseph's Road.

Of course, schools had been found for them and the boy (being the youngest) became a pupil in the old St Saviour's school in Locking Road, adjacent to St Saviour's Church. He still fondly remembers (after 70 years) the year or so he spent in the resort, before returning home safely to Sussex.

Memories flood back, including winning some sort of competition for reciting a poem at the Tropicana! Early morning treasure trails up in Worlebury Woods to find a picnic breakfast waiting for hungry lads. And, of course, an abiding memory of mud, mud, glorious mud when attempting to swim or paddle in the sea. However, the one memory that stood the test of time was the church where the lads went to worship every Sunday. The one thing the boy always remembered about the church was its bright interior, no stained glass but possessing very uncomfortable wooden chairs on which to sit.

Fast forward 52 years that same young boy now in his mid-fifties and a Church of England priest is nervously approaching the doors of All Saints Church in Weston-super-Mare. The purpose of the visit? Nothing less than being interviewed by the Church Wardens and Council Members of the Church and the sister Church of St Saviour's as their prospective vicar.

Guessed who the young boy was? It was myself and that return visit in 1994 not only brought back memories of wartime Weston but also heralded 12 glorious years as the Vicar there. It also brought me into contact with Bishop Mervyn Alexander. Coincidence perhaps? No, because I firmly believe it was part of God's plan for me and I can't thank Him enough for my years as a Westonian." [One of the authors, AAC, was also evacuated to Weston-super-Mare with his mother to his grandparents' in Milton.]

Fr Peter Clarke

"My journey into the Catholic Faith

Sheila Berry reflects on her new life in the Catholic Church – she wrote this piece on the first anniversary of her reception into the Church.

I have been an Ordinariate Catholic for one wonderful year. A year of awakening in a new world, deepening my faith and knowledge. The depth and breadth of the Catholic Church is a wonder to me. I praise and give thanks to God for all that has happened.

My journey has been so calm and peaceful. It began in October 2009. Michael, my husband died on 26th July 2009. I was desolate. Our marriage had been so very, very happy. Michael's funeral was held on our 49th Wedding Anniversary. That morning in

Chapter 2

October 2009 the one o'clock news was on the radio. I was not listening, until my attention was caught by the announcement. The Pope was going to introduce an Ordinariate for Anglicans. I certainly did not understand the word "Ordinariate" but as I listened I felt my anguish lifting and a flow of warm joy filled my being. I knew then that God wanted me to become a Catholic.

With this wondrous knowledge, I quietly waited for what would happen next. In December 2010, I received a letter from Fr Peter Clarke inviting me to a meeting for anyone who was interested in joining the John Henry Newman Group Ordinariate [Blessed John Henry Newman was an Anglican Priest before he converted to Catholicism]. (Fr Peter had spoken to me a little while before this letter and knew my feelings.) I joined, retiring as Church Warden of All Saints with St Saviour on March 20th 2011 (Michael's birthday) and continued my peaceful progress.

By courtesy of Richard Austin

Sheila Berry with Fr Peter Clarke outside St Joseph's

Members of the John Henry Newman Group were advised to attend their local Catholic Church. One morning soon after this I went into Our Lady of Lourdes and just sat down appreciating the serenity of that beautiful church.

Fr Martin received my friend Sybil Gwynne-Jones and me with his warm lovely calmness making us feel secure and welcome. We attended preparation classes happily and met others also being prepared and so the journey continued.

We were received and confirmed as Ordinariate Catholics on 23rd April 2011 on Holy Saturday night, a moving and beautiful Mass.

Chapter 2

Now we feel so content and very, very blessed having Fr Martin as our Parish Priest. Fr Peter Clarke, our John Henry Newman (Bristol) Group Pastor, with Ann [his wife] supporting us all as ever and Mgr Andrew Burnham – so admired and loved as our former Bishop of Ebbsfleet.

Sybil Gwynne-Jones, Christopher Press (who was confirmed and received at Epiphany 2012 in St Joseph's Church) and me are always telling each other how blessed we are."

Sheila Berry

Another writes anonymously

"I had never been a regular churchgoer, going mainly for births, marriages and deaths, but when I was invited to go with a friend to All Saints with Saint Saviours Anglian Church I decided to join her. This is a delightful Church with a lovely atmosphere, but before the service started I told my friend that "I didn't do the churchy bit at the altar."

I had no intention of getting involved with the Church. I had some difficulties following the service in the missallette but at the appropriate moment I read the recommendation to receive a blessing by taking the missallette with me to the altar. Out of the blue I sensed a voice coming from my left shoulder saying, "Are you always going to sit on the fence?" Without a thought I found myself getting up from the pew and approaching the altar with the missallette. I received a blessing, and from that day I regularly attended Sunday Church for a blessing until I was Confirmed after receiving instruction from Father Peter Clarke.

I attended this Church regularly for about ten years. It was during the second interregnum, when there was a lot of division in both the Church of England and my local Church over the direction that the C of E was taking, that I became unsettled. During the periods of the two interregnums there were many months without a parish vicar to guide and encourage us, although there was always a vicar to take the Sunday service. Father Peter had retired some time before and was now joining the Catholic Church through the Ordinariate of our Lady of Walsingham, taking some of the congregation with him.

I then started to look for a new spiritual home and I visited various C of E churches in Weston and Bristol and even a Baptist Church where some friends went, but I found them all uninspiring. When a work colleague told me that Father Peter was preaching at Saint Joseph's Church I felt drawn to my old preacher and decided to go to the Church to hear him, although I knew that I did not want to get involved with the Catholic Church, which felt foreign to me. Unfortunately (probably fortunately) my colleague had omitted to tell me that Father Peter was only preaching once a month, so that when I went to the next Sunday service I was surprised and horrified to find that he was not part of the entrance procession. I was sitting half way down the aisle and looked hopefully back to the entrance door, but it was too far away to make a discrete retreat. There was nothing I could do but resign myself to putting up with the Catholic service.

The opening prayers seemed fairly familiar and I started to relax a little, and when it was time to go for communion I was happy to go for a blessing. After the service had ended I realised that I had found my spiritual home in the last place I would have thought of. As I was leaving I met Eilis, who asked if I was local to the parish and I said no.

She then asked if I was a Catholic and I again said no, but I was going to be one. After the next Sunday's service, Father Peter introduced me to the Ordinariate and to Father Martin at Our Lady of Lourdes for my instruction into the Catholic faith.

I am now a Catholic and take an active part in not only parish life but also the Ordinariate."

Anon

The services in Polish

St Joseph's has a weekly Polish Mass celebrated by Fr Wieslaw (William) Garbacz, who lives in the Presbytery. He ranges from Weston to Taunton and Yeovil. St Joseph's Church will just about hold 150 people, mostly young ardent Polish Catholics, energetic and hard working. Reminiscent of the Polish fighter pilots and exiled Poles staying here to make new lives in a foreign country after the Second World War, and becoming very successful.

Sometimes this young congregation swells up to 250. This large number is catered for by a loudspeaker in the narthex and three closed circuit televisions, one in the Church, one in the Church Hall and one in the Church grounds. How they all manage to go up to Holy Communion must be a wonder to behold. Perhaps the question of enlarging St Joseph's may come to the surface once more.

What prompted Fr Garbacz to come to Britain was a series of 10 programmes describing how the young polish immigrants were coping with British life and customs. He immediately recognised a need for more Polish priests, and he contacted the Bishop of Warsaw with a view to be one of them. At first the Bishop was opposed to the idea because Fr Garbacz was a German speaker who celebrated Masses for the Germans amongst the Polish community who had stayed after the War. Fr Garbacz was one of the few priests who could provide this service.

Not discouraged, he approached the Bishop again, who eventually relented, giving him leave of absence for five years. Fr Garbacz attended a course of English lessons for a year, before being sent for three years to London. After that he came to St Joseph's, where Bishop Declan Lang gave him permission to hold Polish Masses there. He built up a huge congregation of eager young Polish people who were seeking their fortune in this country. Not all of them could get into the church, but such was their keenness that they kept attending.

Apart from the 9.30am Mass at St Joseph's on Sunday, he celebrates Masses at Bridgwater (18.30 on Saturday) and on Sunday he goes to Taunton at 12.30 and Yeovil at 16.30. He carries out all the visiting of the sick in hospital and at home for all four parishes. There are weekday Polish Masses every day at St Joseph's.

Zdrowaś Maryjo (The Hail Mary)

Zdrowaś Maryjo, łaski pełna, Pan z Tobą, błogosławionaś Ty między niewiastami, i błogosławiony owoc żywota Twojego, Jezus. Święta Maryjo, Matko Boża, módl się za nami grzesznymi teraz i w godzinę śmierci naszej. Amen.

Chapter 2

Parish Priests at St Joseph's Church

1858 - 1862	Fr William Pippett	Was transferred to Arno's Vale as Chaplain to the Convent.
1862 - 1878	Canon Maurice J Power	Died 1878
1878 - 1898	Fr John Peter Bouvier	Sometime after he became Monsignor, he retired to his native Normandy.
1898 - 1917	Canon Eustace Baron	Died in 1917.
1917 - 1935	Canon John Lyons	Went to be Parish Priest of Corpus Christi and died in 1958.
1935 - 1959	Canon Joseph T Judge	Died in February 1959 aged 74.
1959 - 1967	Fr Henry John Carter	Left to go to the Parish of St Mary's, Bath and died 1982.
1967 - 1970	Canon James Rea	Moved back to Ireland to be with his sister and brother and died in 1971.
1971 - 1986	Fr Matthias McManus	Retired to a flat in the Boulevard in Weston.
1986 - 2000	Fr James Stirrat	Moved to Ireland.
2000 - 2001	Interregnum of six months *	
2001 - 2007	Bishop Mervyn Alexander	Went to St Angela's Nursing Home in Clifton, Bristol, where he died in 2010 aged 85.
2007 - 2013	Mgr Gabriel Leyden from Corpus Christi *	Went to St Joseph's, Home of the Little Sisters of the Poor, Cotham Hill, Bristol.
2013 – 2017	Served by Fr Richard Dwyer from Corpus Christi *	Went to St Catherine's, Frome
2017 -	Served by Fr Kevin Hennessy from Corpus Christi *	
2007- 2015	Fr Martin Queenan OLOL*	Went to St George's, Warminster
2015	Fr Alexander Redman OLOL*	

For all those priests in the list above who have died may they rest in peace.

* No parish priest appointed to St Joseph's at this time.

Chapter 2

The Church of Corpus Christi

The 1870 Education Act of Parliament decreed that all children should receive a Primary Education. The Catholic Hierarchy restored in 1850, had a vision of the Catholic faith being spread through a national network of schools. Priests were encouraged to build schools before churches, a practice that still applies today.

Some thirty years later, Canon Barron of St Joseph's had recognised a need for a central school and a much larger church to cater for the increasing population of Weston, but he died in 1917 before he could find such a site, leaving £800 for such a project. Fr John Lyons, his successor at St Joseph's, was determined to complete what Canon Barron had started. The free school called St Joseph's reopened in Oxford Street. A year after the school moved to a place between the Plantations and Meadow Street. In 1905, it moved to the floor above Barclay's Bank in High Street thence to No. 3, Connaught Place in 1916, and then on to St Helier's in 25 Beach Road in April 1919. The place was made suitable for a school, which admitted children on 8th September, the feast of Our Lady's birthday. The same year, Fr Lyons worked diligently in securing one of the larger rooms in St Helier's Catholic School, St Joseph's, for Sunday Mass, which was more central than St Joseph's Church. Sunday Mass began on 16th November. He obtained temporary accommodation next door to St Helier's in Carlton Street after much well-prepared persuasion. The disused stable and decrepit coach houses were demolished to be replaced by a new building on the old foundations. The work was completed in July 1921, and on the 31st of that month, the feast of St Ignatius Loyola, the new chapel was opened and called Corpus Christi.

Only two months after opening this Mass Centre, a site was being considered for a possible school and church, both of which would be called Corpus Christi. Land was purchased in Ellenborough Park South. On this land was a house called "Montibello", which would be suitable for a presbytery. Until that time it was rented out. As in many cases churches have been spawned from Mass Centres. Eventually in 1930, both the little Chapel in Carlton Street and St Helier's were sold. Fr Lyons had worked so hard to get a suitable place for a church. He became a Canon in 1924.

On the octave day of the feast of Corpus Christi, the contract for the erection of the new church and presbytery was signed. John Bevan, F R I B A, of Bristol, was the chosen architect and Messrs Hendy and Sons, of Bristol were the contractors.

On 8th September 1928, Our Lady's birthday, Bishop Dr George Burton of Clifton laid the foundation stone of Corpus Christi Church in Ellenborough Park South, the only church in Weston to be built in the Byzantine style. Unlike the beginnings of St Joseph's, the ceremony was performed in the most public manner and in accordance with the full ceremonial of the Church.

The new church was opened on 6th June 1929 (the Octave of the Feast of Corpus Christi) by the Bishops of Cardiff and Menevia, exactly one hundred years since the Catholic Emancipation Act had been past. On the previous night the Right Rev Mgr Provost William Lee V. G. blessed the building. He was to become the future Bishop of Clifton. He had always taken a great interest in the developments in Weston-super-Mare - a very suitable choice.

Chapter 2

Sadly, Bishop Dr George Burton was too ill to officiate so his Grace the Archbishop of Cardiff took his place and celebrated the first Mass. With equal kindness Bishop Francis J Vaughan came from his Diocese of Menevia to preach the sermon. Abbot John Chapman O. S B was the distinguished representative of Downside. The Clergy, both Secular and Regular came from nearly every parish in the Diocese, joined by those from Corpus Christi, to be present at the event. Over 250 people attended a very happy luncheon after Mass.

The new church and presbytery cost about £16000, leaving a debt of £3000. Canon Lyons moved from St Joseph's to be the first Parish Priest. In 1931, Corpus Christi School was opened by the most Rev Francis Mostyn and run by the Sisters of La Retraite. It was where what is now the Presbytery. By 1934, the debt on the Church and School had been paid off so that the church could be consecrated. It was a great achievement for Canon Lyons and his parishioners.

On Wednesday 6th June 1934, several parishioners and visiting Catholics stood in the gardens in front of the church to see the Rt Rev William Lee Bishop of Clifton, the Rt Rev Francis J Vaughan Bishop of Menevia and the Rt Rev John Francis McNulty Bishop of Nottingham and their attendants, including the Rt Rev Bruno Hicks OSB the newly-Blessed Abbot of Downside, coming out of the church to conduct the blessing of the outer walls of the building. Other clergy present were Dominicans, Carmelites, Jesuits, Benedictines, and Franciscans. This occurred at shortly after 9.30.

The relics had been consecrated on the previous day in preparation for the consecration of the church. When the blessing ceremony had been completed, Bishop Lee bearing the relics followed by two other consecrating bishops, attendants and the congregation walked in procession around the church before all entered for the consecration ceremony to begin.

Bishop William Lee placed the relics of St Peter, St Paul, St John the Evangelist, St Andrew and St Philip in the High Altar, with assisting clergy Rev Canon T. O'Riordan and Rev Mgr Canon P Long and Rev Denis Foran as MC.

Bishop Vaughan placed the relics of St Agnes and St Cecilia in the altar of the Lady Chapel with assisting clergy Rev Canon Iles and Rev Canon J Noonan and Rev P Power (curate at Weston-super-Mare) as MC.

Bishop McNulty placed the relics of St Agatha and St Barbara in the altar of St Peter's Chapel with assisting clergy Rev Canon J Casey and Rev L McEnery with Rev C A Gryce as MC.

The Pontifical High Mass started at 1 pm, an hour later than planned. Canon Rev C W Davey of Bridgewater celebrated this Mass, with Rev Canon H Sugden as Deacon and Rev Canon P Murphy as Sub-Deacon with Mr D Cockram as MC. The Deacons-at-the-Throne to Bishop Lee were Rev Mgr Canon H V Lean VG, Rev Cannon T O'Riordan and Rev Mgr Canon P Long. The cantors were Messrs J R Bradley and C Evans. Canon J Lyons wrote a full-service booklet with an explanatory preface and copious footnotes for the parishioners. The whole proceedings took over four hours.

After the ceremonies, many attended a public luncheon at the Grand Atlantic Hotel, when Canon J Lyons presided and following the repast gave the toast "Pope and King". There followed many more toasts and speeches. As Canon Lyons had moved from St Joseph's to be Parish Priest of Corpus Christi, it was announced that the new Parish Priest for St Joseph's was Fr Joseph T Judge.

Chapter 2

When he became Mgr Lyons he liked his parishioners to refer to him as Canon. He became as much loved at the new church as he had been at St Joseph's. He had lost none of that capacity for making friends: he was the essence of friendliness and good humour. He was indifferent to whether he was dealing with clergy of other denominations and he co-operated in the activities that were for the common good. However, one blow to ecumenism was when Canon Lyons in 1924, the year he became a canon, had a fiery dispute with the Vicar of All Saints, Reverend J Wilson-Steele.

In December 1936, the order of nuns called the Poor Servants of the Mother of God purchased a large house (Totterdown Hall) in Hutton Road, Oldmixon, in the Parish of Corpus Christi. Their mission helping educationally challenged girls and young women began in July the following year. Priests from Corpus Christi travelled out to them for Holy Mass.

*

RAF Locking was opened in 1937 initially as a Training Unit about a mile away from RAF Weston airport. It became a Technical site for the RAF's Number One Radio School until its relocation to RAF Cosford in 1999. According to the RAF Locking Information Handbooks, there were three small chapels on site, one was the Catholic Chapel of Holy Cross situated on the first floor of the Scarf Block off Bowen Road and adjoining the Parade Ground. This too was served by the friars from the Clevedon Friary, who also provided pastoral care. Services were conducted there on Sundays, weekdays and Holy Days of Obligation. In 1974 negotiations with the Anglican Diocese enabled Holy Mass to be celebrated in the Church of St John at the far end of the Parish, which continued for several years.

These Friars originally came from Amiens in France, escaping the religious persecution from 1880. They took up refuge in the disused Dominican Convent of St Catherine in Park Place, Clifton, offered to them by Bishop Clifford. They moved to Clevedon between 1881 and 1882, where they served the Catholics from Portland House in Wellington Terrace. The first Mass was celebrated in this Friary on 14th July for a congregation of only five, being the total Catholic population of the town. Soon a larger house for the increasing numbers of friars arriving was purchased, formerly called the *Royal Hotel*, for the sum of £3800 with money received from friends back home. This former hotel stood on the property currently occupied by Friary Close. Masses were held in the bar of this hotel from 14th February 1883. In 1884 *The Tablet* reported that a fire had destroyed a room over the cellar, which was the Chapter room and private chapel of their Friary. By then the community present had grown to 37. They had scarcely arrived when they decided to build a small church in Portishead, which was served by a priest from Clevedon until 1906.

As the congregation slowly increased in Clevedon, it was decided to build the present church in the grounds of the Friary. The foundation stone was laid on 16th February 1886. The architect was Canon Scholes and the builder James Hillier Kitch. The church was constructed in the Early English style using local stone with a Bath-stone dressing at a cost of £3000. Most of the money came from the Tertiaries of Amiens in thanksgiving for the hospitality given to the French Franciscans. The first public mass was celebrated a year later, and the church was consecrated in July 1887.

The brightly coloured stained glass windows depict a variety of images: many portray Franciscan saints such as St Bonaventure and St Duns Scotus, while others picture the Baptism of Our Lord, the Descent of the Holy Spirit and Veronica wiping the face of Jesus. The two side chapels are dedicated to St Francis of Assisi and Our Lady.

French Friars served the people of Clevedon, Portishead, Nailsea and surrounding villages until 1902, when they could return to their native land, leaving English Friars to take over the Parish of the Immaculate Conception. Portishead continued to be served from the Friary until 1907, when the new church and parish was given over to the Diocese. In 1925 a generous legacy of £18000 from a parishioner, Mr Erasmus Smith, enabled the English community to transform the interior of the old hotel into a suitable Friary.

In Yatton a Mass Centre was set up in a private house, until the congregation grew too large when in 1935 an arrangement was made with the Claverham British Legion who let their wooden hall for Masses on Sunday mornings and Holy days. During the War in times of petrol rationing, a local car hire firm drove their priest to Holy Mass, but for other religious duties such as catechism classes and similar the friars had to cycle regular twenty-mile round trips. In the early 1960s, the wooden hall was sold to the Parish. This became the Chapel-of-Ease known as St Dunstan and St Anthony named after Franciscan saints.

In Nailsea a regular Sunday Mass was held in the Royal Oak Hotel until a small hut was purchased in 1936 to be used as a Mass Centre until the Primary School was built in 1980, when Nailsea became its own parish. The villages of Yatton, Congresbury, Claverham and Wrington continue to be part of this parish.

In 1937 the church in the grounds of the Friary was rewired at a cost of £1600, and it was decided to knock down the old *Royal Hotel* and build a new Friary next to the church. This gave rise to some resentment when the plans for demolition were broadcast. This project eventually went ahead with the new building being opened in 1978. Some of the land was used for housing.

*

On 21st and 22nd July 1938, the Catholic Women's League (CWL) of Corpus Christi arranged the Summerland Fête over two afternoons opened by Mrs Blanche Kelson. Mgr Lyons, who presided over the fête, said he was certain that Mrs Kelson needed no introduction: she was well-known in the town not merely because of the high civic office she held; not because she was the daughter of a distinguished Westonian whom everyone knew, namely Mr Henry Butt; but because of the geniality of her nature and her readiness to do all she could to assist everybody, no matter what their creed or station in life might be...

Canon Lyons observed that when he was in hospital recently, Mrs Kelson had come to see him at least once a week. Her visits had always brought him great cheer, and she had never come empty-handed... After mentioning Drs H T M. and Richard Alford were to judge the baby competition together with Miss Lucy Bere, he said he was glad the Matron of the Hospital was present because he wanted her to take back to the staff of the institution his best thanks for the way in which they had looked after him whilst he was in their care. Weston had reason to be proud of its hospital.

Bouquets were presented to Mrs Kelson by little Miss Irene Lawrence and to Miss Bere by Master Raymond Flood.

Chapter 2

The title of the Fête was perhaps a precarious one in a year notable for its unseasonable weather, but this time the organisers were lucky: on the opening afternoon, the sun shone brilliantly from an azure sky broken by a few wandering snow-white clouds. Everyone was in bright summer attire as they meandered, pausing only before well-laden stalls to make their purchases. Others sat at tables to take tea; still others tried their skill or chanced their arm at sideshows – all was fair and bright.

The Fête held on the grounds of Corpus Christi School in Ellenborough Park was as ambitious as usual for the purpose of raising money to help pay for the new church that was nearly complete at Milton.

The baby show on Thursday afternoon arranged by Mrs P D O'Connell and Mrs Coole featuring 90 to 100 babies was extremely successful, followed at 6.00 pm by a comic dog show arranged by Mr G Miller, which went down very well. In the evening Mrs O'Connell organised a concert in the schoolroom. The following afternoon pupils from Corpus Christi School rendered an appealing entertainment under the direction of Mother Mary Joseph, followed in the evening by a whist drive organised by members of the St Vincent de Paul Society.

Then everything changed. The outbreak of war with Germany in 1939 meant that any ambition to create a new separate parish in Milton was temporarily set aside, with the general anxiety about aerial bombing and its possible consequences. The pupils of La Retraite were evacuated to Hertfordshire, while their buildings were requisitioned as a Red Cross hospital until May 1946. They re-opened as La Retraite on South Road, with Pen Maria and Saltaire (renamed St Teresa's) used as dormitories.

Weston-super-Mare might have become a military target because of its Airport, its RAF Radio and Radar School at Locking and the Shadow Aircraft Factory being built at Oldmixon. Until 1941 though, the Luftwaffe was not established in France, and there was relatively little seen of it in the West of England, which was therefore regarded as a haven for Americans (who were not then in the war) and school children evacuated from the London area, including one of the authors.

Owing to wartime security there are few detailed records, but we know that on the 14th August 1940 the first bombs in Weston almost hit the Tropicana, then on the 30th August houses were damaged in Albert Quadrant, but there were no local casualties until on the 3rd September bombs fell in Worle High Street killing three people. Soon after a whole stick of bombs destroyed the boating lake in Ashcombe Park. This may have been an attack on the nearby Waterworks facilities, but it was typical of events in the wide area around Weston where bombs and incendiaries fell here and there at random from German bombers terrified by RAF Beaufighters, or in one case, so confused as to land on the partly-built Lulsgate runway. That was amusing but, on the 25th September, there was a major raid on the Bristol Aeroplane Factory north of Filton with many workers killed, and Westonians expected an early attack on the partly-built factory at Oldmixon.

Instead, on 4th January 1941 though, in freezing weather, there was a full-scale night raid for nine hours concentrated on the town centre, the High Street, the Boulevard and the Manor House in Grove Park; and on the Bourneville Estate with 27 houses destroyed, and heavy damage to St Paul's Church, Walliscote Road, and Wadham Street Baptist Church. Thirty-four people died with 35 injured. None of these targets had any obvious military value.

Chapter 2

After that things were, for a year and a half, fairly quiet in Weston with no deliberate air-raids, although there were many attacks on South Wales and on Bristol, which could be seen and heard from Weston. In April 1942, there was even a public display on the beach of Army equipment, with a Polish Spitfire Squadron showing off its skills in the skies above. However, at the end of June on two clear moonless nights the Luftwaffe returned to the town centre causing much destruction, with 102 civilian deaths and 3500 houses damaged. It was reported by Germany that all their bombers got home safely. On the other hand, there was no damage to the Oldmixon Aircraft Factory, which managed to turn out 3,336 Beaufighters during the war.

A bomb destroyed Lance and Lance Ltd. at Lance's Corner (now Argos), as seen from looking down Waterloo Street across High Street, after the air raid of June 1942. One of the traffic lights close to the building was intact. The other street signs had their tops blown off. The roads were on fire: the wooden blocks that had the appearance of small bricks or cobbles when they were laid down to make up the road surface caught alight in various places around the town during the bombing raids.

These were the main war-related events of the 1939 - 45 period, in which the Catholic Parishes of St Joseph's, and Corpus Christi (with Our Lady of Lourdes) got off lightly as far as these events go. Catholics were just as likely as others to be killed or injured in the air-raids, or to have members in the Armed Forces during those war years, with all the anxieties that implies. We had no churches bombed (La Retraite and Totterdown Hall were also unharmed), fortunately, and when peace and normality returned, gradually we could continue with civilised and Christian life, thanks be to God. It had though been a close-run thing at times, even in quiet Weston-super-Mare.

The closest shave that occurred to Catholic property was when a time-bomb was reported in the garden at the rear of Corpus Christi church. Roads were closed to all traffic and those living in the vicinity had to be evacuated until the bomb squad successfully defused it.

When prisoners of war were billeted near Weston, Mgr Lyons thought nothing of paying them visits in their camp on his push-bike. A letter from Germany received some ten years later records how much the prisoners enjoyed his visits. He was most unpretentious.

By Courtesy of Weston Mercury

Lance and Lance bombed in the prolonged air raid at the end of June 1942.

Chapter 2

During and after the war was a difficult time for the church's finances, with expenditure greater than income despite the numerous fund-raising efforts. After a couple of year's occasional illnesses, Mgr Lyons left in 1948, moving to St Teresa's Nursing Home, Corston, Bath, as Chaplain to the Poor Servants of the Mother of God, and died there in 1951. Fr Denis Ryan took his place as Parish Priest.

In April 1946, Daniel Patrick Cotter died at Dale View, Banwell. He left his home in Cardiff to become one of the oldest members of the Catholic community in Weston-super-Mare, and certainly one of its most generous benefactors. He was 71 years of age and came to Weston-super-Mare thirty years before. He was primarily responsible for establishing a Chapel-of-Ease in Carlton Street; followed by Corpus Christi Church at Ellenborough Park Road South in 1929, before making a gift of land at Milton Road/Baytree Road crossroads on which stands the Church of Our Lady of Lourdes.

He conducted his whole life, methods of business and general conversation in such a way that displayed a great devotion to Christ. He held strong convictions but his sincerity, general good humour and friendliness commended him to all. In pre-war days, he made an annual pilgrimage to the Grotto at Lourdes, where he worked as a Brandcardier on behalf of the invalids taken to bathe in the famous curative waters. Was it this devotion to Our Lady of Lourdes that inevitably caused the Church at Milton to be named after Her? In his home parish in Weston he was President of the local Vincent de Paul Society and one of the original members of the Knights of St Columba.

The son of the deceased, Fr Anthony Cotter, a priest at the Pro-Cathedral in Clifton, was the celebrant at the Requiem Mass at Corpus Christi. Those taking part were the Bishop's Vicar General Mgr Canon J Lyons, VG (Corpus Christi), Mgr Long (Pro-Cathedral), Deacons-at-the-Throne; Fr T Hughes, (Pro-Cathedral, Master of Ceremonies); Fr P Barry (Knowle, Assistant M C); Fr R Morris (Deacon) and Fr G Smith (Sub-Deacon); Frs C Hookway, M Reedy of Keynsham, J T Judge of St Joseph's, D Lucy of Filton, J P Buckley the Bishop's Secretary, J Kehoe of Cheddar (choir), Fr Richard (RAF Locking), Fr P J Heatherman (Cheddar), Mr W Bradley and Mr R Osborne (representing the Knights of St Columba).

Among the congregation were Mr R Knowles, Mr and Mrs C A Stokes, Mr and Mrs S W G Garner, Mr and Mrs T Sanders, Mr Stock, Mrs Godley, Mrs Mason, Mr P D O'Connell and a number of sisters from the Poor Servants of the Mother of God at Totterdown and the Sisters of La Retraite.

The mourners included Mr Lawrence Cotter, Dr Michael Cotter, Miss Patricia Cotter and Miss Gwen Cotter (sons and daughters). This was a measure of the people who loved, respected and would miss the deceased. The funeral took place at Cardiff Cemetery on Thursday, the following day.

After the sad loss of Daniel Cotter, work continued to build a school close to the church and central to the town. For this Etonhurst was bought in 1953. Then the late Miss Conroy generously donated her garden; a parcel of land was bought from Clifford House later. This meant that the greater part of the required land was secured.

In 1956, the new Bourneville Estate was being built, including a Mass Centre. With the population growing rapidly, the Catholic Church was offered the Community Hall by the Council, which was accepted, although the site was far from ideal. Church vestments had to be taken from Corpus Christi each Sunday for the priest to be dressed for Mass. On one occasion, the priest opened his case to find, to his horror, that he had brought his dirty laundry instead.

In 1959, there were difficulties in maintaining the private school. It put a heavy burden on the church's finances. Canon D Ryan was very anxious to keep the school, but rising costs were aggravating the problem. It was a constant struggle to raise money for maintaining the building and paying the salaries. Without the considerable devotion of the Sisters of La Retraite, the school would have been lost. The parishioners built up a thriving football pool with the help of the town's non-Catholics. The annual Garden Fête became more picturesque, entertaining and profitable with the introduction of themes such as Spanish fiesta amongst others.

Canon D Ryan was a very unworldly and holy priest, nevertheless he was very kind and sensitive to the cares of all around him. He visited his parishioners on foot or on bicycle. He lost many a good night's sleep through worry about them and about the finances. Eventually his health gave way and he suffered several bouts of illness between 1954 and 1958, so much so that he was forced to resign to go home to Ireland, where he died in October in 1963.

In 1959, he was succeeded by Canon J P Leahy, who combined wonderful enthusiasm with great talent. The great hurdle preventing a school opening on the site was that the Local Education Authority would block it because there was no provision for a sports field. Canon Leahy dealt with the matter by buying Ellenborough Park. A great deal of work was necessary to make it suitable for a playing field and for sport.

The park consisted of two parts separated by Walliscote Road. The part opposite the church had a small pond, which had to be filled in, and several copses in the middle. These copses contained some large mature trees that had to be cleared, leaving some trees around the edge. The part on the other side of the Walliscote Road was left unused but nevertheless had to be kept tidy with the grass being cut occasionally. Railings and walls enclosed both parts. Maintaining the unused part became expensive and onerous and much later was sold for a nominal amount to the Council, who kept it as a recreation area for the community. Mgr Gabriel Leyden managed this transfer.

Canon Leahy enlarged the site by including the old presbytery and took up residence on the left-hand side of the church. He laid the Foundation Stone in 1961, on the Feast of Pentecost. The building cost was £42000 plus the cost for the redecoration of the church, the debt being met entirely by the generous donations and fund-raising efforts of the parishioners and their friends. The school opened the following year.

In the 1960s, La Retraite saw some expansion with the purchase of Dunmarklyn, which was used for extra dormitory accommodation, together with the construction of a dining hall annexe to the main building. This was accompanied by a rapid increase in numbers and in academic and cultural achievement. The large sixth form saw an increasing number of girls going to university. Later, the growth of Church-affiliated comprehensive schools in the Bristol area meant that Catholic secondary education was becoming more widely available, with an attendant decrease in the need for private Catholic schools. The writing was on the wall.

On 8th April 1960, an Ordination of a Westonian, Rev Michael House, took place, the first ordination at Corpus Christi. The unusual aspect of this ordination was that he was at London University training to become an Anglican Minister, but at the end of his course he was converted to the Catholic faith and studied for the priesthood.

Extra seating was provided in the side aisles to accommodate a possible record congregation. During the Solemn Pontifical High Mass, at one period, the ordinand lay prostrate on the floor, and later, had his hands anointed with oil. The ceremony of ordination recalled the scene at the Last Supper when Christ gave to those he had chosen the power to offer sacrifice. Moreover, it recalled the first Easter Sunday when He confirmed on them the power to forgive sin. Father Mervyn Alexander acted as commentator during the service, which naturally was in Latin. The Bishop of Bath, the Right Rev J E Rudderham, imposed hands on the ordinand and then presented him with the chalice and paten, while saying, "Receive the power to offer sacrifice to God and to celebrate Mass, both for the living and the dead." As the Mass continued, the ordinand was vested by the Bishop with the stole of his priesthood, followed by the anointing of his hands with oil in the sign of the Cross. The newly ordained priest, using the power confirmed on him, concelebrated the Mass with the Bishop.

The assistant priest to the ordaining prelate was Rt Rev Mgr Canon P Long, V G, while Very Rev Canon J Rea and the Very Rev F Rynn were the Deacons-at-the-throne. The Rev Fr W Ryan was deacon of the Mass, with the Rev Fr M C Roche as sub-deacon. The MC to the Bishop was the Rev Fr W O'Callaghan and the MC for the Mass was the Rev Fr T J Hughes. The assisting priest to the ordinand was Rev Fr J P Leahy (Corpus Christi) and the choir was under the direction of the Rev Fr M Meehan. The other present clergy were: Rev Frs H J Carter, D Soran, M Reidy, R Norris, J Mulholland, A Urrutia and M Gibson. A fourteen-year-old Corpus Christi School pupil, Sheila Wga, was organist.

Fr Michael House gave his blessing to the congregation of Corpus Christi on Sunday evening. Fr J P Leahy gave the address. It was understood that the new priest would be appointed to a church in the Clifton diocese.

The following Monday morning, Fr M House said High Mass for the first time, when children of Corpus School sang and Sheila Wga was again the organist. The deacon for the Mass was Fr M Gibson, with Fr H J Carter as sub-deacon, Fr M C Roche was M. with Fr J P Leahy as assistant priest.

Since then there have been two more ordinations held at Corpus Christi: Fr Eric Foxwell in 1978; and a former pupil at Corpus Christi School, Fr Robert Corrigan in 1989. In both cases the services were in English rather than Latin, and no commentator was necessary.

A rally was held in Ellenborough Park, Weston-super-Mare, in August 1961 in honour of the Forty Martyrs. Several thousand pilgrims from the Diocese of Clifton on a lovely summer's day listened to Fr Caraman as he addressed the assembly before the arrival of Bishop Joseph Rudderham of Clifton, proclaiming that in the cause of these Forty Martyrs more miracles had been granted in the last few months attributed to them than in the history of any cause since medieval times. At present twelve cases of cures were under examination like those at Lourdes. He said that there will be even more striking ones, and that people will turn to the church by signs and wonders. That is what we are praying for. The sick received a special blessing with the skull relic of blessed Cuthbert Mayne. The wound made in his skull when a stake was driven in to it was clearly visible.

Chapter 2

A corps of trumpeters from the nearby No. 1 Radio School from RAF Station, Locking, sounded a fanfare, while airmen from the station formed a guard of honour for the Bishop's procession, as it wound its way into the park and up to the high altar erected beneath an open-air awning. Nearby, on the beach and promenade, holiday makers were having fun completely oblivious to what was happening in the park.

The trumpeters again sounded out a fanfare at the instant of Consecration as the Bishop celebrated Pontifical Mass. Fr Caraman remarked that the occasion was not a mass-meeting, nor a demonstration, but a gathering to hear Holy Mass celebrated by the Bishop in honour of the English and Welsh Martyrs, and to give thanks to them, and to petition them for our own needs and for all the needs of those who are dear to us. Special honour was given to those among the forty who had associations with the diocese.

Nearby, a Rally Exhibition was held in Corpus Christi Junior School. On display were the skull of Blessed Cuthbert Mayne; several vestments from the penal days; a newly-discovered portrait of Blessed Ralph Sherwin, which was on show for the very first time; a first edition of Campion's Decem Rationes; and the Westminster Chasuble, worn at Westminster Abbey in the time of Catherine of Aragon, which attracted great interest. A "Pedlar's Vestment" designed to avoid detection was loaned to the exhibition by the Duke of Norfolk, which proved to be an outstanding attraction.

Three of the martyrs had associations with the West Country. Blessed Alexander Briant was born in Somerset and put to death at Tyburn in 1581 (canonised by Pope Paul VI in 1970). Blessed Swithin Wells, a school master for many years at Monkton Farleigh, Wiltshire, was sentenced to hanging outside his own house in 1591 (canonised by Pope Paul VI in 1970). Blessed Davis Lewis, a Jesuit, died on the gallows at Usk in 1679 (canonised by Pope Paul VI in 1970). Next to his grave is the tomb of the man who betrayed him and later repented.

*

There are three stages to canonisation: in the first stage the person is referred to as "venerable"; in the second stage "blessed"; and finally, "saint". When enough information about a possible saint has been collected, the process to canonisation may begin at least five years after the candidate has died – this was waived for Pope John Paul II and Mother Teresa of Calcutta. If a recommendation to the Pope is made that the candidate be made a proclamation of the Servant of God's heroic virtue: i.e. the Servant exhibited the theological virtues of faith, hope and charity, and the cardinal virtues of prudence, justice, fortitude and temperance to a heroic degree, the candidate is said to be "heroic in virtue", and is referred by the title "Venerable". A Venerable has no feast day, no churches may be built in his/her honour, and the Church has made no statement of the person's probable or certain presence in heaven. Prayer cards and other materials may be printed to encourage the faithful for a miracle wrought by his/her intercession as a sign of God's will that the person be canonised. At some point permission is granted for the body of the Servant of God to be exhumed and examined. A certification ("non cultus") is made that no superstitious or heretical worship or improper cult has grown up around the servant or his/her tomb and then relics are taken.

Beatification is a statement by the Church that it is "worthy of belief" that the person is in heaven, having arrived at salvation. What happens next depends on whether the Venerable is a martyr or a "confessor" – a confessor has borne witness to their faith by how

Chapter 2

they lived their lives. For a martyr, the Pope has only to make a declaration of martyrdom: for a confessor, it must be proven that a miracle has taken place by his/her intercession: performing a miracle in response to the Blessed's prayers i.e. that God has shown a sign that the person is enjoying the Beatific Vision by God. This almost always involves a miraculous cure.

This allows beatification, giving the Venerable the new title of Blessed. A feast day will be designated, but its observance is normally restricted to the Blessed's home diocese, to certain locations associated with him/her, and/or to churches or houses of the Blessed's religious order, should he/she belong to one.

To become a saint depends on whether the Blessed was a martyr or not. For a Blessed who was a martyr only one miracle is needed (i.e. normally an additional miracle after that granting beatification), but for a Blessed who was not a martyr, normally at least two miracles must have been performed after his/her death. Canonisation is a statement by the Church that the person certainly enjoys the Beatific Vision. The saint is assigned a feast day, which may be celebrated anywhere within the Catholic Church, although it may or may not appear on the general calendar or local calendars as an obligatory feast, parish churches may be built in his/her honour, and the faithful may freely and without restriction celebrate and honour the saint. This is just a brief introduction to the rules leading to canonisation and now we return from Ellenborough Park across the road to Corpus Christi.

*

The new school was proposed to replace the rather out-dated building at the junction of Ellenborough Park South and Walliscote Road. This school was demolished to be replaced by a new presbytery and six flats. The first dramatic event occurring at the new presbytery was when a small black baby wrapped in a shawl was left on the steps. The note on it said that the mother could no longer care for it. The abandoned one was taken into the new presbytery and given a home. Regrettably, we are not told the name that was given to the little black kitten.

The new school was designed to accommodate 200 infant and junior pupils. It had taken over 60 years of hard work from planning to completion at a great sacrifice to the Catholics of Weston, the nuns of La Retraite and the clergy. In 1962 the new school was opened by Bishop Rudderham assisted by Fr William Ryan and Fr Richard Norris.

Canon William Ryan returned to Corpus Christi in 1963 as Parish Priest. He was born in Charleville, County Cork in 1913; he trained for the priesthood at All Hallows College, Dublin and was ordained in Roscrea Abbey in May 1937.

In 1966, the mural painted above the confessional by artist Jean Clark was commissioned with money from the Edwin Austin Abbey Memorial Trust Fund. This shows Christ granting forgiveness to a sinner. The Stations of the Cross were painted the following year.

In 1967, a temporary altar table was installed facing the people to conform to changes decreed by Vatican II. Mass had been celebrated in English since 1964, and now not only could people understand the Mass but they could see it clearly. This year was the first time that Holy Week services were completely in English.

Canon William Ryan showed his appreciation of all women who had worked in the parish with the window to St Margaret Clitherow. The windows in the Lady Chapel depict various incidents in the life of the Mother of God. The glorious round window above the choir, of the Last Supper, is what the celebrant sees when he raises the host and the chalice during the Eucharist: a link with the event 2,000 years ago.

The organ in the choir loft was built toward the end of the 19th century by Messrs Wadworth of Manchester. It was originally in the Bible Christian Church, Barry Dock, South Wales. It was moved into Corpus Christi in 1965. It is said to be one of the finest in the West of England.

The same year, Fr Martin Fitzpatrick attended to the moving of the altar table from the back to the front. The whole area was redecorated.

In 1970, he became a member of the staff at the Clifton Pro-Cathedral. He was a very popular Assistant Priest with young people: he introduced a "Pop" Mass for teenagers and inspired a strong interest in the Parish Youth Club. In addition, He introduced popular House Masses. Every fortnight he drove the Meals-on-Wheels van with the Parish Priest, Canon William Ryan. The Parish greatly missed him.

*

One very important innovation introduced by Vatican II was the inauguration of deacons. Deacons are ordained ministers within the Church, who perform various ministries usually at parish level. The Permanent Diaconate was re-established after Vatican II. Deacons have a special attachment to the Bishop, who lays hands on the candidate during the ceremony, saying:

> "In the first days of your church, under the inspiration of the Holy Spirit, the apostles of your Son appointed seven men of good repute to assist them in their daily ministry so they themselves have more freedom for prayer and preaching. By prayer and the laying on of hands, the apostles entrusted to those men the ministry of serving at table."

The Permanent Diaconate can be conferred on married men. Among the tasks of a Deacon are: to assist the Bishop and priests in the celebration of the Divine mysteries, in assisting and blessing marriages, the proclamation of the Gospel and preaching, presiding over baptisms, and dedicating themselves to various ministries of charity.

During the liturgies of the Church, Deacons wear different vestments from the priest. The stole is traditionally worn over the left shoulder so practical work could be carried out without the "scarf" getting in the way. The Dalmatic is simpler than the priest's chasuble to permit freedom of movement whilst serving the people.

*

In 1971, the Community Hall in Bourneville was demolished. The Vicar of St Andrews Anglican Church kindly allowed Sunday Mass to be celebrated in his church. What a wonderful act of charity! This stopped in 1979 when the parishioners from Oldmixon and Bourneville were bussed to Corpus Christi.

In 1971, Sisters of La Retraite closed the School and Convent in South Road owing to the re-organisation of local education. The La Retraite School amalgamated with the school at Burnham-on-Sea, which from earlier days always was a Catholic stronghold, while the much-loved Convent was sold by auction to a property developer. Five Sisters went to live at 11 Walliscote Road, offering an open door to parishioners, and travelling the country giving retreats and Spiritual Direction to laity, clergy and religious. Two of the sisters, Sr Elisabeth and Sr Bernadette were teaching in the Parish School. The latter took her final vows at Corpus Christi in 1975. In November 2017 the nuns remaining in Walliscote Road were moved to the Monica Wills New Care Home in Keynsham, Bristol.

Donated to the Church by Angela Sleep by courtesy of the Western Daily Press

The Feast of Corpus Christi June 1981. All the children of Corpus Christi School had just attended Mass, which also was the funeral Mass for one of the pupils. Afterwards the whole school evacuated to the beach until lunch time. It was a lovely day. Mrs Angela Hannon (now Sleep), in the photograph, was looking after a group of children. Left to right: Fiona Greaney, the White sisters, Joanne Faulkner, Kieran and Kelsey Venn and Adam. Mrs Hannon was the batsman.

Since St Mary's Convent opened, it played a notable part in the life of Corpus Christi parish, contributing enormously to its spiritual and well-being for 37 years. In 1974, it became evident that because of a lack of vocations the Convent and Home would have to close. For 36 years, the nuns had lovingly cared for some sixty mentally handicapped girls and women as well as diligently and quietly working in the parish, giving generous help, support and encouragement to the priests. For several months before their convent and home finally closed, Sister Mary St Catherine and Sister Mary Borgia bravely remained to complete the closure. The Convent was leased out to be adapted for the care of alcoholics, with an agreement that the Chapel would be available for Sunday Mass for the people of Oldmixon. The Sisters left the Parish an extremely valuable piece of ground for any future developments.

Canon William Ryan retired as Parish Priest in 1982, whereupon he went to live in St Bonaventure's, Bishopston, Bristol, where his great friend and former curate, Fr Martin Fitzpatrick was Parish Priest. Canon William Ryan went to work in the parish straight away, making many friends there. In 1993, when Fr Fitzpatrick became a Canon, returning to Corpus Christi as Parish Priest, he persuaded Canon Ryan, now in his eighties, to join him as his assistant. Thus, for a third time, Canon William Ryan returned to Weston, a place of which he was very fond, where the parishioners and others were delighted to see him. He was as strong as ever, as he strode straight-backed along the promenade, a hand in pocket while he prayed the Rosary as he went. He loved a game of golf but gave up in his late eighties because he had run out of partners.

Local charities started to use Corpus Christi to raise funds and the musicians and singers appreciated the excellent acoustics, which was an source of extra income to the Parish.

In 1995, there were big changes in the layout and decoration of the Sanctuary, when the Parish Priest, Canon Martin Fitzpatrick, instigated the moving of the altar table from the back to the front, followed by the redecoration of the whole area in cream, grey and terracotta. In most modern churches, the tabernacle is placed to one side of the main altar so that people can sit somewhere to pray, the Corpus Christi tabernacle was not moved from the centre of the main altar because the church is named after the Body of Christ.

In the same year, Canon Martin Fitzpatrick instigated walks and trips for the parish. Probably very good for the parishioners' fitness. The very important Tradecraft Monthly Sales began, with its great commitment to the Third World with a donation of 10% of income to various projects.

In the new millennium, the Weston winds and damp had penetrated the church, which required the roof to be mended and the walls of the Lady Chapel and sanctuary damp proofed and redecorated. The heating system was completely overhauled. During this work, the workmen found a newspaper under the floor boards dated 1929, showing that the system had not needed too much work carried out on it since that time.

In the year 2000, Canon Fitzpatrick tragically died of heart disease, which had plagued him in recent years. Canon William Ryan finally retired in 2004 and went to St Angela's Nursing Home in Bristol, where he died on his birthday in 2006 aged 93.

By courtesy of David Pluck

The Church of Corpus Christi

Chapter 2

Fr Timothy Barry, (Fr Tadgh to his Irish friends) retired as Parish Priest from Our Lady and the English Martyrs Parish, Burnham-on-Sea, to retirement flats at Corpus Christi. In 2001, he was appointed an Honorary Canon and continued to celebrate Masses at Our Lady and the English Martyrs Church; at the little chapel in the Burnham Nursing Home, where many of the nuns were in care; at Corpus Christi and Our Lady of Lourdes, until he was very seriously ill. After what seemed a very long time, he recovered, played golf again, and returned to Weston to work until he was critically ill again and died on 7th January 2008 in Bristol.

The 75th anniversary of Corpus Christi fell on the Feast of Corpus Christi, June 10th 2004. A history book and story of the Parish was published at the beginning of June and a week of celebration began on June 6th with a pilgrimage from St Joseph's Church, Camp Road, stopping off at Carlton Street, where the first mass centre was set up, and then on to Corpus Christi. The pilgrims wore bright colours or National costumes and carried multi-coloured balloons.

On June 7th, there was a tea party for the members of the Corpus Christi Friendship Club. Local author and historian, Sharon Poole gave a talk at Corpus Christi Primary School on June 8th. A Vigil and Taizé music and song for young people was held at the Church the following evening, and on June 10th, the feast of Corpus Christi, there was a special morning Mass followed by a picnic in Ellenborough Park and a carnival. At 7.30 pm, the Bishop of Clifton, the Right Reverend Declan Lang, was the principal celebrant at a Mass in the Church, after which the parishioners moved on to a simple American supper in the Parish Hall. The festivities did not end then, because on June 11th there was a reunion at the school for pupils from 1939 – 1967. A Summer fair and fête was held at the School in the afternoon the following day, and finally, on June 13th, a family picnic was held in the morning in Ellenborough Park. In the afternoon, the elderly and housebound were taken to the Church for a service of healing and Benediction.

Throughout the week there was a flower festival in the Church with the Parish flower arrangers helped by the members of the Weston and Burnham-on-Sea flower clubs, while pupils at Corpus Christi undertook a project on life in the 20s and 30s together with an art exhibition. A plaque was put up in the Church listing the names of the priests who had served the Parish in the last 75 years. This was unveiled on the Feast of Corpus Christi.

In 2007, Clifton Diocese launched a new book for Somerset's Polish worshippers. The Clifton Diocese Directory contained details of all Polish masses and priests in Bristol, Gloucester, Somerset and Wiltshire. As well as church information, the directory gave practical details about organisations that could be greatly helpful to Polish migrants. It was available in all parishes. Mgr Gabriel Leyden observed that Polish people are increasingly contributing to our local communities and parishes. They bring an opportunity for us to welcome fellow Catholics and give us new viewpoints from which we can better understand our faith. In return we can offer them a concise collection of useful contacts and full details of Polish pastoral care in our areas and put them in touch with appropriate organisations.

In 2012, Mgr Leyden celebrated 45 years of life in the priesthood at a special service on 23rd February. The following year he retired to be replaced by Canon Richard Dwyer, whose Induction Mass was held on 22nd May.

Chapter 2

Parish Priests (in red) with their Assistant Priests

Canon John Lyons	1929 - 1948	He retired to be Chaplain of the Convent of the Good Shepherd, Ashwick Hall, near Marshfield. Eventually moving to St Teresa's Nursing Home, Corston, Bath, as Chaplain to the Poor Servants of the Mother of God, where he died in 1951.
James Murtogh 1929 - 1932, Patrick Power 1932 - 1936, Michael O' Brien 1936 - 1940	William J Ryan 1937 - 1944, Patrick McGovern 1940 - 1942, Richard Norris 1942 - 1948	Gerard Smith 1944 - 1946, Jerome Dennehy 1946 - 1950
Canon Denis Ryan	1948 - 1958	He died in Ireland in 1963.
Jerome Dennehy 1946 - 1950, Daniel O'Callaghan 1948 - 1953	John King 1951 - 1952, Edmond Murphy 1952 - 1957	Michael Roche 1953 - 1963, Dermot Grehan 1957 - 1958
Canon Joseph P Leahy	1958 - 1963	He died 1996.
Michael Roche 1953 - 1963	Dermot Grehan 1957 - 1958	Michael Meehan 1958 - 1963
Canon William J Ryan	1963 - 1982	Retired to St Bonaventure's, Bishopston, Bristol then in 1993 returned to Corpus Christi. He died in 2006.
Martin Fitzpatrick 1963 - 1971, Francis Nugent 1964 - 1965	Thomas O'Donovan 1965 - 1969, John Ainslie 1971 - 1975	Brendan Monahan 1975 - 1977, Gregory Grant 1977 - 1981, Michael Saunders 1981 - 1984
Fr John F O'Connor	1982 - 1992	He died in 1994.
Michael Saunders 1981 - 1984	Raymond Matus 1984 -1989	
Canon Martin Fitzpatrick	1993 - 2000	Died 2000
Canon William J Ryan 1993 - 2004	Canon Timothy Barry 1997 - 2008	Went to St Angela's Nursing Home, Clifton, Bristol and died on his 93rd birthday in 2006.
Mgr Gabriel Leyden 2000 - 2012		Retired to St Joseph's Home of the Little Sisters of the Poor, Cotham Hill, Bristol.
Deacon Stephen Munday 2000 -	Deacon Pedro Gregory 2003 - Canon William J Ryan 1993 - 2004	Canon Timothy Barry 2001 - 2008

Chapter 2

Canon Richard Dwyer 2013 - 2017		Went to St Catherine's, Frome.
Deacon Michael Roberts 1999 -, Deacon Stephen Munday 2000 -	Deacon Pedro Gregory 2003 - 2016	
Fr Kevin Hennessy 2017 -		
Deacon Michael Roberts 1999 -, Deacon Stephen Munday 2000 -	Deacon Pedro Gregory 2003 - 2016	

For all those priests in the list above who have died may they rest in peace.

Looking at the table, it is interesting to note how many Assistant Priests there were, and these were often augmented by retired priests who were still able to take on some duties such as celebrating mid-week Masses, but where have they all gone? Currently there are two Parish Priests, Fr Alexander Redman of Our Lady of Lourdes and Canon Richard Dwyer of Corpus Christi, who being an Expert in Canon Law is taken away from his Parish duties two days a week to give his expert opinion. These two share the work of St Joseph's aided by Deacon Tom Moffatt of St Joseph's, and Deacon Michael Roberts (ordained at Corpus Christi 1999), Deacon Stephen Munday (ordained at Corpus Christi in 2000) and Deacon Peter Gregory (ordained at Corpus Christi in 2003). These deacons had permanent jobs, for instance, Stephen Munday a father-of-six, worked in the Information Technology Department of the Weston Area Health Trust. God, please make us grateful for the few priests that we have.

St Joseph's has a large young Polish community, whereas a group of Syro-Malabars have Holy Mass celebrated in their own Rite at Corpus Christi on the 1st and 3rd Sunday of the month at 3pm.

The Syro-Malabar Catholic Church is one of the twenty-two Eastern Catholic Churches in full communion with Rome. It is the second largest after the Ukrainian Church and the largest of the St Thomas Christian denominations. It is an Apostolic Church that traces its origin to St Thomas the Apostle, who landed at Cranganore (Muziris) in 52AD, founding seven Christian communities in Kerala (West coast of South India). St Thomas was martyred in 72AD at Mylapore, near Chennai (Madras). The early Christian Community in India was known as the St Thomas Christians, or Nazranis, meaning those who follow the path of Jesus of Nazareth. Their vernacular language is called Malayalam.

In this country the Syro-Malabar Catholic Church is set up in the same way as the Ordinariate, with its own liturgy, but in full communion with Rome. The Rev Fr Paul Vettikattu is the Syro-Malabar Coordinator for the South West Region.

Now it is time for the history to focus on the little village of Milton quickly growing.

Chapter 2

CHRONOLOGY

79 AD	Vesuvius erupted and burying Herculaneum.
105	The origin of consecration is attributed by some historians to Pope St Evaristus.
200	Tertullian, the Christian author from Carthage describes Christians "praying in the direction of the rising sun".
231	Origen wrote in De Oratione 32.
314	The church at Tyre was consecrated.
335	The Church of the Holy Sepulchre at Jerusalem was consecrated.
410	When the Romans left Britain.
506	Council of Agde.
517	Council of Epaone in 517. The first legislation against wooden altars.
563	The First Council of Bracara in 563.
1229	Henry III (1216 -72) made the first of 4 pilgrimages to Walsingham in 1229, 1232, 1235 and 1242.
1234	Weston was referred to as Weston-propre-Worle.
1311	Weston was called Weston-juxta-Worle.
1348	The earliest known reference to Weston-super-Mare is in the register of another Bishop of Bath and Wells, Ralph of Shrewsbury.
1493	The Pynson Ballad was printed by Richard Pynson.
1545 - 63	The Council of Trent.
1568	The mineral calamine was discovered in Worlebury Hill.
1581	Blessed Alexander Briant was born in the Somerset and put to death at Tyburn.
1591	Blessed Swithin Wells, a school master for many years at Monkton Farleigh, Wiltshire, was sentenced to hanging outside his own house.
1600	Weston had its own Manor held by William Arthur of Clapton.
1679	Blessed Davis Lewis, a Jesuit, died on the gallows at Usk.
1688	The Western District was established consisted of the whole of Wales and the present Catholic dioceses of Plymouth and Clevedon.
1696	The Manor was sold to John Pigott of Brockley.
1778	The Papist Act.
1779	An Armada. Lord George Gordon became the President of the Protestant Association of London.
1780	The Gordon Riots began.
1789	King George III followed the Sea Cure in Weymouth and set up a fashion.
1791	The Reverent Leeves of Wrington built his own seaside cottage on the dunes, a fragment of which survives as "The Old Thatched Cottage Restaurant 1774". The Catholic Relief Act.
1803	The Worle and Tickenham Enclosure Act was passed.
1806	Franciscan fathers came on a mission to Weston-super-Mare.
1810	The population of Weston was only a 100. The first hotel was built in Weston.
1812	The winter population of Weston-super-Mare was only 160.

Chapter 2

1815	The Weston Enclosure Award was completed.
1820s	Weston Woods were planted by the Lord of the Manor.
1822	Weston's first guidebook for holidaymakers was published. The population was 735.
1829	the Catholic Emancipation Act.
1830	Bishop Peter Baines, the Vicar Apostolic, bought the Prior Park Estate near Bath.
1841	Brunel's Bristol and Exeter Railway finally reached the terminus in Regent Street.
1842	The Improvement and Market Act was granted on 13th May.
1845	Potato Famine in Ireland.
1847	Potato Famine in Ireland.
1850	A limited number of trains were pulled by steam locomotives through the junction to Weston. Pastor Pascal O' Farrell secured Greenfield Cottage at Knightstone as a presbytery and the Weston mission commenced.
1851	Horses continued to be used to pull certain trains from Worle Junction until 31st March. With the approval of Bishop Hendren, the Jesuit Fathers from Bristol rented the Old Assembly Room, in Regent Street.
1854	The first resident priest was Fr Van de Voorde.
1858	The first priest-in-charge was Fr William Pippett. Mass was celebrated for the first time at St Joseph's on the 4th Sunday of Advent. The Jesuit fathers had started a mission for 30 Catholics.
1862	New goods facilities were built at Locking Road. Fr William Pippett was transferred and Canon Maurice J Power became the new Parish Priest of St Joseph's.
1865	The number of parishioners at St Joseph's had increased to 59.
1866	On 22nd July, a large passenger station was opened adjacent to the goods yard.
1867	Birnbeck Pier was completed.
1870	The 1870 Education Act.
1875	A third rail was introduced to each line so that standard gauge trains could reach the station as well. The Bristol and Exeter Railway obtained an Act of Parliament to construct a new loop line through the town.
1878	Canon Maurice J Power died and Fr John Peter Bouvier became the new Parish Priest of St Joseph's.
1879	No broad gauge trains were used on the branch.
1880	A court case forced the Great Western Railway Company to pay 5% interest to the affected property owners. Fr Bouvier reported that an old maid had £60 in store, which will be given to him on the express condition that a sacristy shall be built almost at once.
1881 - 82	The Friars from Amiens in France arrived in Clevedon, where they served the Catholics from Portland House in Wellington Terrace.
1883	The Friars purchased the *Royal Hotel* for the sum of £3800. Masses were held in the bar there from February 1883.

Chapter 2

1884	Weston gained a through railway station when the present station and loop line opened into the town on March 1st.	
1886	Even more sidings and an engine shed were constructed on the North side of the line near the station. The Friars built a church in the grounds of the Friary. The foundation stone was laid on 16th February.	
1887	The first public mass was celebrated in the church, which was consecrated in July.	
1891	Weston-super-Mare was beginning to grow rapidly and had nearly doubled.	
1893	The Smyth-Pigott family donated the side chapels, while Fr Bouvier was the Parish Priest.	
1897	Weston, Clevedon and Portishead Light Railway opened.	
1898	Fr John Peter Bouvier retired from St Joseph's and Canon Eustace Barron replaced him. In June, Canon Barron wrote to the Mother Superior at Burnham-on-Sea to ask her to send nuns to Weston to open an elementary school and a day school. Mère St Césaire, the Superior General, and some of her Sisters came to Weston on 1st July 1898 to meet Canon Barron at his request.	
1899	Rossmore in Atlantic Road was rented by the nuns in June. On October 2nd, the nuns' elementary school opened with one pupil.	
1901	Bishop Brownlow allowed the nuns to take in up to a dozen pupils as boarders, on condition that they needed sea-air for their health.	
	In 1901 Canon Barron borrowed money from Bishop William Brownlow's Fund to build the present presbytery West of the Church, which connects to it by way of a lobby.888	
1902	French Friars served the people of Clevedon, Portishead, Nailsea and surrounding villages until they were able to return to their native land, leaving English Friars to take over the Parish of the Immaculate Conception.	
1903	Nine girls were seen at Mass under the care of the Sisters of La Sainte Union at Bath. The Nuns of La Retraite felt sufficiently confident to open a Secondary School in South Road,	
1904	The Grand pier was opened. Miss Georgina Barham of Weston had promised Canon Baron £3000, but instead, she gave the money for the purchase of the Bishop's House. The day school had closed and there were only three boarders at Rossmore.	
1905	When Mother Imelda arrived from London, the elementary school was still very small.	
1907	The elementary school was transferred to a better house. It had 30 pupils although the day school was still closed. On Christmas Eve, a woman in floods of tears arrived at the Convent asking for shelter. Portishead continued to be served from the Friary, until the new	

Chapter 2

	church and parish was given over to the Diocese.
1908	The nuns could extend the property in South Road, by buying Fortfield.
1909	Two more postulates left for Angers (London).
1910	In September, Mr Ibbs left very suddenly and the sisters hoped and prayed for his house for a boarding school. In October, Bishop George Burton asked the nuns to open a secondary school for girls in Weston.
1911	Mr Ibbs' school became La Retraite. In the summer of Canon Barron spent time in hospital with pneumonia.
1912	Ashcombe Park had just received the bowling green ahead. After difficult and protracted negotiations, Fr Palmer was appointed as Chaplain for the school children on 5th January. R.M. St Pacome fell ill on 15th January and died on 26th March at the age of 59.
1914	The Piggots held the Manor until 1914 when the estate was sold. A new terminal station was opened called Locking Road Station to deal with excursion traffic.
1914 - 18	Weston played an active part in the First World War.
1916	The free school called St Joseph's reopened in Oxford Street before it moved to the floor above Barclay's Bank in High Street thence to Connaught Place in 1916,
1917	Canon Eustace Barron died and Canon John Lyons became the new Parish Priest of St Joseph's.
1919	The free school moved to St Helier's in 25 Beach Road. Fr John Lyons made temporary arrangements for Sunday Mass to be said in one of the bigger rooms of the Catholic School at St Helier's.
1921	The Chapel-of-Ease in Carlton Street called Corpus Christi was opened.
1922	The Rev Hope Patten was the Anglican Vicar of Walsingham who started an Anglican Shrine of Our Lady of Walsingham,
1924	Fr Lyons became a Canon.
1925 - 29	Roald Dhal was sent to St Peter's Boarding School.
1927	The Winter Gardens and Pavilion were opened.
1928	The Bishop of Clifton laid the foundation stone of Corpus Christi Church in Ellenborough Park South.
1929	The new church, Corpus Christi, was opened on 6th June 1929 by the Bishops of Cardiff and Menevia.
1931	The first mention of the picture the Adoration of the Shepherds in the Stable at Bethlehem but no one knew where it had come from. A shrine church on the site of the Shrine Church destroyed by Henry VIII was built at Walsingham. Corpus Christi School was opened by the most Rev Francis Mostyn and run by the Sisters of La Retraite.
1934	The debt on the Church and School of Corpus Christi had been paid off so that the church could be consecrated.
1935	Corpus Christi and St Joseph's Parishes separated. Canon John Lyons left St Joseph's to become Parish Priest of Corpus

		Christi while Canon Joseph T. Judge replaced him.
	1936	Weston Airfield was officially opened in June. In December, the order of nuns called the Poor Servants of the Mother of God purchased a large house (Totterdown Hall) in Hutton Road, Oldmixon. In Nailsea a small hut was purchased for use as a Mass Centre.
	1937	The town was granted Borough Status. RAF Locking was opened initially as a Training Unit about a mile away from RAF Weston airport. On 21st and 22nd July, the Catholic Women's League (CWL) of Corpus Christi arranged the Summerland Fête over two afternoons.
	1939	The second World War: the pupils of La Retraite were evacuated to Hertfordshire while their buildings were requisitioned as a Red Cross hospital until May 1946. A new separate parish in Milton was temporarily set aside.
	1940	Weston, Clevedon and Portishead Light Railway closed.
	1942	Weston was bombed over two consecutive nights. A bomb destroyed Lance and Lance Ltd. at Lance's Corner (now Argos) in June.
	1946	The nuns re-opened as La Retraite on South Road, with Pen Maria and Saltaire (renamed St Teresa's) used as dormitories. In April, Daniel Patrick Cotter died at Dale View, Banwell. He was a great benefactor to Corpus Christi and Our Lady of Lourdes, giving the latter the original parcel of land to build a Chapel-of-Ease.
	1953	Etonhurst was bought with a view to building a new school close to Corpus Christi and the town centre. Then the late Miss Conroy generously donated her garden and a parcel of land was bought from Clifford House later.
	1956	The new Bourneville Estate was being built, including a Mass Centre.
	1959	Canon Joseph T. Judge died and Fr Henry John Carter replaced him at St Joseph's. There were difficulties in maintaining Corpus Christi as a private school. Canon D. Ryan retired owing to ill health to be succeeded by Canon J P Leahy.
	1960	On 8th April, an Ordination of a Westonian, Rev Michael House, took place, the first ordination at Corpus Christi.
	1960s	La Retraite saw some expansion with the purchase of Dunmarklyn, which was used for extra dormitory accommodation, together with the construction of a dining hall annexe to the main building.
	1961	Canon J P Leahy laid the foundation of the new school after having bought Ellenborough Park and re-organised the site around the Church of Corpus Christi. A rally was held in Ellenborough Park in August in honour of the Forty Martyrs.
	1962	Corpus Christi School was opened by Bishop Rudderham assisted by Fr William Ryan and Fr Richard Norris.
	1963	Canon William Ryan returned to Corpus Christi as Parish Priest after Canon J P Leahy retired.

1964	Locking Road station closed on 6th September. Mass was celebrated in English for the first time at Corpus Christi.
1965	Corpus Christi bought an organ, originally in the Bible Christian Church, Barry Dock, South Wales.
1966	The mural painted above the confessional by artist Jean Clark was commissioned. The lines and engine shed on the North side near the 1886 station were finally closed on 30th June.
1967	Fr Henry John Carter left to go to St Mary's Parish in Bath to be replaced by Canon James Rea as Parish Priest at St Joseph's. A temporary altar table was installed facing the people to conform to changes decreed by Vatican II.
1968 - 73	The arrival of the M5 motorway to Worle.
1970s	The title "Lord of the Manor" was sold.
1970	The Gospel was read facing North from ancient times until this date. Fr Martin Fitzpatrick became a member of the staff at the Clifton Pro-Cathedral.
1971	Canon James Rea retired to Ireland and Fr Matthias McManus became Parish Priest at St Joseph's. The Community Hall in Bourneville was demolished. The Vicar of St Andrews Anglican Church kindly allowed Sunday Mass to be celebrated in his church. The Sisters of La Retraite closed the School and Convent in South Road owing to the re-organisation of local education.
1972	There was a need to serve the town's gasworks by rail until this date. The loop line was singled on 31st January. The bay platform (Platform 3) was downgraded to the status of a siding.
1974	St Mary's Convent closed because of a lack of vocations.
1975	Sister Bernadette took her Final Vows at Corpus Christi.
1978	Fr Eric Foxwell was ordained at Corpus Christi.
1979	When Catholic services were stopped at St Andrews Anglican Church, the parishioners from Oldmixon and Bourneville were bussed to Corpus Christi.
1980	The Primary School was built after which Nailsea became its own parish. The villages of Yatton, Congresbury, Claverham and Wrington continue to be part of this parish.
1981	Worle was the fastest growing suburb in Britain.
1982	Canon William Ryan retired as Parish Priest. Fr John F. O'Connor became the new Parish Priest.
1984	The rate of new building in Worle had lessened.
1986	Fr Mathias McManus retired and died. He was replaced at St Joseph's by Fr James C Stirrat.
1989	A former pupil at Corpus Christi School, Fr Robert Corrigan was ordained.
1990s	The Church of Corpus Christi began to be used as a setting for concerts both sung and orchestral.
1992	Fr John F. O'Connor retired.

1993	Fr Fitzpatrick became a Canon, returning to Corpus Christi as Parish Priest. He persuaded Canon Ryan, now in his eighties, to join him as his assistant.
1995	The SeaQuarium, a new pier on Weston beach, was opened. There were big changes in the layout and decor of the Sanctuary, when the Parish Priest, Fr Martin Fitzpatrick, instigated the moving of the altar table from the back to the front, followed by the redecoration of the area,
1999	In the late 1990s the site of the former parish hall was redeveloped with housing; and in February Fr Stirrat had the current church hall built. The Technical site for the RAF's Number One Radio School was relocation to RAF Cosford. Deacon Michael Roberts was ordained at Corpus Christi.
2000	Fr James C Stirrat retired from St Joseph's. Canon Fitzpatrick of Corpus Christi died of heart disease and Mgr Gabriel Leyden became the new Parish Priest. Deacon Stephen Munday was ordained at Corpus Christi.
2001	Bishop Mervyn Alexander became the new Parish Priest at St Joseph's.
2002	Deacon Tom Moffatt was Ordained as a Deacon on 13th July.
2003	Deacon Peter Gregory was ordained at Corpus Christi.
2004	Canon William Ryan finally retired. The 75th anniversary of Corpus Christi fell on the Feast of Corpus Christi, June 10th.
2007	Bishop Mervyn Alexander retired owing to ill health and thereafter St Joseph's had the Parish Priests from Corpus Christi and Our Lady of Lourdes sharing responsibility for the Parish. In October, the Traditional Anglican Communion presented to the Holy See a petition for the full union with the Catholic Church. Clifton Diocese launched a new book for Somerset's Polish worshippers.
2008	In July, Cardinal Levada responded to their formal request for full union.
2009	On 20th October, Cardinal Levada announced the institution of the Personal Ordinariate. The Apostolic Constitution enacting the introduction of personal Ordinariates for former Anglicans was released on 9th November. In December, Cardinal Levada responded to each of the bishops of the Traditional Anglican Communion who had signed the October 2007 petition.
2010	The Traditional Anglican Communion arranged some discussions, planning to give formal response after a meeting of bishops at Eastertide.
2012	Mgr Leyden celebrated 45 years of life in the priesthood at a special service on 23rd February.
2013	Mgr Gabriel Leyden retired to be replaced by Canon Richard Dwyer, whose Induction Mass was held on 22nd May.
2015	Pope Francis raised the sanctuary of Our Lady of Walsingham to the status of a minor basilica on 27th December.
2017	Canon Richard Dwyer was replaced by Fr Kevin Hennessey, who on 15th November was inducted as the new Parish Priest of Corpus Christi Church

CHAPTER 3 - THE CHURCH OF OUR LADY OF LOURDES IN THE PARISH OF CORPUS CHRISTI

3.1 THE DEVELOPMENT OF MILTON AS WE KNOW IT

It was not until after the end of the 1914 - 18 war that Milton began to develop into the populous residential area we now know. In 1914 Milton Road was extended by the then Axbridge Rural District Council from Baytree Road corner to connect to Worle High Street. A commemorative stone set into the boundary wall of our Church, adjacent to this road, records this development. In 1922 the Milton Rise Council houses were built and in-fill development of private houses, bungalows and more council houses continued apace.

Up to the late 50s Seabrook Road, then the last road before Worle, and Gillmore Road were all termed "Un-adopted", which meant that they were not metalled. The surface was rough with stones and weeds growing between them, making it very difficult to walk up and down with a pram or a pushchair, and riding a child's scooter was impossible. Eventually the Town Council adopted the two roads, so that they duly received their tarmac surface, except for that part of Gillmore Road, its east end, leading to the little path up to Spring Hill, which to this day may still be "un-adopted". Consequently, when it was eventually finished, the householders either side of that part of Gillmore Road had to pay for the work. It may still be their responsibility.

Sue Maguire

The Commemorative stone in the church wall – Milton Road.
The missing words are "THIS ROAD".

Chapter 3

Unlike Weston and Worle, Milton could only expand by in-filling, sandwiched as it is between these two much larger areas. Had the Church of Our Lady of Lourdes been built much later, after the great expansion of Worle outwards to the motorway, the church might have been situated there.

3.2 THE BEGINNINGS OF OUR CHURCH

In 1923, to meet the needs of our growing district, a wooden Chapel-of-Ease was erected in Milton, near where our Church stands. This made journeys to Mass much easier for elderly people who had no transport. It was affectionally called "The Hut". The land on which it stood was given by Daniel Cotter, a member of Corpus Christi Parish. It was dedicated to Our Lady of Lourdes. There is another postcard picture of it on the outside of the back cover. This card was sent in 1923. Both pictures show the north and west sides of the building.

The Chapel was constructed of wood and placed on a concrete plinth. It faced east-west with the altar at the eastern end and positioned on the two parking spots to the left of the handicapped drivers parking spaces, but farther away from the wall facing Baytree Rd. It was surrounded by allotments, which over the years were gradually vacated and replaced by lawn. Between the 1920s and 1930s a number of these kind of chapels were made similarly, not only this Catholic one but several throughout the town for the different denominations. The Anglican Chapel of St Peter's at the Locking Road end of Baytree Road was of a similar construction. The estimated size of our building is 24ft long, 14ft wide and 10ft high.

Photo by Sandys Photographic Service Ltd., Weston-super-Mare

The Milton Chapel of Our Lady of Lourdes as it was in 1923

Fr John Lyons blessed the church the evening before the first Mass was offered officially by the Rt Rev William Lee, Bishop of Clifton, on 29th July 1923. Priests from the Parish Church of Corpus Christi said Mass on Sundays and Holydays, with Catechism on Sunday afternoons for the children taken by the Nuns of La Retraite, and an Evening Service of Rosary and Benediction.

In the background of the picture above, there is a hedge marking the edge of the Church's land, with another farther south beside the narrow-gauge railway line of the Weston, Clevedon and Portishead Light Railway (1897 – 1940), which was originally conceived and built in the 1880s as a standard gauge tramway to link these coastal towns. From its terminus at the junction of Milton Road and Ashcombe Road, along what is now called "Colonel Stephens Way", the line travelled between the Milton and Locking Roads to Milton Road Station, Bristol Road Station out to Worle Town Station (close to Worle Recreation Ground) and beyond. It crossed Baytree Road to the south of our little chapel going through the main gates of what is now Baytree Road Recreation Ground. The main Bristol to Taunton railway line runs to the south of the site of this light railway. Colonel H F Stephens took over this light railway in 1911. He ran several similar railways and was known as the "Light Railway King".

By courtesy of Trisha Roberts

The "Hut" in June 1977 being used as a storage area after the building of the new Parish Hall in 1970.

Chapter 3

In the picture above, the wedding guests are milling about in front of the church. Behind them is the "The Hut" previously used as a Chapel, then a Parish Hall and now awaiting to be dismantled. The gable-end cross was removed some years before and "The Hut" has received a vent towards the front that was not there originally. The congregation must have been much hardier in those days. The new presbytery has not yet been built and in the background the Lombardy poplar trees planted in Baytree Road Recreation Ground are clearly visible. In the foreground there is still lawn between the path to the church and the "Hut".

Very few people had cars in those days so that the priests, who were no different in that respect, cycled back and forth from Corpus Christi on their push-bikes, carrying their vestments with them.

By 1933 it was becoming obvious that the "Hut" was going to be too small to deal with the increasing Catholic population of Worle so that more land adjoining Daniel Cotter's gift was purchased for £560. This land adjacent to Daniel Cotter's gift was on the corner of Milton Road and Baytree Road upon which our present church stands.

Early in 1938 when Mgr John Lyons was Parish Priest and Fr W Ryan was Curate at Corpus Christi, Bishop William Lee of Clifton gave permission for the building of our present Church. The building was 75 feet in length and 25 feet 6 inches wide, which would hold a congregation of 300. It was built in the Gothic style in Taunton Vale cream bricks laid in stretcher bond with firestone dressings, with dun-coloured Bridgwater tiles, and was completed in 1938 at a cost of £4000.

Bishop William Lee with Fr (later Canon) William Ryan, Fr M. O'Brien and the architect, Mr Willman of Taunton, were present at the laying of the foundation stone on Wednesday 20th April 1938. It was quite a simple ceremony, with only those intimately connected with the Church watching. The Bishop officiated, laying the stone while blessing it. He blessed other parts of the edifice, and offered prayers. Mgr John Lyons Parish Priest of Corpus Christi, who had been in hospital for some weeks but was well enough to leave, was allowed to sit patiently watching the ceremony.

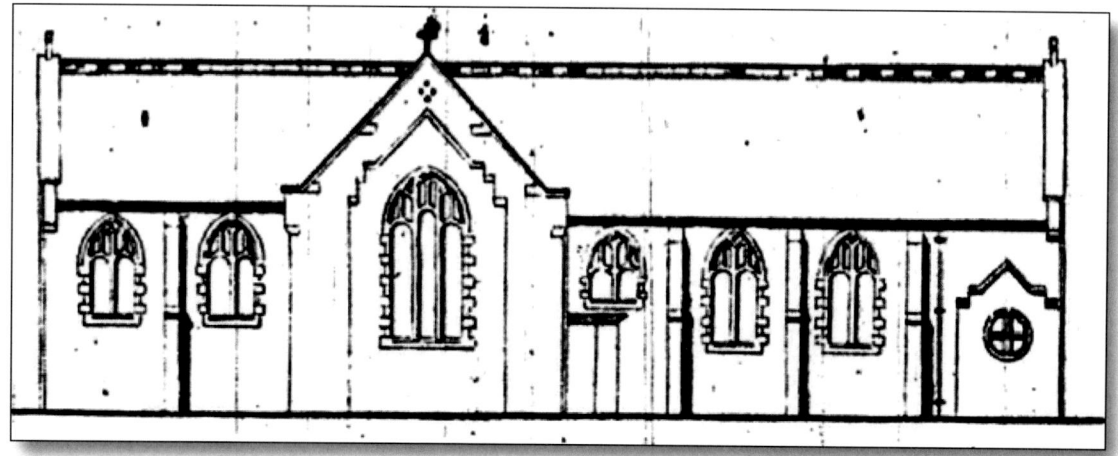

By courtesy of the Weston Mercury

The Church of Our Lady of Lourdes elevation to Milton Road.

By courtesy of Weston Mercury

The Milton Church Our Lady of Lourdes in July 1938, showing that the Church is still in construction with a pile of sand in the foreground right and a builder up a ladder at the extreme left.

By courtesy of David Pluck (19/11/2010)

A modern photograph of Our Lady of Lourdes, where apart from the traffic lights and the Savage family trees, the north side of the building looks the same in 2017 as it did in 1938.

Chapter 3

Sue Maguire 2017

The Foundation Stone on the eastern wall of the church on the right-hand side.

Sue Maguire 2017

A modern photograph of the entrance porch together with the statue of
Our Lady of Lourdes, the narthex windows, the three-light windows above and
the gable end cross.

Chapter 3

By courtesy of David Pluck (19/11/2010)

The statue of Our Lady of Lourdes above the entrance porch.

The photograph lower left (P106) was taken after the old oak wooden fence had been replaced on the north and west sides of the church by the brick wall with metal gates by Fr Martin Queenan. Above is a photograph of the statue of Our Lady of Lourdes directly above the entrance. Since this photograph was taken, Brian Griffin, who does much of the current work on the church, has restored the statue to its natural stone colour, including Our Lady's blue sash.

In a similar way to St Joseph's, the design of the church allowed for future extensions in the form of a chancel, sacristy and south transept. The planned extensions would result in a cruciform shape. The window tracery was of a free perpendicular character. The west elevation has a large three-light window above the entrance doors, which were both framed by a shallow recessed gabled arch. On the other side are circular narthex windows with mullions and transoms forming crosses.

The opening of our Catholic Church in Milton marked yet another milestone in the development of Weston's most progressive suburb: Worle was becoming dwarfed. Such was the situation in 1938. The Church was intended to serve Worle, Banwell and Locking as well as the burgeoning Milton. The architects were Messrs. Roberts and J H H Willman, ARIBA of Taunton and the contractors were the well-known firm of J Dyer & Son of Weston. We are told the contractors were glad of the work as it was at a time of economic recession, reflected in the very reasonable costs of the building. The steelwork was fabricated and erected by Burton Constructional and Engineering Co. Ltd. of Burton-on-Trent. The inside of the church was simple and quite in keeping with Catholic Gothic architecture. It was free from wall designs but the altar was thought very artistic.

Many people on passing the growing building, which dwarfed the old "Hut", became fascinated and some gave contributions to the cost of this new church. One of these from an outside source gave £1000, whilst another generous supporter gave a loan of £1000 interest free. There were other smaller donations for the interior furnishings and vestments. This left a shortfall of £1500, which eventually would have to be paid. The plan was to use the obsolete wooden hut as a youth club and other activities, which would help to generate money to repay the debt. It was still standing when the new presbytery was completed in October 1982 when it was used by the builders to store their materials.

In a semi-private ceremony on Wednesday evening, 31st August 1938, Mgr John Lyons VG, Parish Priest at Corpus Christi, who had worked tirelessly to guarantee the project would go through successfully, solemnly blessed and dedicated the new church. Assisted by Rev M O'Brien and Rev W Ryan and attendants, he walked around the outside of the Church three times sprinkling Holy water on the walls and then the altar and finally the interior walls. A small congregation in the church and outside watched the ceremony, accompanied by soft organ music and the sound of the traffic in Milton Road. People passed by oblivious to the sacred ceremony being carried out, and totally unaware that the following day, Thursday, there would be a magnificent opening ceremony consisting of the first sung Mass, a Mass of thanksgiving, celebrated by Dr William Lee, the Bishop of Clifton. The Pontifical High Mass would follow next day.

After the ceremony, Mgr John Lyons, in a brief address, said how glad he was to see such a good number present, and hoped as many as possible would attend the Mass of Dedication the following morning at 11 am to show their gratitude to God for such a beautiful church, "which we may regard as a further manifestation of God's blessing upon us in Weston-super-Mare." The Mass of Consecration would celebrate the opening of the Church with the Pontifical High Mass to follow on Friday 2nd September.

By courtesy of the Weston Gazette

The ceremony of blessing the church, which was carried out by Canon John Lyons on the Wednesday evening, 31st August 1938 (when photography in poor light was tricky)

Chapter 3

By 11am on Friday morning a huge congregation had arrived watched by a crowd of local people standing on the pavement outside amazed at the colourful spectacle they were witnessing. The congregation was so great that many could not gain admittance and had to kneel in the porch, whilst the organ loft was filled with visitors. The Mayor, Alderman Henry Butt JP, and Mrs Kelson, the Mayoress, were present, as were many Catholics from other parts of the Diocese. Shortly after 11.00am, the visiting clergy who had robed up in their multicoloured vestments in the temporary wooden chapel adjoining the Church, processed into the new Church, going from the old to the new, watched by the fascinated crowds outside, followed by the Bishop, who conferred his blessing as he proceeded down the aisle, accompanied by the Nuns from La Retraite Convent singing "Ecce Sacerdos Magnus".

By courtesy of Weston Gazette

The first Pontifical High Mass at Our Lady of Lourdes celebrated by Bishop William Lee on Friday 2nd September 1938. The photograph shows the old altar set against the East wall. The Priest says Mass with his back to the congregation so that all worshippers are facing the same way.

They offered the Mass up that morning in thanksgiving for the great benefits God had bestowed upon them in Weston-super-Mare in having a third church. Later in his address, Bishop William Lee, said he was pleased to see present that morning both the Mayor and Mayoress of their beautiful town, and to welcome them, for it was proof that they appreciated the efforts of the Catholics in their midst and that they had a true and full civic sense by paying and giving encouragement to each and every section of their community.

The Bishop then commenced the Pontifical High Mass assisted by Mgr Canon J Lyons VG. The Deacons-of-the-Throne were Provost C W Davey (Bridgwater) and Canon R A Iles (Taunton); Fr M O'Brien was the Deacon of the Mass and Fr F W Ryan, Sub-Deacon, whilst the duties of the MCs were discharged by Rev Denis Foran (Bishop's Secretary), and Mr John Charlesworth. Other clergy present were Mgr Canon B Lean (Burnham-on-Sea), Canon J J Casey (Minehead), Canon O'Riordan (Bristol), Rev J T Judge (St Joseph's), Rev Vellasis (Oratory at Burnham-on-Sea), P O'Beirne (Chard), T Cambourne (Southwark Diocese), J Murray (Minehead), Fr Raphael (Guardian at Clevedon), and Fr G H Richards. The choral parts of the Mass were sung by the Nuns of La Retraite Convent and the Proper by the men of the congregation.

After the Mass, a private lunch was held at the Grand Atlantic Hotel, and in the evening, there was Benediction at the Church of Our Lady of Lourdes.

By courtesy of Weston Gazette 3/9/38 digitally mastered by John Sach

After the Pontifical High Mass on 2nd September 1938.

Chapter 3

Sue Maguire 2017

Brian Griffin obtained this statue of Our Lady of Lourdes, and Fr Alexander Redman blessed it on the Feast Day of Our Lady of Lourdes, 11th February 2017. The Holy Water Font is the first object you see on entering the narthex of the church, where people dip their fingers to make the sign of the cross.

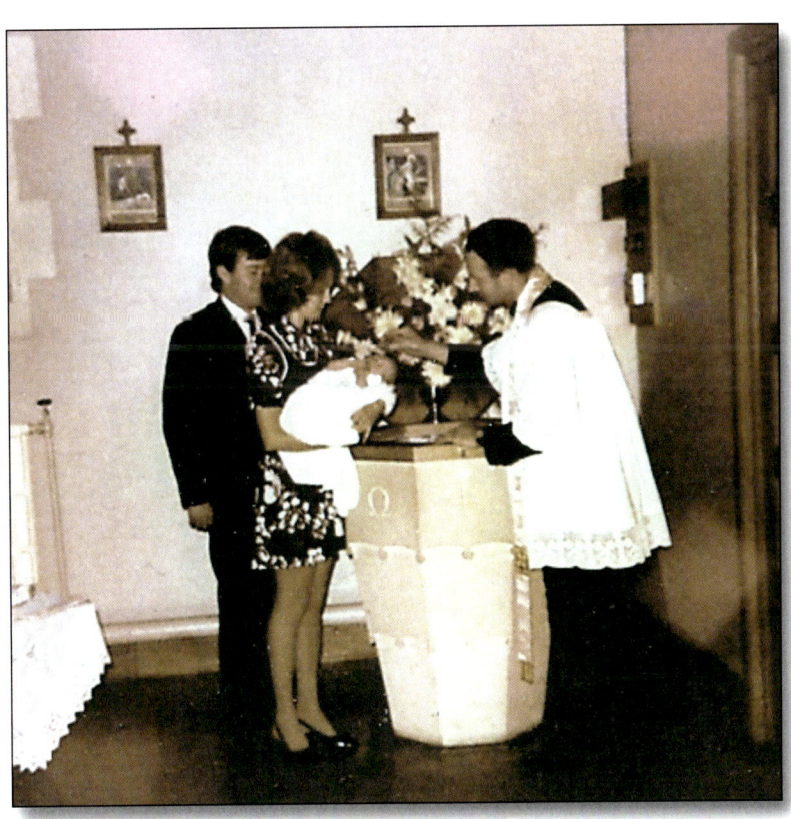

By courtesy of Jim and Sue Maguire 1972

The Christening of Charles Joseph Maguire on 27th August 1972, conducted by Rev Michael O'Sullivan and showing the stone font, situated where the Sacred Heart Statue of Our Lord now stands. The Stations of the Cross and the Holy Oils cabinet have since been replaced. Jack V Kingston was the Sacristan at this time.

Chapter 3

Before Vatican II the Sacrament of Baptism was quite often carried out on a Sunday afternoon about 3pm. Prayers were said in the narthex before entering the church, followed by the Sacrament of Baptism conducted just inside the church where the font would be situated, which in our church was to the right of the entrance doors where the statue of Our Lord currently stands. Once the baptism has been completed, the child becomes a full member of the Church.

The current practice is to conduct the Baptism during the Mass after the Homily, which is often directed at the children in the congregation, who are brought forward to get a better view. Instead of the congregation following by reciting the Apostles' Creed, all the members, including the parents and the Godparents retake their Baptismal Vows.

On the south side was a chamber containing the heating apparatus. The semi-circular roof trusses were concealed with plaster, which blended in well with the whiteness of the ceiling, as seen in the photograph of the organ loft taken from in front of the sanctuary.

The four-bay nave has pointed reinforced concrete transverse arches whose apex is just below the ceiling at collar-beam level. The sanctuary has crossing diagonal ribs forming a kind of rib vault.

Undated press cutting digitally mastered by John Sach

The above is an early picture taken before the south transept has been built.
There is a door leading from the sacristy directly into the sanctuary.
In the picture below this is hidden by the lady in the white coat.
There is another door leading into the sacristy opposite the
doors of the confessional.

Anon 1971

A wedding in 1971 celebrated by Fr Mervyn Alexander, still showing the church as it was when it was built in 1938, except for the colour scheme. The East window is hidden by the wall of the sacristy, which is parallel to the line of the pews, with the hymn number board attached to its edge. At first this is difficult to visualise. This gives a small corridor to the sacristy door, opposite which are the two doors of the confessional. This corridor is lit by the window over the confessional. The altar is against the East wall.

The sanctuary light hangs from the ceiling. Two windows lit the large sacristy.

A view across the church into the North Transept displaying the Lady Chapel showing that the sacristy in the North Transept has been removed and the East window is in full view. This allows for a Lady Chapel with additional pews. The South Transept has been added, containing a small chapel, additional pews and the new smaller sacristy. The altar has been moved forward and the alcoves are a relatively new feature. There were no changes to the church building between its opening in 1938 and 1976 for reasons that will become evident later.

The sanctuary light, now positioned on the wall near the tabernacle, was donated by Miss Eleanor Hussey, Sacristan, in memory of her parents.

Sue Maguire 2017

Chapter 3

By courtesy of David Pluck (19/11/2010)

Statue of Our Lord originally positioned at the left-hand side of the altar.

By courtesy of David Pluck (19/11/2010)

Statue of Our Lady originally positioned at the right-hand side of the altar.

Sue Maguire 2017

Part of the four-bay nave.

Sue Maguire 2017

The diagonal crossing ribs over the sanctuary.

Chapter 3

There is a wood block floor and all furnishings are carried out in light oak. When these oak pews are rubbed with linseed oil, they darken and the oil brings out the beautiful grain of the light oak in a startling way. The beautifully carved altar of white freestone was set off to advantage by the red carpeting of the original sanctuary.

Sue Maguire 2017

The wood block floor from the nave continues unchanged through the door of the sacristy and into it. The broken pattern reveals where the walls of the sacristy used to be. There is another door leading into the sacristy from the sanctuary, there is no mark on the floor to confirm its position.

Chapter 3

Sue Maguire 2017

The organ gallery showing the semi-circular roof trusses. On the balcony is a reproduction of a painting by Sassoferrato.

Sue Maguire 2017

The reproduction of the Virgin Mary by Giovanni Battista Salvi da Sassoferrato 1650.

Above the narthex is the organ gallery where a reproduction of a painting attributed to Sassoferrato hangs. Giovanni Battista Salvi da Sassoferrato (1609 – 1685), also known as Giovanni Battista Salvi, was an Italian Baroque painter known for his archaic commitment to Raphael's style. Some of his paintings are at the Benedictine Convent of San Pietro in Perugia (1630). This painting was damaged during Fr O'Sullivan's time and was repaired.

Our Church continued to be served from Corpus Christi throughout the Second World War, which began a year later in 1939. Although Weston-super-Mare was bombed quite heavily at times during the War, there was very little damage to Catholic churches or church property. Life continued as normal, and afterwards when the war was over, the clergy were still riding back and forth on bicycles from Corpus Christi to Milton.

Meanwhile the development of Milton as a residential area continued and the former wooden chapel saw sterling service as a parish social centre and fund raising base. What Catholic parish did not rely on Salvage Drives (collecting salvage for sale – a throwback to the war), Dances and Bingo Sessions to raise the necessary funds in those days? Paul Spindler eventually persuaded the organisers that prizes should be given at these events, which raised a great deal of income. Rose Wakley was a very intelligent and well-organised woman who carried out a great deal of work for the Parish. Paul used to mow the lawns for the priest, but when Fr O'Sullivan came he took over that duty as exercise, which he believed would be good for him.

Starting on 30 September 1961, for a fortnight, there was a mission run by two Franciscans, Fr Antony Rickards OFM and Fr Dunstan Baker OFM, who held instructional Mass and evening mission services at two churches in Weston, Our Lady of Lourdes and Corpus Christi, aiming to teach non-Catholics about the Catholic faith and to help others who are Catholic. Fr Antony was from Somerset and had been with the missions mainly in India. He was a member of the Clevedon community of the Franciscan Order. Fr Dunstan had run courses for non-Catholics in London. He joined the RAF during the war and afterwards took Holy Orders.

Although many parishioners, particularly children, found Fr Roche a bit frightening, one parishioner, Dorothy Tuckett did not. She would often go to him to suggest some new collection for a good cause. He would quietly listen and then, saying nothing, would simply stick his hand out. They achieved quite a lot in good causes.

The two similar brass nameplates marked Power to reserve their places were given to the Church by two spinster sisters, Marie Agnes (born 1879) and Winifred Mary (born 1889). They owned a millinery and gown shop at 34, Hill Road, Clevedon, from 1940 to 1965. Now 34 Hill Road is a large building in Clevedon that currently belongs to ATC Recruitment with a restaurant above.

Sue Maguire 2017

Chapter 3

Sue Maguire 2017

They lived not far from the Church, in Gillmore Road. Marie died at home the year after they sold the business, aged 87. Her sister, Winifred, continued to live in Gillmore Road until 1978, when she moved into Ryddenwood Nursing Home in Lower Bristol Road, Weston, where she died in 1987 aged 97.

On the end of one of the back pews is a brass plaque for Francis Ferguson, who died in Weston-super-Mare General Hospital in April 1972 aged 67. He was born in Liverpool in 1904 and married Agnes McAvady in 1927 in Oldham, Lancs. He was a retired Aircraft Engineer. They had three sons, Peter, Roy and Paul. Peter was the informant on Francis' death before he himself died in Clophill Bedford in 1982. Agnes died 6th December 1982.

Sue Maguire 2017

On the end of the opposite pew is a brass plaque for Edward Oatley, who was born in Wells in 1915, and died in the Royal Hospital in September 1971. He was ten days short of his 56th birthday. He was still working for the Bus Company as a District Traffic Superintendent. He married Margaret O'Dowd in 1941 in Wells, and they had five children - all born in the District of Wells - Maureen, Ita, Bernadette, Kieran and Christopher. Margaret died on 16th February 1991 aged 75. She lived at Homechime House, Prior Road, Wells.

Mr Christopher Oatley was one of the new members elected to the Parish Council in March 1974. He lived in 16 Cherrywood Rise, Worle. He oversaw transport arrangements for the Glastonbury Pilgrimage in 1974. He was a member of the Social Committee but left the Parish before April 1975.

Chapter 3

Sue Maguire 2017

Sue Maguire 2017

At first it was believed that the brass nameplate "Weakley" referred to Rosina Wakley, but Fr Martin Queenan assured us that the two names were different. One of the congregation then told us that Rose used to sit towards the back of the church and not in the pew marked "Weakley". After several weeks of asking if anyone could remember a family or a person called Weakley, it became obvious that the person or persons were completely forgotten, which seemed a shame.

A cursory glance through the telephone book revealed that there was only one person in there with the surname Weakley. In 1938 there were only nine householders in Weston named Weakely on the electoral roll, surprisingly Brigid appeared on it when she was 21. It is astonishing how successful a cold call can be. The person referred us to his aunt, Gillian Wall, née Weakley, who had made a family history of some of the Weakleys. In the past this group of families lived in the Kewstoke and Norton areas, which is where the Weakely nurseries used to be. The family supplied groceries to the local hotels in the region of Dauncey's at the North end of the promenade.

It was at Dauncey's or a nearby hotel where a young Irish woman, Brigid Malone, had come to work, and probably where she met Leonard John Weakley when he made deliveries. The story goes that they fell in love. The Weakley families were mainly Anglican but, nevertheless, they married at St Joseph's on 3rd February 1951. They were both born in 1928. Fr Daniel O'Callaghan (1948 – 1953), who celebrated the Wedding service, was a priest from Corpus Christi, while his Parish Priest was Canon Denis Ryan (1948 – 1958). The Parish Priest of St Joseph's was Canon J T Judge (1935 – 1959).

Chapter 3

Leonard and Brigid, who had two children, Geraldine and Paul, lived at the Elms, 110 Kewstoke Road from 1953 to 1980. Leonard died in 1982. In 2009/10 Brigid was in Nashley House Care Home and died on 1st April 2011. According to Gillian Wall, she had a Requiem Mass at Our Lady of Lourdes, but we have not been able to check this. She maintains that Brigid attended Our Lady of Lourdes but was not sure whether the children went there. Brigid Weakley is a possible candidate for the nameplate. However, they are not the only Catholic Weakleys who could lay claim to it.

Joyce Deakin was the housekeeper to both Fr Alexander and Fr O'Sullivan over 35 years. She made up two scrap books. In Book 1, why should she have sandwiched the political shenanigans of the Engineering Union members between the reports of Fr Mervyn Alexander becoming a Bishop in 1972 and various newspaper cuttings from 1975? More importantly, why should it be of interest to us?

The story was about a 35-year-old toolmaker living in Gowerton, Swansea, called John Weakley. With a colleague, Graham Healy, they had just won a High Court action over the retention of postal balloting. This legal action had resulted in the AEUW reversing its decision to drop postal balloting.

Weakley looked destined to reach the top echelons of the Union when he first made his name in the international sphere in the mid-seventies by taking on the powerful Union President, Hugh Scanlon in the High Court. The Union's ruling National Executive Committee was deadlocked 26 – 26 at its Annual Conference, and Scanlon was going to use his casting vote in favour of the Left, who were then opposing Labour's pay policy. Weakley persuaded the High Court to exclude Scanlon from voting at the union conference. It was the first of many victories for the right-wing led by Duffy, Weakley and General Secretary John Boyd. By taking control of the Union Executive in the late 1970s, the Right played an important rôle in stopping the rise of Tony Benn and the Left in the Labour Party in the early 80s.

John Weakley became a full-time Union official as the District Secretary in South Wales in 1977, and within two years he was on the ruling National Executive Council, eventually becoming its longest serving member. He was also the longest serving member of the TUC Council. It was believed that he was destined for better things but in 1986 Bill Jordan, his junior, became the Right-wing's official candidate to succeed Terry Duffy as President. Weakley never reached the top: he was a shrewd negotiator, but better known as a backroom fixer rather than a high-profile leader.

The interesting point for us is that above the clip picturing him in the scrapbook, Joyce had written, "John was a very good altar boy for many years at Our Lady of Lourdes, Milton."

Frank Bailey, when he was working for Bristol Aerojets, met John Weakley on 7 or 8 occasions when the Union man had business with the Management. Frank met him unexpectedly the last time, when Anita and he were invited by the Queen to the Buckingham Palace Garden Party. John Weakley was there with his wife. Although they were aware that they were both from Weston, neither knew the other aspect they had in common was Our Lady of Lourdes.

Charles Michael Weakley and his wife, formerly Mary Horgan, married in 1931 in Swansea. Charles was born in Bridgend on 6th Jauary1906, while Mary Horgan was born in 1905. They moved into 2 Jubilee Place, Milton, in 1943 with their two children, Terrence Charles who was born in Swansea in 1932 and Patrick John (known as John) was born 20th March 1940, again in Swansea. They attended Our Lady of Lourdes Church; John was confirmed at Corpus Christi in 1948 as they all were then; and they have a strong claim to being the family who had the brass nameplate put on the second large pew from the front on the right-hand-side facing the altar.

The family lived at the same address until 1963 with John apprenticed as a toolmaker in Bristol for British Aerospace, who gave him his initial career, after which he left home and married Margaret Susan Coles in 1963 at Corpus Christi on 29th September. Between 1972 and 1982 they lived at 5, Brookside, Bishwell Park, Gowerton, Swansea. He was a moderate shop steward at British Leyland's Llanelli factory. They had no children.

His older brother, Terrence Charles, died in 1967, and Mary died on 21st November 1970 aged 65, both still living at 2, Jubilee Path. Charles died on 4th January 1980 aged 74. He was still living in the same house.

John Weakley outlived them all and died on 23rd January 1995 in London aged 54. His death certificate lists his occupation as a Trade Union Executive.

Memories of two parishioners in the 50s and 60s

To end this chapter, we mention two memories that encompass this period and naturally lead into the next chapter.

Paulo Francesco Radmilovic (Raddy) by Joan Dunne

"I worked for Mr and Mrs Radmilovic at 'The Imperial' in Weston-super-Mare from 1960 to 1963 a couple of evenings a week. They were wonderful years and 'The Imperial' or 'The Imp', as it was affectionately known, was the most popular pub in Weston and I never remember any drunkenness.

Mr and Mrs Radmilovic always kept a lovely vase of flowers in the entrance hall and I remember her standing there welcoming all the customers and staff alike when they arrived. All the customers were well known to them and the pub was used a lot by RAF personnel as well as local people. How well dressed we all were then. I feel so proud to say I was a part of it.

Mr Radmilovic (of course we always addressed them by their surnames in those days) was a quiet, dignified man, and I do remember that Mrs Radmilovic's daughter-in-law, Peter's wife, had a lovely Christian name, Hermione, unusual then. I believe they had a granddaughter called Georgina. Their home was in a flat above the pub, but they moved to Worlebury when he retired.

There were 4 bars, the front lounge and TV room, middle bar and public bar at the back, known as 'Jacko' bar, again no drunkenness ever, just good companionship and laughter. I served Acker Bilk and his band in the middle bar. I remember he did enjoy his whiskey!

Chapter 3

By courtesy of Joan Dunne 1961

This picture was taken outside the Imperial, "The Imp", in 1961 showing Joan Dunne (née Petheram) on the left with Ruth and another member of staff in front of Mr Radmilovic. (Joan Dunne was Consort Lady Mayoress of Weston-super-Mare in 2015.)

Meals were served on the premises and lovely steak pies were sold. We used to buy ourselves one after our shifts.

My name then was Joan Petheram, a lot of people here still call me that. I moved away from Weston in the mid-60s after marrying a serviceman but, on a trip home once, I remember meeting Mrs Radmilovic in Grove Park and we chatted about all the old customers at 'The Imp' – happy memories. I believe Mr Radmilovic was in good health then.

I know very few people in Weston would have known Mr and Mrs Radmilovic so I am proud to have had that privilege. I would say this to their grandson if I met him that it was an honour to work for them. All the time I worked there, I never knew how famous he was."

Paulo Francesco Radmilovic – A Local Report

"Paulo Radmilovic has won more gold medals than any other British water sports athlete and, until Steve Redgrave collected his fourth gold in 1996, had more gold medals than any other British Olympian. 'Raddy', as he was widely known, was born in Cardiff, Wales, in 1886 and proved his athletic prowess early on, winning selection for the National water polo side at the tender age of 18. He was an international swimmer from the age of 16 until he was 45. He moved to Weston in 1904, and all his Olympic successes came while he lived in our town.

A first taste of Olympic competition came in 1906 at the Intercalated Games, which is no longer officially recognised as an Olympics. Raddy finished fourth in the 100m freestyle and fifth in the 400m. His most successful games came in London in 1908. It was there he won gold in the Water Polo Final against Belgium, and was drafted into the 4x200m relay squad at the last minute, to take another gold medal. He was also part of the winning water polo team in Stockholm in 1912, and it would be his goal again in 1920 at Antwerp. He also competed in both the 1924 and 1928 Games, before retiring from the Olympics aged 42. In a remarkable career spanning two decades, he won numerous English and Welsh titles, before running The Imperial Hotel, in South Parade, for many years, with his wife, Madge. They had three children, Anne, Peter and Paul.

By courtesy of Weston Mercury 1907

By courtesy of Weston Mercury 1907

Paulo Radmilovic 'Raddy', Weston's 4x200 relay Gold Medal Winning Olympic Swimmer – 1907

Raddy in action – diving (1907)

Raddy continued to be involved in water sports as a referee throughout his time in Weston and had a long association with the Weston Swimming Club. He was also a keen golfer, boxer and snooker player, and he and his wife lived at Selwood House, Worlebury.

In 1967, he was the first British swimmer to be inducted into the International Swimming Hall of Fame. He died a year later, aged 82, in October 1968. His Requiem Mass was held at Our Lady of Lourdes and he was buried in Milton Road Cemetery. He was a humble and quiet man and if you had met him you would know of his achievements only from others.

A blue plaque recognising the achievements of one of the country's greatest Olympians has been unveiled in Weston, and the ceremony was attended by local dignitaries, also Paulo's grandson, Simon Siddall. Paulo Radmilovic, known as 'Raddy, won four gold medals in water polo and swimming while he was living in the town. The plaque has been unveiled at The Imperial pub, in South Parade, which Mr Radmilovic used to run. Weston Town Council has paid for the plaque, and it is the first of 13 that will recognise famous names from the town's history.

By courtesy of Weston Mercury 2017

Paulo Radmilovic's grandson, Simon Siddall, with 'Raddy's' plaque.

Weston by Maureen Spicer (née Fay)

"I was born in 1949 and throughout my childhood lived in the Milton area of Weston-super-Mare. Our Lady of Lourdes was always considered our home parish. However, for much of my childhood the priests serving Our Lady of Lourdes church came from Corpus Christi and resided in the presbytery there. This situation did not change until Our Lady of Lourdes acquired its first presbytery, a house on the Milton Road, close to the church. I am not sure when exactly this happened, but I suspect I must have been at secondary school by then.

Weston was served by the Catholic Primary School, Corpus Christi. La Retraite Convent provided primary school education but was a fee based school. Both myself and my brothers, Patrick and Kevin, attended Corpus Christi school until we reached secondary school age. This would have been the case for a number of Catholic families living in the area. Our friends of primary school age were often those we met through a combination of school and parish life. Once we reached secondary school age both my brothers went on to attend secondary schools in the area, but these were not Catholic schools as there was no local Catholic secondary education for boys in Weston. I went on to attend La Retraite Convent. My memories of Our Lady of Lourdes Parish were predominantly formed when I was under 11 years of age. Some of the families we became friendly with through links with school and parish life included the Macey family, the Quan family, and the Slattery family (who in later life ran the Lamb Inn in Worle), to name but a few.

Looking back, it is striking how closely our lives revolved around the school, the church and the activities that took place within both. I distinctly remember the old church hall which, when we were children, was the venue for Sunday school parties, the showing of silent movies, together with various church events and meetings etc. I understand that the old church hall was used as the original church prior to the present church being built. My brother Patrick remembers the time when the area between the old church hall and the present church was used for sports day events for the children. This once grassed area has long since disappeared to tarmac for car parking and the old church hall demolished to make way for the present presbytery and newer much larger church hall.

My mother, Bridget Fay, was a very active member of the parish, taking part in the CWL (Catholic Women's League), together with the Legion of Mary, regular church cleaning, helping out with jumble sales, and making refreshments during the bingo evenings that took place in the rooms above the old co-op on the Milton Road. In addition, she was a regular visitor of the elderly and sick within the parish and also took up the role of catechist at Sunday school sessions within the parish.

My father, James Fay, worked for the nuns (The Poor Servants of the Mother of God) at Totterdown Hall, the convent at Oldmixon. I used to visit Totterdown Hall with my father where he worked managing and maintaining the convent gardens. The convent and grounds provided an idyllic environment within which I played happily on many occasions as a young girl. I believe there was only one entrance and that was via the main gates followed by a drive to the convent, off the road on the Oldmixon side (Hutton Road). I cannot recall any other entrance to the grounds.

Dad worked at the convent virtually all his working life until he suffered bouts of illness that eventually led to his untimely death in 1969, at the age of 53. Dad also played an active role within church activities and was a 'pools' collector when this fund-raising activity was run in the Corpus Christi Parish.

As young children, we used to attend church three times on a Sunday. Morning Mass took place at 8.30am and 10am Catechism (Sunday school) took place in the afternoon and finally Benediction in the evening. As a young girl, I was allowed to climb up the wooden stairs to the choir stalls at the back of the church where I joined the choir for Benediction each Sunday evening. I must have been quite small as I can remember peering over the balcony to see the congregation below. I suspect that the choir tolerated me rather than I being an asset for my singing voice! Both my brothers were altar boys. Patrick remembers one day when he was serving with another altar boy and discovered the book he was using had several pages missing, which unfortunately held vital clues and instructions on what his duties were during various parts of the Mass. Luckily a parishioner attending the Mass approached the altar rails and relayed instructions to the altar boys which, on this occasion, saved the day.

Chapter 3

The priests I remember most from my childhood are Fr (Edmund) Murphy and Fr (Michael) Roche. They were a big part of both school and parish life and I have fond memories of them both. Fr (Mervyn) Alexander (our then future Bishop) was Parish Priest as I was approaching adulthood. I remember him as a gentle and very kind man. As Parish Priest, he officiated at my wedding to Terry in 1970.

Although Fr (Henry) Carter was not a parish priest at Our Lady of Lourdes, I have clear memories of him as Parish Priest of St Joseph's Church. As teenagers, we were in total awe as he rode his motor bike around the town. My brother Kevin remembers him as legendary for saying Mass quickly, with the weekend evening Mass often taking just twenty minutes.

My First Confession, First Holy Communion and Confirmation all took place at Corpus Christi Church, while I was a pupil at Corpus Christi School. The school played a big part in the preparation for the sacraments.

There were also several events that took place in the Corpus Christi Parish, such as the annual Summer Fête held in Ellenborough Park. This event always felt very much a celebration across the parishes.

There are several people I remember as active members of Our Lady of Lourdes. These include Miss (Mary) Porter, Mrs (Rose) Macey, Miss Drake, Mrs Wilkins, Mrs Westbury, Mr & Mrs Brooks, and Mr & Mrs Murphy. There were many other active people in the parish, those I have mentioned are just a small number that I can remember. Mr Brooks was either choir master or church organist - perhaps both.

When I was in my late teens, my dad was worried about me cycling to the Technical College and bought me an NSV Quickly motor cycle, which was always breaking down and ending up with Mr [Harold] Macey who would fix it, until the next time. We cycled everywhere in those days: the whole family had push-bikes. Mum was still cycling to Mass every day when she was in her eighties. We had to confiscate the bike eventually for her own safety. The traffic along Milton Road had increased alarmingly since she was young. She died in 2004.

If my memory serves me correctly, Mr Murphy used to film parish event(s) - probably using a cine-camera at the time. Mr Murphy lived in Westbrook Road, close to the church. I believe there may have been some footage of the May Queen procession and celebrations when I was May Queen. I would have been about 8 or 9 years old at the time. Kevin, my brother, served as an altar boy on the day. It was quite a parish event! If this film exists and if there are any others like it, is it possible that these are held within parish archives? If so, then this would capture images of parishioners from years gone by and could also be of great interest to today's parishioners and the 'history of the parish project'."

*

In the early 50s there were many push-bike families; priests biked to church, children biked to school, fathers biked to work, nearly everyone biked everywhere; there were few motor vehicles, making the roads much safer for cycling than now. The schools provided cycle sheds to which the children locked their valuable mobile possession, while behind them some of the bolder school children indulged in the dangerous act of smoking. This lack of mobility meant that people had less choice than we do, money was tight and rationing was still in force for a while, so that people remained at home, went to local clubs or societies, sent children to Sunday School, even if they were not religious - Sunday afternoons were sacrosanct. Of the priests in the two dioceses only Fr Henry Carter of St Joseph's had a car, but everything changed in the 60s once the motorways arrived and people had more money.

By 1964, it was decided that the growth of Worle and Milton justified Our Lady of Lourdes having its own parish. There was sufficient money in the coffers and enough priests to serve Milton.

CHRONOLOGY

	1886	Paulo Radmilovic was born on 5th March.
	1914	Milton Road was extended from the corner of Baytree Road to Worle High Street.
	1914-18	The first World War.
	1922	The Milton Rise Council houses were built.
	1923	Daniel Cotter gave land at the corner of Baytree Road and Milton Road to Corpus Christi to build a Chapel-of Ease called Our Lady of Lourdes. Fr John Lyons blessed the building the evening before the first Mass was offered officially by the Rt Rev William Lee, Bishop of Clifton, on 29 July.
	1930	St Peter's Anglican Chapel was built at the south end of Baytree Road.
	1933	Land adjacent to that of Our Lady of Lourdes was bought for £560. The growth of Weston and Worle justified the building of a larger Our Lady of Lourdes in Milton when the money was available.
	1938	Bishop William Lee of Clifton gave permission for the building of our present Church. He was present, with Fr William Ryan, Fr M O'Brien and the architect, Mr Willman of Taunton, at the laying of the foundation stone on Wednesday 20th April. Building was rapid and the blessing of the church was carried out by Canon John Lyons on the Wednesday evening, August 31st. The following day there was a Mass of Thanksgiving. The Pontifical High Mass was celebrated on Friday 2nd September. The former Chapel-of-Ease was used as a Parish Hall.
	1940	Weston, Clevedon and Portishead Light Railway closed (1897 – 1940).
	1961	Two Franciscans, Fr Antony Rickards OFM and Fr Dunstan Baker OFM ran a Mission for a fortnight starting on 30th September.
	1965	The present Anglican Church of St. Peter's was being constructed to replace the small chapel, which then became their Parish Hall.
	1968	Paulo Radmilovic died on 29th September. The rapid growth of Worle caused by the motorway justified plans for extension of Our Lady of Lourdes in Milton when money was available.

CHAPTER 4 - THE PARISH OF OUR LADY OF LOURDES

4.1 Fr William O'Callaghan – Parish Priest 1964 - 1967

By courtesy of the Weston Mercury 25th Feb. 1967

On Sunday 18th October 1964, Our Lady of Lourdes, Milton, became an independent parish separate from Corpus Christi, and Fr William O'Callaghan LCL was appointed our first Parish Priest. He was born in 1925, a native of County Cork in Ireland. He was ordained at St John's Waterford in 1948, studied Canon Law in Rome for two years, and then in 1950 was appointed first as a curate at the Pro-Cathedral in Bristol and then in 1952, he went to the Parish of St Nicholas of Tolentino as a curate before becoming Secretary to Bishop Joseph Rudderham in 1954. He spent 10 years there before coming to Milton. In his duty as Secretary to the Bishop, he became very familiar with Milton, celebrating Mass several times.

He left in 1967 to go to be Parish Priest at The Immaculate Conception, Stroud, and later to St Anthony's, Henbury and finally St Joseph's at Portishead. He was always good company with his amusing and kind observations of life and will always be remembered for his faith, sincerity and care of the sick. He had a great devotion to Our Lady and did much to promote the Legion of Mary. It was no surprise when he was appointed Canon of the Cathedral Chapter. His housekeeper, Mary, was a great blessing to him, nursing him through bouts of sickness and through to health until when he retired he could boast of a long period of good health, until he eventually fell ill and died in 2003.

Funds did not permit the immediate building of a presbytery, but fortunately a house in Milton Road just opposite the church had become available at a reasonable price. Sufficient land was available on the other side of the church in Baytree Road for a presbytery when funds allowed.

The Rev W J Ryan, the Parish Priest of Corpus Christi, told the Mercury reporter that the parishioners of Milton had been looking forward for a very long time to the day when they would have their own parish. In preparation for this event, there had been some improvements to the church, with the installation of a new tabernacle and a new organ.

Separating Milton from Corpus Christi meant that the latter would lose one of its curates, Fr Francis Nugent, who was to move to Swindon. This would leave Fr Ryan with Fr Martin Fitzpatrick at Corpus Christi.

Chapter 4

When Fr O'Callaghan arrived, the financial arrangements he had to accept were:

1. Milton Parish would be responsible for £10,000 of the remaining debt for Corpus Christi School.

2. Corpus Christi Parish would contribute £1000 towards the cost of 253 Milton Road recently bought as a temporary presbytery.

3. Corpus Christi Parish would lend £1000 towards furnishing the Presbytery.

4. Milton Parish would retain the income from offertories, the bingo, and its proportion of the football pool.

This immediately put the Parish of Our Lady of Lourdes finances under pressure, and consequently there were no changes to the church building between its opening in 1938 and 1976. This has enabled us to use many modern photographs to illustrate points where we have found no photographs taken at the actual time.

Sue Maguire October 2017

The original Presbytery at
253 Milton Road.

Sue Maguire October 2017

Many Catholic priests, it is said, would walk through walls to get out of the pouring rain to and from church. The truth is in the text below.

During the war years there was little opportunity for fund-raising projects apart from the "regulars" mentioned, but after 1945/6 a Milton Presbytery Building Fund had been built up in the Diocesan accounts amounting to £1830, which was paid towards the purchase price of 253 Milton Road.

In those days, parts of the church grounds were still used as allotments. Efforts were made to get the holders to vacate their plots. It took time! The land was given over to lawn.

Chapter 4

You will notice that there is a path leading directly away from the north-east corner of the church towards the wall, and across Milton Road to the old presbytery, at number 253. The oak fence had a gate cut into it by Fr O'Sullivan in 1974, two years after he arrived, and concrete slabs were put across the lawn, probably by him. Until then the priests had to walk around the perimeter fence in all weathers to enter the church grounds via the front gates.

When the new presbytery was built in 1982 on the other side of the church, and the oak fence was replaced by a wall in 2004 by Fr Queenan, the concrete slabs across that section of grass became redundant, and no gate was needed in the wall. The slabs are also in danger of being removed.

Now that Our Lady of Lourdes had become a parish in its own right, the congregation had to take over positions and responsibilities. Below is a summary of some of the early meetings, sadly, not from the very beginning, but almost.

The first of the Men's Meetings recorded in the archives was held in the Parish Hall on Tuesday 5th October 1965, with Gordon Brooks as Chairman, the Secretary was Clement Smith and members present were Messrs Corrigan, Phillips and Jack Kingston. Mr Fovargue sent apologies. Rev Dr Mervyn Alexander visited. Regrettably there was lack of support for these open meetings so that it was decided to discontinue them in their present form. In future, Fr William O'Callaghan invited specific members of the congregation to serve on particular committees when he felt it necessary to hold a meeting. It was hoped that this method would encourage members of the congregation to take a fuller part in parish affairs. The minutes of an earlier meeting (not extant) were accepted, and it was decided that in future the Parish Priest would be Chairman thereafter. Gordon Brooks, who always had a rather severe countenance, was the organist and choir master. By profession he was an Estate Agent, who eventually had his own agency at 56 Severn Road in 1968. He was always a prominent member of any meeting.

The arrangements for the next recorded meeting, on Wednesday 23rd March 1966, saw Fr William O'Callaghan as Chairman, with Clement Smith as Secretary, and the members present were Messrs Gordon Brooks, P. Groves, Jack Kingston, Phillips, Clement Smith, Fovargue, D. O'Connell, Fitzgerald and M. Tasnier. Messrs John Savage, Keys, R. McCarthy and P. Groves sent their apologies. John Savage, a woodwork master from St Brendan's Catholic School (now St Brendan's Sixth Form College) in Bristol did a great deal of the church's maintenance.

The beginnings of organisation saw rotas for the Holy Week readers and for the ushers and the collectors, leading eventually to the introduction of monthly rotas for these duties to be given to the Parish Priest. In 1966, the Society of St Vincent de Paul was formed and five members attended the conference every Sunday; a date was set for the Garden Fête; and the allotment holders were to be asked to vacate their plots, which surrounded the church and hall, as soon as their notice expired.

Miss G Drake was responsible for the church brass in April 1974. She was welcomed to the Parish Committee in 1969 and was Sacristan in 1967.

The church finances were not healthy: had it not been for the success of the bingo and the income from the football pools the Parish would have been insolvent. The Committee decided to circulate details of the parlous state of the Parish finances to all parishioners to encourage them to increase their contributions to the "Envelope Scheme" and to inspire others to join it.

By courtesy of Weston Mercury 25th February 1967

Before he leaves to take up an appointment in Gloucester, parishioners of Our Lady of Lourdes, Milton, presented to Rev W O'Callaghan a new lectern to recall that he was their first Parish Priest. It was formally presented by the Sacristan, Miss G Drake (sitting second left). Gordon Brooks in glasses is standing directly behind the lectern.

John Sachs

When Father William O'Callaghan left in 1967, a light-oak lectern was purchased for the church to commemorate his time as first Parish Priest.

The presentation plate attached to the new lectern set on the sanctuary of Our Lady of Lourdes Church in Milton, and recalling that Father William O'Callaghan served as its first Parish Priest from 1964 to 1967.

4.2 Fr Edward Hickey – Parish Priest 1967 - 1967

By courtesy of the Archives of the Bishop of Clifton

Fr Edward Hickey came to Weston at the beginning of March to succeed Fr William O'Callaghan. Fr Hickey was a teacher before he was ordained in 1934. He made his name through his work in the field of education in the Diocese. For some years, he was the Clifton Catholic Diocesan Religious Inspector of Schools, was a member of the Board of Diocesan Inspectors of Schools and Clifton Catholic Diocesan Schools Commission representative for the area of the Gloucestershire County Local Education Authority.

During the war, he served as a Chaplain in the Forces. Later he became Parish Priest in Chippenham, followed by Parish Priest in Stroud for 12 years before coming as a replacement for Fr O'Callaghan.

By reputation he was a lively and friendly person who was an excellent raconteur with a flair for imaginary anecdotes, which made him very popular. He never bored his audiences, whether they be clergy on retreat, or his own parishioners. Sadly, our parish did not benefit from this because he was Parish Priest for only a very short time in 1967 – about two months.

When he arrived, the Chairman of the Parish Council, Bert (Herbert) Wilson either noticed or had been told to keep an eye on him. Bert Wilson was Chairman of the Parish Council for 8 years.

Fr Hickey's early departure was a shock to the Bishop, leaving a hole in our Parish. During an interregnum, priests from Corpus Christi and friars from Clevedon gave the services until a new Parish Priest could be found.

Fr Edward Hickey's obituary states: "Ted's ill health compelled him to pass the next two years on sick leave." When he returned he took up his last appointment as Chaplain to Prior Park Preparatory School, Cricklade, and to have the pastoral care of the small Catholic Community in town. Regrettably his illness returned in 1972 and he retired to St Angela's Convent in Clifton, Bristol, operated by The Sisters of the Temple, where he died peacefully on 5th December 1977.

There was already some lay participation in practical matters within the church, and efforts were made to encourage this. A St Vincent de Paul Society group had been formed in 1966 with five members and this continued until 1992. The parish started a Catholic Women's League in 1968.

The covering letter dated 4th August 1967 was sent to Fr William Ryan, Parish Priest of Corpus Christi, possibly because Fr Edward Hickey had already left Our Lady of Lourdes owing to sickness.

Telephone 33072　　　　　　　　　　ST. AMBROSE, LEIGH WOODS, BRISTOL, 8.

4th August, 1967.

Dear Father Ryan,

<u>re erection of Milton Parish</u>.

Will you kindly post up the enclosed in your Church porch, together with a note to the effect that parishioners are invited to make their comments, and if no objection is received within fourteen days then the decree will become law. You could explain to your people that this is a canonical procedure.

With all good wishes,
Yours sincerely,

W. J. Mitchell
Bishop's Secretary.

Corpus Christi, WESTON.

Chapter 4

JOSEPH
Dei et Apostolicae Sedis Gratia
EPISCOPUS CLIFTONIENSIS

Since the spiritual needs of the people of the Parish of Corpus Christi in the Town of Weston-super-Mare in the County of Somerset in this Diocese cannot be adequately attended to because of its large territory and the smallness of its Church,

Having duly consulted our Cathedral Chapter and all interested parties, as the law demands,

WE, JOSEPH RUDDERHAM, by the grace of God and the favour of the Apostolic See Bishop of Clifton,

By virtue of these Letters do hereby divide the territory of the said Parish of Corpus Christi and do erect the Mission Church of Our Lady of Lourdes, Baytree Road, Milton, Weston-super-Mare, which hitherto has belonged to the Parish of Corpus Christi, as the Parochial Church of a new Parish of Milton.

The limits of the said new Parish of Our Lady of Lourdes, Milton, shall be those already agreed and acted upon by the Parish Priest of Corpus Christi, Weston, and by the resident Priest-in-Charge at Milton. Maps shall be drawn up and we reserve to ourselves the right to make any alteration in the boundaries of the Parish.

The Parish shall belong to the Deanery of Christ The King, Bristol.

The endowment of the New Parish shall consist in the voluntary offerings of the faithful, in the stole fees to be paid according to our Diocesan laws and customs, and in the Church buildings and other property belonging to or to be acquired in the future by the Parish.

The new Parish Church shall enjoy all the rights and privileges attached by Common Law to a Parish Church, and the rights and obligations of the Parish Priest for the time being shall be those determined by Common Law and by our Diocesan law and customs.

All things to the contrary notwithstanding.

Given at Clifton, this Third day of August 1967.

+ Joseph
Bishop of Clifton.

By order of my Lord Bishop.

W. J. Mitchell
Secretary.

By courtesy of the Archives of the Bishop of Clifton

Letter outlining the Parish Boundary of Our Lady of Lourdes.

4.3 Fr Dr Mervyn Alban Alexander – Parish Priest 1968 -1972

By courtesy of the Archives of the Bishop of Clifton

Fr Dr Alexander was born in 1925 in Highbury, London. He trained for the priesthood at the Venerable English College in Rome and was ordained in Rome in 1948 at the Leonine College. He continued his theological studies at the Pontifical Gregorian University, Rome, obtaining a Doctorate in Divinity in 1951. When he finally returned to England, he was appointed as Assistant Priest in the Cathedral Parish, Clifton, Bristol, where he served from 1951 to 1964. He acted as the Chaplain to the Bristol Maternity and Homeopathic Hospitals, and in 1953 served as part-time Chaplain to the University of Bristol. He was appointed as full-time Chaplain in 1964. In 1967, he was appointed as Parish Priest at Our Lady of Lourdes, taking up his appointment the following year. The first thing he did was to buy a dog named Tessa. She was a mongrel, an Old English Sheepdog with a few bits extra. She was big, shaggy and very affectionate.

When Fr Mervyn Alexander moved into the presbytery he advertised for a permanent housekeeper. Joyce Deakin applied for the position and was appointed in 1968. She had lived with her parents in a Council house they rented in Milton Brow. When they died, Joyce continued living there. She married and had a son. Her husband, William, was killed during the Second World War and she brought up her son, Alan, alone. After Alan had grown up and left home, Joyce saw that the new Parish Priest wanted a housekeeper to live in and she successfully applied for the position, but she still maintained her house in Milton Brow.

While in Weston, Fr Alexander was Chaplain to various groups of doctors, nurses and teachers. He was Chairman of the Diocesan Religious Education Centre and a leading member of the Diocesan Ecumenical Movement as well as being Chairman of the local Council of Churches. He instigated a Parish Mission with the Franciscans. He was a keen golfer, as a number of the local Catholic priests were.

Fr Alexander quickly became very popular. He particularly liked children, who used to grab his hands and pull him every which way while the priest was trying to have a serious conversation with their parents. Tessa was the same when she took Father for a walk.

Fr Alexander greatly encouraged the idea of a Parish Council with free and open discussion. When he arrived, he changed the structures of the meetings: they were no longer Men's Meetings chaired by Mr Gordon Brooks or the Parish Priest but Parish Council Meetings. The first meeting of these was held in the Church Hall on Friday 5th July 1968. Fr Dr Mervyn Alexander presided and from then the President was the Parish Priest. Those present were: Mrs Cosker, Joyce Deakin, House, Rae Kirkham, R McCarthy and H Townsend; the Misses Kingston and M Prescott; Messrs D O'Connell, P Groves, Gordon Brooks, Jack Kingston, A E F Lambourne, R McCarthy, B F Mullin,

J Barber, John Savage and Clement Smith; with apologies from Mrs Brooks, Mrs Groves, Misses J Wilkins and M Tasnier.

Fr Mervyn Alexander addressed the gathering, suggesting that the offices of Chairman, Vice-chairman and Secretary should be created, and he called for nominations. Mr D O'Connell was elected as Chairman, with Mr P Groves as Vice-chairman and Mr Clement Smith as Secretary. Fr Alexander immediately vacated the Chair in favour of Mr D O'Connell. The Council decided that Fr Alexander should invite Mr Fitzgerald to be the Council Treasurer. In this way, the new meetings were introduced.

Women had their roles: Miss M. Prescott had been involved with the combined parishes' Garden Fête. She had also been involved with organising flowers for the altar, a job that had become the province of Mrs Brooks. This led to a discussion of the formation of separate committees to be a permanent feature of the Council. Each committee would be involved with a particular task or tasks, such as dealing with newspapers and repository and church and brass cleaning ('should it be paid' was asked).

In the next meeting of the Parish Council on 6th September 1968, matters arising were settled, Miss J Wilkins agreeing to assist with secretarial duties, Miss Linda Smith would assist with the repository while the altar flowers were in the hands of Mrs H Townsend. In addition, elections to the various committees were held. Mr H Wilson gave a report on the results of the three Parishes' Fête during which £1065 was raised, while the raffle raised £400; Mr J Barber gave a report on the repository; and the report on the Church Grounds was left to the Parish Priest. In the following meeting (13th December), Mr M Tasnier reported on welfare; Mr H Wilson reported on social; Mr J Savage reported on Church fabrics; there was no report on Liturgy as Mr and Mrs Groves had moved; Mr J Barber apologised for not reporting on Ecumenical; and Fr Alexander reported that Mr Fitzgerald would continue to deal with the cash counting and the bills, and would attend committee meetings in an advisory capacity. The following committees were set up: Finance, Management, Liturgical, Social and Fête, Ecumenical, Welfare and Church fabrics and grounds. As time went by short-lived committees were formed to deal with specific projects. One very important one was building the new Parish Hall.

The Finance Committee was responsible for managing the "Liquidation of the Parish Debt", a Covenant Scheme with the use of Offertory Envelopes, and a collection box for World Poverty relief(Cardinal Heenan had suggested 1% of Parish income for this cause).

Fr Alexander had shaped the administrative structure of the Parish Council with the Parish Priest as President, a Chairman and Vice-chairman, and each committee with a Chairman who reported to the Parish Council on progress since the previous meeting. In addition, there was an Annual General Meeting with a review of the year's work and future planning.

Comparatively recently, Pope John Paul II stated that councils should be concerned with the spiritual life of the parish rather than the fabric of the church and its grounds. A Parish Pastoral Council should support the work of the Parish Priest. Bishop Declan later formed a policy that the councils should be Pastoral Councils concerned with the welfare of the Parish. The sole legal requirement for parishes is that each must have a Finance Committee accountable to the Diocese.

Apart from setting up the various committees, the Parish started its own branches of the Catholic Women's League (1968), the St Vincent de Paul Society (1966), the Knights of St Columba (1973) and St Margaret's Guild (1973).

The first mention of the Catholic Women's League (CWL) in Milton was in the Welfare Committee meeting of December 1968 when Mrs H Townsend was elected as Chairman. A request was made for their members to liaise with the members of the Society of the St Vincent de Paul (SVP). A 1969 report stated that The Old Folks' Party of 20 people was a great success as was a Children's Party held in January 1969. The CWL and SVP worked together as the years went by. The SVP carried out the Parish visiting and joined with the CWL in organising parties, charitable works and fund-raising. One of these concerned donating a silver Communion paten to the Hospital chapel, as reported in the Weston Mercury. Many social events such as skittles evenings would be arranged by the CWL. In 1975, the CWL jointly of St Joseph's and Our Lady of Lourdes had arranged a very successful Old Folks' Party. Twenty of these partygoers came from our Parish.

In 1979, when Mrs Helen Salt was Chairman, there were far more details of the CWL activities: various members supported Junior Catechism Camps both locally and nationally; a fund was set up. A Cheese & Wine event for the "Year of the Child" raised £185; also a bring-and-buy morning was held, and a jumble sale that brought in £55.

The members in 1979 were still quietly very active in various charitable works. In 1982, Mrs Wyn Bray who was new to the Parish, said there were 30 active members who assisted in many outside charities, e.g. muscular dystrophy and Cheshire Homes; members still met on the third Tuesday of each month. A coach trip to Worcester, and a Wine and Buffet Fair were being arranged.. As usual they were assisting in the First Communion Breakfast and in the Fête.

There was a trip to Prinknash Abbey in 1985, and in 1986 the CWL raised a £100 in the March Jumble Sale. In April, they donated £100 to the New Hospital Fund. The photograph from 1998 shows that the CWL was still going strong.

Kath Reynolds was Chairperson in 1996 and in 1997 Monica Morrison was secretary and Anita Bailey was Treasurer. She handed that position over to May O'Reagan, but the CWL was drawing to a close in Milton: the coach trips were becoming increasingly expensive and the younger women of the Parish did not want to take over responsibility for organising the CWL as in the past. Far more women were working full time than ever before, yet still had to run a family. The CWL stopped functioning in Our Lady of Lourdes around 2002. After that people in the Parish in the form of a Social Committee arranged the visits, such as the one to Weymouth in 2001.

In April 1966, Fr O'Callaghan announced that a St Vincent de Paul Society, consisting initially of five members, met every Sunday in the Parish Hall. The ethos of the Conference was person-to-person work associated with the Parish, such as visiting the sick, aged and lonely. St Vincent de Paul is the Patron Saint of all charities, prisoners, leprosy and spiritual help, and St Vincent de Paul Conferences.

In 1973 there were 8 members making Parish visits. Whereas the CWL arranged social visits, the SVP arranged trips of a more spiritual nature, such as the one to Downside Abbey and another to an organ recital at Clifton Cathedral. They also arranged a successful Senior Citizens' Party. Mr Tasnier reported that by 1969, the St Vincent de Paul Society was beginning to flourish, so that a youth section had been introduced. Nineteen boys received invitations to join, with Mr R McCarthy elected as President at Milton, with the earlier honour of being elected President of the West Somerset Particular Council of the Society in a meeting at Our Lady of Lourdes in December last.

This print was kindly donated by Kath Reynolds

June 1998 the Big Sheep Outing.

Tony and Sue Inganni

A Parish visit to Buckfast Abbey and Weymouth.

Mr Basil M Fuller was the representative of the SVP and another member was Mr D Reagan. Mr Basil Fuller was a member and often Chairman of the Ecumenical Committee and a representative on the Diocesan Ecumenical Conference. He often attended ecumenical meetings with Miss I M McGuire, such as the East Group Church Fellowship Meetings and discussions at Milton Vicarage and at the Milton Baptist Church Hall. They attended the South West Ecumenical Congress in Bristol in April 1973.

In 1975, the Welfare Committee reported that the membership of the St Vincent de Paul Society had increased, a car rota system was currently bringing five parishioners to church and in January 1982, Mr J Murphy of the SVP reported that there would be a Church door collection to send a handicapped child to Lourdes. The SVP continued their work, which was not always reported to the Parish Council.

The Knights of St Columba is a non-political Catholic fraternal service organisation dedicated to the principles of Charity, Unity and Fraternity and exists to support the mission of the Catholic Church. It is essentially for men.

The first mention is in the AGM of 2nd March 1973 under the sections on Social and Fête Committees along with the CWL and SVP. Mr J. Rimmer reported that the membership in 1979 was 27 in all three parishes.

Mr Bernard Bray of KSC reported that there would be a sponsored parachute jump to raise funds to send a child to Lourdes. The three organisations often helped in this way. In addition, Mr J. Murphy reported that the KSC were raising money to build houses in India or Guyana. Bernard Bray was Chairman in 1984 when the KSC helped two boys to go to Lourdes. The KSC showed films such as the Appearances at Garabandal and on Our Lady of Fatima. The KSC helped the CWL with Summer Fêtes and with breakfasts for the children who had just received their first Holy Communion. The KSC organised the Glastonbury Pilgrimages. During these pilgrimages, the blue CWL banner was always held high during the processions. Mr Rimmer was no longer in office as Branch Secretary. Reporting in 1981, Fr O'Sullivan said that the KSC met every month in St Joseph's Hall and were organising a Flag Day. The membership while Mr Bernard Bray was Chairman was about 30 to 33 in all three parishes. The KSC members were selling off the souvenirs after the Papal Visit. In 1984, new laws of a moral nature were to be introduced in Parliament. If any of these should offend Christian moral principles parishioners should complain to their MP. Bernard Bray would issue some guidelines.

The last mention of the SVP was in 2002 when Fr Martin Queenan wanted to form a Congregation of the Society, and the KSC ended in 1992. However, social functions carried on in which these three groups, formed or unformed, probably assisted. There was a regular pattern of a November Bazaar, a Summer Fête, a Summer Barbecue and a Winter Quiz Night for the intention of raising money for charity or the needs of the Church. There was an annual Carol Service at St Peter's until we had our own.

St Margaret's Guild promotes and practices the spirit of prayer, service and love. Members serve spiritual and practical needs of the sick, home bound and bereaved. The only specific mention of the Guild in our parish was when Mrs Joyce Deakin reported on 13th September 1973 that at the last AGM (2nd March 1973) it had been decided to discontinue the Guild in its present form, though members intended to meet informally at each other's homes.

The youth of Milton were served by a Youth Club, which was first mentioned on 5th July 1968 regarding getting someone responsible for collecting money for the newspapers after the 10.00am Mass. There may have been an existing Youth Club while Our Lady of Lourdes was part of Corpus Christi Parish. The support fluctuated over the years, but when it was most popular there were as many as 34 members (1976). The Parish Hall, the former "Hut", was used for scouts, the Youth Club and for other events organised by the CWL.

In 1977, Aidan Reynolds was the Youth Liaison Officer with help from Frank McVeigh and Frank Bailey on a rota basis, when the club was split into 2: 12 – 14-year olds and over 14s. By 1979 the club membership had reached 45. After 1979, the Youth Club was called a Youth Group. Mr John Slattery was appointed Chairman of the Youth Group. By 1981, Tony Inganni reported that the youth group had only 8 or 9 attending and the Deanery Youth Group was in the red, so that Tony organised members of the Youth Group every Sunday Evening for table tennis, with 12 attending.

Chris Simpson, Chairman of the Social Committee, and Aidan Reynolds used to organise barn dances in the Parish Hall. John Brock, the Head of the Music Department at Broadoak School, his wife, and his brother provided the music, while Dick Whitt, who had his own radio programme, called out the moves. Ray Salt ran the bingo sessions. Other members of the CWL were May O'Reagan and Rita McVeigh.

Chris Simpson used to bring his barbecue to the Church grounds to cook for the Parish barbecues. He had a brother, Fr Romuald from Douai Abbey, Berkshire, who occasionally would celebrate Holy Mass at our church when he was on holiday in Weston and Fr O'Sullivan was away.

By 1982, the Youth Group was functioning well again but the Deanery Youth Club had folded. Mr Day, a teacher from Worle School, took over the Youth Group in 1982, reporting that numbers were increasing with a membership of about 20 with 14 regular visitors. A committee within the membership had been formed. In June 1983, Mr Day had to resign from looking after the Youth Group owing to a change of job and other commitments. Miss Eleanor Hussey took over the Youth Group and decided that it would be open all summer. By 1984 she was assisted by Mrs Wilson. The "Living Your Faith Week" was a great success as was the disco. The youth also helped with the Fête. The membership was running at about 19. In 1985, the membership had risen to 25 and it was intended to get together with Corpus Christi to arrange a Deanery Youth Club. By July 1985, it had been realised that there was a problem in the whole Diocese: the youth showed a lack of interest, with low attendance at Mass and Youth Clubs.

In 1986, Mr M Greaney decided to split the Youth Group into under and over 16 in the hope of drawing more members. Membership increased to 15-20 members. By 1990 more volunteers were required to organise and run the Junior Group, while the Senior Group had attracted insufficient numbers to make it viable. Far more members were involved with "A Levels" than before. By 1993 there was no Youth Group and the following year there were no volunteers either.

The Slattery family, John (mentioned above with regard to the Youth Club), Dympna, Sean, Anthony and Seamus ran the Public House in Worle called the Lamb Inn for many years as landlords. John was the chief altar server to Bishop Alexander at his Episcopal Ordination. Dympna signed the Pledge at the age of sixteen and, despite working in a pub, was always teetotal. She was very involved with the Parish, and they were both very generous in providing items of children's clothes and for the raffles. She often used to lead the singing when we were without an organist. When Dympna first came to Weston, she was the manageress of the Lions Tea House.

*

Appearing in the accounts of 1967, the late Mrs Edith Wright left a legacy to the church for the building of a new Parish Hall. There were 2700 one-pound shares and £1300 in cash. The shares were sold, and the proceeds, together with the cash were invested in the Diocesan Trust, which a year later came to £3754. The income from the investment amounted to £4.10s.0d. per week. She died on 3rd February 1965 aged 75 and lived at 14 Chelswood Avenue, Weston-super-Mare. She was the widow of Henry Robert Wright who died 25th February 1953. No children are mentioned.

Mr John Savage produced a plan for the hall. He had already investigated St Peter's hall: it was a classroom type for 80 pupils and was quoted at about £2000. A Hall costing between £2000 and £3000 could be suitable for ourselves. The Main Hall was to be 43ft by 30ft with a small committee room, kitchen, and ladies' and gentlemen's toilets on either side of the entrance hall. The building was to have full central heating. This was reported in the minutes of the Parish Council meeting held on Friday 7th March 1969.

By courtesy of Weston Mercury 8th May 1970

The new Parish Hall.

Chapter 4

By courtesy of Weston Mercury 8th May 1970

John Savage cutting the lawn surrounding the new Parish Hall.

As the legacy left by Mrs Edith Wright was insufficient to pay for the new Parish Hall and other necessary changes, on Friday 4th October 1969, it was decided to withdraw the money from the Bishop's Trust to use to construct the new Parish Hall and the balance of the money required be raised by interest-free loans from parishioners, from the existing balance available from the Parish funds, and from a short-term bank loan. The new hall would increase the income to the Parish by being let out. Gordon Brooks had suggested that, as a result of the new liturgy and growing congregation, the money would be better spent on extending the church. The main argument for building the new Parish Hall was that it would attract more requests for hire. St Peter's Parish Hall at the Locking Road end of Baytree Road, which had been, until about 1965, their original Chapel, had been almost fully booked. A Parish Hall Committee was to be set up, with Mrs Rae Kirkham reporting.

The known cost of the new hall had reached £5960 of which £3500 had already been paid. The Fabrics Committee required £350 to £375 for the car park and the Management Committee needed about £200 for chairs and tables. Thus, a further £3060 had to be found, some of which was still left in the legacy. John Savage said that the loan scheme and donations had raised £800. Fr Alexander hoped that the whole congregation would work in making the opening of the new Parish Hall a great success. A brass plaque commemorating Mrs Edith Wright's bequest would be put up in the entrance of the new Parish Hall.

In 1970, the new Parish Hall was completed, situated behind the old "Hut" that had sufficed as both church and afterwards as a Parish Hall. It is light and airy inside, with a hedge and lawns, with a car-park to the side, later to be extended. With great rejoicing, it was opened on 30th April 1970.

At the formal opening, the Chairman for the occasion, Mr Herbert Wilson, welcomed the guests and the clergy, Canon William Ryan, Fr Thomas O'Donovan, Fr Edmund Murphy, Fr Michael Roche, Fr Michael Meehan, all clergy who had served Our Lady of Lourdes from Corpus Christi, and Fr Anthony Cotter, son of the original donor of the land whose family lived in the Parish.

By courtesy of Weston Mercury 8th May 1970

Fr William O'Callaghan, Canon W J Ryan and Fr Mervyn Alexander
after the opening of the new Parish Hall – 30th April 1970.

By courtesy of Weston Mercury 8th May 1970

Fr Michael Meehan and Fr Michael Roche (Canon W J Ryan in the background)
with parishioners after the opening of the new Parish Hall – 30th April 1970.

Chapter 4

Fr William O'Callaghan blessed the Hall, and congratulated the present Parish Priest, Fr Mervyn Alexander, with the Parish Council and parishioners on their achievement, which marked a further step in the development of the Parish. Mr Wilson outlined the progress from the original Chapel-of-Ease under the auspices of Corpus Christi to its full development into an autonomous Parish. He added his congratulations to all the parishioners who had helped towards the new hall, especially the planning and supervision work of Mr John Savage. He described how the Parish Meetings, which commenced in 1965, developed into a Parish Council, and he urged that from this the parishioners should consider having elections for members of future councils. Members of the various committees gave brief outlines of their work.

Sue Maguire October 2017

A brass plaque in the new hall celebrates the legacy of Mrs Edith Wright.

At the time of writing the provenance of this painting is unknown together with when the painting was obtained, either as a gift or a purchase. The same is true of the reproduction of the Sassoferrato hanging from the organ loft, and the originally supposed Pittoni that used to be at St Joseph's.

Sue Maguire October 2017

A picture of the Blessed Virgin Mary above the doors leading into the Parish Hall from the passage.

In January 1971 a playgroup booked the Parish Hall for mornings at £5 per week and the caretaker, Mr Prescott, was to be paid 10s. for clearing up afterwards. This was soon increased to £1.10s. for clearing up afterwards and preparing the Hall for special functions. This income from hiring out the Hall would help in paying off the debt to Corpus Christi.

In the meeting of Friday 13th November 1970, it was reported that Fr Alexander had been elected Vice-president of the Weston-super-Mare Council of Churches. This ecumenical work had begun in 1968 in Milton when 3 representatives were required to attend the three meetings per year of the Weston Council of Churches. Mr J Barber, Mr B F Mullin and Mrs Martin volunteered. Mr J Barber mainly reported to the Parish Council on progress. By January 1970, three or four representatives had attended the Inter-Church Conference and the 1970 Unity Octave was to include Victoria Methodist on 20th January, and for Milton and Worle at Milton Methodist on 22nd January. Fr Alexander announced that an ecumenical group had started at St Peter's and Milton Methodist Churches, which it wished to enlarge to all local churches. Fr Alexander mentioned the possibility of a new Catholic Primary School this end of the town.

In the same meeting, Fr Alexander spoke on the National Conference of Secular Clergy being held in Yorkshire in June. The topic was "The Organisation of Parishes and the Relations of Priests to Laity", i.e. Parish Councils. He was one of the four priests invited to speak. He asked the meeting for opinions on how collegiality can best be achieved.

The suggestion was made of conforming to Vatican II to accommodate the priest to face the congregation while celebrating the Holy Mass. Until this point there had been insufficient money to bring the altar forward and facing the congregation, which would mean a new altar and demolition of the existing one. This money had been allocated to the new hall.

Mrs Macey reported that the bingo sessions were badly supported by our Parishioners. Prizes were asked for but only six prizes had so far been forthcoming.

In 1971 a Constitution for the Parish Council was ratified and the Council continued to fulfil its important role in sharing in the development of the Parish as a thriving Catholic Community. It was involved in the re-ordering of the Church necessitated by Vatican II, and it did not take too kindly to the drastic re-ordering of the sanctuary recommended by the Diocesan Liturgical Commission. It expressed reservations particularly about the moving of the central Tabernacle to the side and maybe wisely, it hesitated. Meanwhile the new Clifton Cathedral was being built and the Weston Parishes had retiring collections to contribute to the furnishings.

It was learned later in the year that Fr Dr Alexander was to become the first Auxiliary Bishop of Clifton in 122 years. He would be installed at St John's Presbytery, Bath, where he would become the first bishop to live in that city for a hundred years.

It was with great regret that the Parish bade him God-speed as he commenced his new and onerous duties as Auxiliary Bishop. He was later to become Diocesan Bishop when Bishop Rudderham retired in 1974. His first job as Bishop was to give his seven-year-old niece, Barbara, her first Holy Communion. The final act of Fr Alexander was to leave his Old English Sheepdog with a bit extra, Tessa, for Fr Michael O'Sullivan to look after: she was an integral part of the Parish.

By courtesy of Weston Mercury 14th April 1972

Fr Dr Mervyn Alexander's farewell social evening. Before he left our Parish in April 1972, a cheque for £250 was presented on behalf of the parishioners and a clock was given by the alter-boys.

Undated news cutting

Fr Dr Mervyn Alexander's farewell address in the Parish Hall.

By courtesy of Weston Mercury 14th April 1972

Presentation by Bert (Herbert) Wilson to Fr Mervyn Alexander before he leaves to become a Bishop. Joyce Deakin and Miss Drake also attended.

Bishop Mervyn Alexander, Titular Bishop of Pinhel.

By courtesy of the Archives of the Bishop of Clifton

Chapter 4

By courtesy of Weston Mercury 28th April 1972

Milton Priest Ordained Auxiliary Bishop of Clifton on Friday 28th April 1972.
The picture was taken during the homily given by the Archbishop of Birmingham,
the Most Rev George Patrick Dwyer.

The homily was preached by the Most Rev George Patrick Dwyer, Archbishop of Birmingham. Among the clergy attending the service were Catholic priests from many parts of Britain, the Anglican Bishop of Bristol, the Rt Rev Oliver Tomkins, and the Bishop of Bath and Wells, the Rt Rev Edward Henderson. Fr Dr Alexander took the title of the Titular Bishop of Pinhel – an ancient town in northern Portugal.

4.4 Fr Michael O'Sullivan – Parish Priest 1972 – 2002

By courtesy of Weston Mercury 2002

Fr Michael O'Sullivan, who also came from County Cork, studied in seminaries in Ireland and was ordained in Kilkenny Cathedral in 1956, before coming to Clifton Diocese where he served in Bristol, Warminster, Salisbury and Cheltenham before coming to be our Parish Priest, and uncharacteristically staying for the next 30 years.

The large boisterous dog, Tessa, originally owned by Fr Dr Mervyn Alexander, was very pleased to welcome the new Parish Priest, Fr Michael O'Sullivan. The startled priest, however, was not quite so keen, although he fulfilled the important responsibility of caring for his new charge admirably until Tessa died; she was never replaced.

In 1971 Sisters from La Retraite had moved into 11 Walliscote Road. When the Sisters went to look at the property before they had the keys, a young Sister decided to borrow a ladder and climb to an upstairs window to get in, watched by the neighbours.

Sister Pauline Mahony moved to assist while the builders finished the work needed before the other sisters came down. There was no electricity or gas, but the neighbours were very generous. The hotel almost opposite the house offered meals, and on the first day that Sister Pauline entered the building she noticed someone staring at the builders about their business, so Sister Pauline took a kettle over to the house for the lady to fill it and boil it for her, which she gladly did. When the Sisters eventually took possession of the property, they celebrated Holy Mass with the Poor Servants of the Mother of God in their chapel at Totterdown Hall, Oldmixon, until it closed.

When they had settled in, the Sisters in Walliscote Road wrote to Bishop Mervyn to ask what new work they could perform in the Parish of Our Lady of Lourdes. The result was that Sister Pauline Mahony and Sister Lonergan travelled to Milton on Saturday mornings to give Catechism to the children to prepare them for their first Holy Communion and the older ones for Confirmation. Later Sister Pauline invited older girls from Bristol to help with the Catechism, which worked very well.

In presiding at the Annual General Meeting on 18th February 1972, Fr O'Sullivan said that he was impressed by the healthy state of the Parish, its Council Committees and Societies. He was amazed at the size of the Parish as he had expected something much smaller. He felt that Worle would be an important and growing part of the district, and was pleased that the Council had this future development in mind.

New officers were elected on the retirement of Herbert Wilson as Chairman and Clement Smith as Secretary, who both received great thanks for their hard work. The new Chairman was Mr P Russell, the new Vice-chairman was John Savage and the new Secretary was Mrs Toynton.

In another meeting on 18th February, the Ecumenical Garden Party organised by Corpus Christi involving other churches such as the Baptist, St Paul's etc. was discussed. At this Garden Party, there would be no draw although it was intended as a fund-raiser. Our Lady of Lourdes Garden Party would be continued with modifications. Earlier a Children's and Old Peoples' Party had been held, which was a great success.

Fr O'Sullivan was to be proved right as the ever-increasing development in "Beating swords into Ploughshares" continued apace. When the war ended in 1945 there was an immediate effect in the Weston and Worle area because the production and repair of military aircraft for the RAF was shut down at Oldmixon and at Banwell. The Bristol Aeroplane Company did its best to keep work going so as to retain its skilled workforce, foreseeing demand for civilian types in peacetime. Firstly, there was an export demand for Hawker Tempest fighters from Banwell, and Beaufighters from Oldmixon. The new Helicopter Division was brought from Filton to Oldmixon to build Sycamores, many of which perhaps surprisingly were ordered for the West German Luftwaffe. Then the Bristol

170 "Freighter" became a success, carrying horses, cattle. and cars, so the BAC gave contracts to Western Airways for 31 of these, many for export, to be assembled in the hanger that today in 2017 still stands, used as a Co-op warehouse, alongside today's Helicopter Museum. Later the same hangar held Britannia airliners flown in from Belfast for electrical fitting-out in the 1960s.

With the onset of the Cold War, development of guided missiles led to the Banwell factory, under a blanket of security, becoming a centre for making rocket bodies, including the Gosling boost rockets for the Bristol Bloodhounds, which stood guard in several countries as well as the UK from 1965 to 1993; one is still "on guard" near the old Weston Airport control tower building, which has been restored. The Banwell factory became Bristol Aerojet Ltd and at one time employed 800 people.

Photos by Chris May

Chapter 4

EMI (Electrical and Musical Industries) Ltd ran another secret employment, which took over the former RAF acceptance hangar near Hutton Moor Lane, when the Air Torpedo Development Unit shut down. No-one officially at least, knows what went on there, but it was said that the work eventually was 'stealthily' transferred to another EMI unit at Wookey Hole.

Meanwhile at Oldmixon the helicopters included the larger Bristol Belvedere for the RAF, and when after 1960 Westlands took over the whole British helicopter industry, more work on Westland Whirlwind and Wessex and the Saunders-Roe Wasp and Scout followed. There was also some non-helicopter work on Fairey Gannet, and when the Falkland Islands were recovered in 1982, it required much emergency working in our neighbourhood. From then on though, aviation declined, as will be related in a later section of this history.

With all this growth, Fr O'Sullivan wanted a primary school in the Summer Lane area (at the back of Summer Lane Veterinary Centre) of Worle where he had singled out a likely plot. The Diocese was not interested although he had some money towards it.

He believed that the important thing to remember was that the Parish is a family and we must all work together as a family. He was pleased to see how well it was working together. After being unsuccessful with the proposed school, he proceeded on a massive and no doubt personally demanding visitation of the Parish, calling on 190 families in his first five months, calling on every fifth family in the town, seeking out lapsed Catholics. He declared if you do that you are bound to fall on a few Catholic families who are not in the fold. He was alarmed that Catholic children who did not attend a Catholic School received only 30 hours of religious instruction in a year. He wondered if the weekly bulletin could be used as an instructional tool for both children and parents. There was a problem that Sister Pauline needed more books for catechism.

The Parish Debt was gradually being reduced mainly by the proceeds of "bingo" and other fundraising events. A generous donation from Corpus Christi Church was also acknowledged. Proceeds from the hire of the new Hall by non-church groups were also a significant source of income.

In 1972 the 3 representatives for the Ecumenical Committee were provided from Mr Basil M Fuller (Chairman), Mrs Williams, Miss McCafferty and Mr J Barber. This was increased at the AGM on the arrival of Fr O'Sullivan to Mr Basil M Fuller (Chairman) with Miss I M McGuire, Mr J. Barber, Mrs M Kelly, Mrs Martin, Miss McCafferty, Mr A E F Lambourne and Mrs Williams. The Weston Council of Churches requested a representative from Our Lady of Lourdes for which Miss I M McGuire came forward. She and Mr Basil M Fuller had attended a Diocesan Ecumenical Conference and had prepared a separate report. This committee shrank to Mr Basil M Fuller (Chairman), Mr A E F Lambourne and Miss I M McGuire later in 1973.

Mr Basil M Fuller and Miss I M McGuire had attended weekly group discussions in preparation for the South West Ecumenical Congress. In addition, he had attended two meetings of the East Group Church Fellowship: one on the subject of "Holy Communion" at Milton Methodist Church Hall and the other on "Spirituality Today" at Milton Baptist Church. They also were present at Group discussions at Milton Vicarage.

Chapter 4

A bulletin from March 1973 shows that there were 3 Masses on Sundays: 8.30am 10.00am and 4.00pm, with Stations of the Cross and Benediction after 4.00pm. Weekday Masses varied from 8.00am to 10.30am, with some evening Masses at 7.30pm. There were no Vigil Masses on Saturday evenings. Confessions were on Fridays at 7.15pm, on Saturdays at 11.30am to 12.00pm, 3.00pm - 3.30pm and 6.30pm to 7.30pm.

Herbert Wilson, the Chairman wrote to Bishop Mervyn Alexander to invite him on Ascension Day (31st May) to view the film of his consecration as Bishop and to receive a presentation This was a great success and Fr O'Sullivan congratulated Mr G Wiltshire on his film of the Bishop's consecration. Consideration was given to forming a Children's play group, and the hall would be an ideal facility for this purpose. A Senior Citizen Group likewise was formed and numerous other organizations used our facilities.

One of the parishioners volunteered to renovate the organ, which he did successfully. Nevertheless, Mr Christopher Manners, who had played this organ at the 8.30am Mass for such a long time was leaving the district so had to retire. Chris Manners was an Anglican at All Saints Church in Weston, who had been working at Percy Olds, organ builders, Clevedon. Mrs Rose Macey also had to retire from her work with the weekly bingo sessions because of family commitments, her husband having died two years earlier.

About 1600 people took part in the South West Ecumenical Congress in the Bristol Cathedral School. It was felt that the Holy Spirit certainly had a hand in the Congress - it came over in the report by the inspiration instilled into its authors - but the message from the Congress was that there was not much evidence of the spirit of Pentecost in people today. The instruction was that to instil this spirit widely it must be done locally.

By courtesy of Weston Mercury 21st June 1974

The first summer fête at Our Lady of Lourdes in June 1974 showing Bishop Mervyn Alexander competing with Fr Michael O'Sullivan. Who won?

By courtesy of Weston Mercury 21st June 1974

Bert Wilson in charge of one of the games.

Not all parish work involved committees and planning, occasionally there was time for play, although being a church function this would undoubtedly involve gathering income, as shown above at the first summer fête opened by Auxiliary Bishop Mervyn Alexander. The afternoon was a great success in raising £500 for alterations and improvements to the interior of the building. Fr Michael O'Sullivan gave thanks to the Anglican Parish of St Peter's farther along Baytree Road for the use of their tables and other accessories.

In 1974, a gate was let into the fence opposite the presbytery, making a short cut to the church, and a new door was fitted to the "Hut". The finances were doing well mainly because of the success of the bingo. The OAPs were given a four-week experimental run of whist drives in the Parish Hall on Thursday evenings, which proved a success and was extended. The Parish Fête generated £489.40 nett profit, which easily paid the £13.50 required for the new boiler in the Hall.

The Weston-super-Mare Council of Churches held a meeting at Corpus Christi School on Wednesday 18th September, which was attended by Fr M O'Sullivan, Miss I M McGuire and a recovered Mr Basil M. Fuller. The Chairman, Mr Scarr regretted that there were still 11 churches not represented.

The Parish Mission conducted by Fr Francis OFM, a Capuchin Friar, took place from October 9th to 20th. The Service of Blessing of young children was held on the first Sunday with a children's Mass on the Saturday. The daily Masses were held at 10.30am and 7.30pm. The East Group attended on Tuesday evening with tea served afterwards. Fr O'Sullivan said that we had been blessed with a marvellous preacher. There was an End of Mission dance that was highly successful and profitable such that the New Year's Eve dance would be restricted to 100 tickets.

Chapter 4

At the end of the year, sadly the St Vincent de Paul Society found that their work of visiting was hampered by a shortage of members; the hiring of the Hall, however, was going well; and the Parish finances were at the healthy level of £4300 in the bank.

Not much had changed between the building of the Church in 1938 and present, in fact the view of the north side of the Church and the front looks the same now as it did then, but partly due to changes decreed by Vatican II, there was going to be a great and rapid restructuring of the main fabric of the interior of the Church. This would be expensive but under the shrewd guidance of Fr O'Sullivan it would be possible, and would not break the bank. This is possibly his greatest achievement and for what he will be remembered. He was a great practical planner and builder of this Church. In 1975, the new doors designed by Mr Duff of glass with hardwood frames arrived at the end of February and duly fitted.

In 1975 plans for an extension on the south side of the Church were discussed. The cost of the extension proposed by the Diocesan Architect was £16000 + VAT. This plan could be modified by moving the Blessed Sacrament. The extension to the south transept would contain a small chapel, a sacristy and a lobby, with a toilet, leading outside. This would mean that the walls of the sacristy in the North transept would be removed to allow for a Lady Chapel. The increased seating would accommodate an extra 56 places. This extension would not maintain the Gothic style of the rest of the building. It was designed by the Rev Robert Townsend ARIBA and built the following year by Bayntun & Son. The architect's fees were 11% of the value. The intention was to keep the cost as low as possible and to repay the debt by the end of 1976. This new extension made room for some more oak pews, which were duly bought. These were half the length of the ones in the nave. Mr Salt and Mr Duff were to assist in the construction of the new side chapel.

Bishop Alexander was in favour of increasing income by extending the number of parishioners giving to the covenant scheme rather than those already in the scheme giving more. Thirty covenants yielded £450 for our Parish in 1974.

The Executors of the will of the late Jack Kingston issued a bequest of £400 towards the Extension Fund. John Victor Kingston was born on 21st July 1898 in Penarth, Glamorgan, as John Victor Kaiser. His German father, Elias, was a jeweller. The family changed its name from Kaiser to Kingston sometime between 1911 and 1917. Jack married Irene Mary Dillon in Cardiff in 1938. She died on 29th March 1963 aged 53. Jack's older sister, Constance Freda, was born in 1895 and lived with him until he died on 30th July 1975 aged 77. He had been employed as a warehouseman. Constance died on 9th February the following year aged 81. One of the silver chalices was given by Jack Kingston, which has been inscribed.

By 1976, Ken Morrison and the Committee produced a prospectus for the Parish Hall with conditions of hire, and income generated was increasing, with bookings from the College of Further Education (4 weekly sessions), the Dancing School (4 sessions), the Youth Club (1 session) and Bingo (1 session). The Hall was considered as one of the best in Weston.

John Savage often helped Fr O'Sullivan with various woodwork projects and he made the hymn board and the holy oils cupboard for the parish. John, Kathie and their family kindly donated and planted three trees: cherry, hawthorn and maple, which are located at the left side of the garden approaching the church entrance. They are especially beautiful in the spring-time. In addition, there are three lovely ornamental cherry trees planted in the back car park border. These were kindly donated and planted by Brian and Margaret Barraclough who also regularly tended the parish gardens until they stepped down about 4 years ago.

Sue Maguire April 2016

John and Kathie Savage's trees: cherry, hawthorn and maple from Westonbirt Arboretum. These were planted away from the Church in November 1997.

Sue Maguire April 2016

Brian and Margaret Barraclough's cherry trees.

Chapter 4

The Lady Chapel in the North Transept.

David Pluck 19th November 2010

By courtesy of Weston Mercury 10th February 1978

The Chapel in the South Transept with Fr O'Sullivan in the foreground.
The small wooden altar in the background was made by Fr Michael O'Sullivan with wood salvaged from a chapel at RAF Locking in 1975.

Chapter 4

Sue Maguire October 2017
The Holy Oils cupboard

Sue Maguire October 2017
The Hymn Board

Both made by John Savage.

Sue Maguire October 2017
An outside picture of the south transept, housing the side-chapel and sacristy.

Chapter 4

The changes demanded by the liturgical provisions of Vatican II had still not been effected. The priest was still unable to celebrate the Mass facing the people. When the Parish finances were in good health, Fr O'Sullivan lost no time in contacting a stonemason to advise about cutting the stone altar away from the wall, although he thought it best for the Tabernacle to remain in the centre, as it still does.

The glass doors separating the Chapel from the main body of the Church were ordered (£346 estimated) and the new pews were nearly ready. The new changes would accommodate an extra 60 rather than 57 parishioners as first thought.

By September, the new altar for the side Chapel was ready but the moving of the main altar forward had only been discussed with no decision made. At the end of November 1975, negotiations with a stonemasonry firm from Taunton were taking place. The tabernacle is set on a canopied stone shelf. The final result was a stone altar with a carving of the Pelican in her Piety and a new timber baptismal font, situated near the light-oak lectern.

The Parish discovered that the Reorganisation of Catholic Schools in Bristol (£344,000 including £51,600 for new buildings) would cost us an extra payment of £900 from our budget. The present commitment was £700 per annum.

There was an emergency meeting on 10th January 1977 to discuss the sudden resignation of Gordon Brooks, the Organist and Choirmaster, who was moving to Kent. An emergency envelope collection was made to thank him for his valuable work in providing the Parish's music over the past few years. Right from the first days of our Parish he had also made a great contribution as Chairman of the Men's Meetings and in committee work in general.

Sue Maguire 1976   The New Stone Altar

Chapter 4

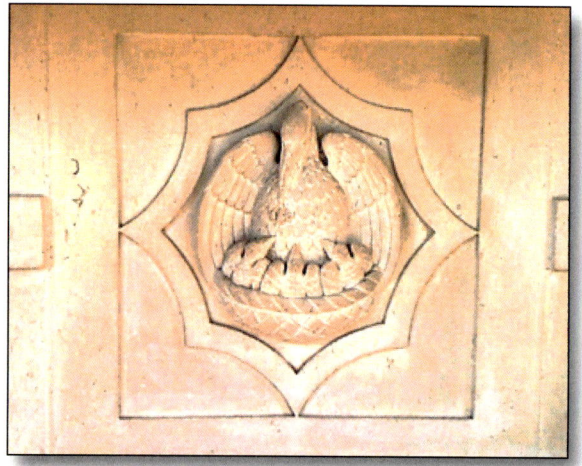

Sue Maguire October 2017

The Altar – Detail of The Pelican in Her Piety.

Sue Maguire October 2017

The Baptismal Font made by Fr O'Sullivan.

Fr O'Sullivan was finding it increasingly difficult to combine his pastoral duties with overseeing and taking part in the day-to-day running of the Parish. Questions were asked of the parishioners about the role of the Parish Council, such as should the Parish Council remove the burden of material activities from the Parish Priest; act as a consultative committee; and to carry out assignments for the Parish Priest? The Parish Council consisted of 15 elected members and representatives of each of the Parish organisations, in total about 20. The committees were Social, Ecumenical, Hall, Fabrics and Youth Club. Later in the year Mrs N. Gurr became the Chairman, after her Mr Ken Morrison, and Chris Simpson was added to the Council.

On 22nd February 1977, negotiations with Stansell (Small Works) Ltd. of Taunton who quoted the cost of moving the altar at about £950 plus VAT, and a meeting was to be set up and the work completed before September. The final cost was £1866.37, which was paid in November. A few months earlier, June 22nd 1977, the lime wood Crucifix cost £230 from Ormsby of Scarisbrick.

In the meeting of 15th September 1977, looking over the last five years since he arrived, Fr O'Sullivan observed that the building work had been completed, the Church redecorated (by Fr O'Sullivan and members of the Parish) and the organ had been restored by a parishioner. He was particularly alarmed at the rapidly increasing population of Worle, and thought that the Church, even in its extended form, still may not be sufficiently large to accommodate this upsurge.

Chapter 4

In 1977, Catholic Secondary Education was being reorganized in Bristol and the parish annual contribution was raised from £700 to £1,600. Plans were begun for the consecration of the Church. During 1977, volunteers redecorated the Parish Hall. Fr O'Sullivan tested three different colours by painting a little of each above the doors for Jan Greaney and Susan Inganni to choose the best for colour and brightness. Fortunately, they chose the same one that he had already bought in sufficient quantities to complete the job. The curtains were chosen and shortened by Susan Inganni and Jan Greaney.

Mr Chris Simpson and the Social Committee in planning for the Consecration of the Church had been told that the legal limit for the Hall was 200 people. It was decided to allow for 250 eating and 300 people for wine. A booklet was to be provided to the parishioners for the Consecration Ceremony.

The great day of the Solemn Consecration of the church by Bishop Mervyn Alexander finally dawned on the Feast of Our Lady of Lourdes, 11th February 1978. By this time the necessary work of re-siting the altar and re-positioning the Tabernacle and statues of the Sacred Heart and Our Lady of Lourdes was completed although the altar rails remained and were removed and stored at a later date.

A large congregation including the Mayor and clergy from the local churches attended the Pontifical High Mass celebrated by Bishop Mervyn Alexander, with Fr Michael O'Sullivan and Canon William Ryan, Parish Priest of Corpus Christi, as Deacons-at-the-Throne. The concelebrants at the Mass included members from the Cathedral Chapter, the Deanery Clergy and past priests of WSM: Friars OFM from Clevedon, Fathers William O'Callaghan (our First Parish Priest), Matthias McManus (St. Joseph's), Michael C Roche (Burnham-on-Sea), D Hayes, SCA (Cheddar), Michael C House (Warminster), P Austin Gurr, OSB, Gabriel Leyden (Bishop's Secretary), Fr. Gregory Grant, Canon Richard Norris and other priests.

Undated news cutting

The Consecration of the Church of Our Lady of Lourdes – 11th February 1978.

Chapter 4

By courtesy of Weston Mercury 10th February 1978

The Consecration of the Church of Our Lady of Lourdes.

During the impressive ceremony, a relic of St Cuthbert Mayne, one of the Forty Martyrs of England, (who was executed in 1577 in Launceston, Cornwall), was carried in procession to the sanctuary and carefully sealed in the altar cavity. Six consecration crosses on the walls of the church were marked with oil of Chrism while the Bishop anointed the altar, which set it and the church apart for God's service.

The Bishop congratulated the Parish Priest and congregation for their wonderful achievement. After the church service, the ladies of the Parish provided refreshments in the Parish Hall.

Early in 1978, it was decided to purchase a new organ as the present one was too old. A suitable organ was available from St Peter's Anglican Church, Burnham-on-Sea for £250. The organ arrived in Our Lady of Lourdes just before Christmas to be installed early the following year. Tony Inganni, John Walcott the organist and Barry Stock and others would do the work. By July Fr O'Sullivan and Edwin Channon the other organist had a meeting with Percy Daniels of Clevedon. The organ console was ready and the work in the gallery would be completed before Christmas, but the assembly work might take up to two months to complete.

Mr Kelly was an expert employed on organ installation and operation. Ken Morrison obtained a Building Surveyor and Structural Engineer to check the floor loadings. The limit was 2 ton and installation planned for Sept/Oct. The old organ was removed and sold. A new organ fund was started. Chris Simpson, who was Chairman over the years 1979 and 1980, had an older brother, Fr Romuald from Douai Abbey, Berkshire, who was an organist. He was involved with some of the work on the organ when he came on holiday to Weston.

Sue Maguire 2017
The 'New' Organ.

Lifting the organ above the parapet into the organ loft was going to be a bit of a performance. First, the old organ had to be removed with everything else to leave the small organ loft completely empty. The new organ was positioned just below the parapet so that it could be hauled up over the parapet and into the organ loft once the organ pipes had been detached.

The 800 to 900 organ pipes were removed from the incoming organ and taken out in the correct order. These were carried up to the organ loft via the narrow spiral staircase to be repositioned in the exact sequence for replacement in the new organ when it was in situ. Blankets were put over the parapet to protect its surface from damage. Ropes were thrown down and fixed to the organ and a few lusty men, huffing and puffing, pulled it up. Then Daniels of Clevedon started to install the organ in the loft and, by 26th September 1978, Fr O'Sullivan said that work was proceeding satisfactorily.

A brass plate was affixed to the organ. Referring to this organ as the new organ is rather a misnomer as it is older than the church. 22nd December 1979: final instalment on the repair and installation of the organ by Percy Daniel & Co Ltd of Clevedon of the organ (total cost £6995).

On 11th January, there was an announcement of the first meeting of a new Pastoral Council at St Joseph's 13th February 1979. On Sunday 29th April, there was a Day's Retreat organised for men at St Mary's Convent, Totterdown, and on Saturday 13th May the women had their turn at St Mary's with a Day of Recollection. Fr O'Sullivan arranged that Fr Francis Hinkman OFM would conduct a Mission from 16th to 23rd September.

Sue Maguire 2017
The Organ Plate.

Chapter 4

In April 1979, it was agreed that the present presbytery (the 3-bedroomed semi-detached house situated across the main Milton Road at number 253) was inadequate, and a new Presbytery, to become 28 Baytree Road, should be built on land adjacent to the Church that Daniel Cotter had given. Tenders were invited and Fr O'Sullivan accepted the lowest of several received. The contract was between Clifton Catholic Diocesan Trustees Regd. and Mr A Warren and Son of Spring Valley, Worle, under the direction of Peter Williams, dated 9/12/81. The tender gave the cost as £41,077.48 and the builder worked to the design by Fr O'Sullivan. This contract was terminated by the employer on 18th October 1982 under Section 7.1.1, because the contractor was bankrupt and failed to proceed with the work. He went bankrupt at the stage when the shell was complete except for the door frames.

As soon as Fr O'Sullivan realised what had happened, he called Tony Inganni to see if he could help to empty the building of the loose electrical cable and pipework and the other paraphernalia left behind which had been paid for. Tony was just off to work at Priddy Electrical Engineers.

Contractors and parishioners completed the work. Tony Inganni had been named on the original contract of 1981, and under the contract an insurance against bankruptcy had been taken out by the contractor. Various other contractors completed the work paid for by the insurance. John Savage and Roy Salt fitted the door-frames, while Tony put in the electrics, and work was completed in 1983. The Chairman of the Finance Committee who had guided this through was Ken Morrison, who had been involved in Parish affairs since he arrived in 1975.

Sue Maguire October 2017

The new Presbytery at 28 Baytree Road to the design of Fr O'Sullivan.

Chapter 4

The photograph taken later (p164, left) also shows part of the boundary wall and gates surrounding the church and the presbytery, which were eventually completed in 2004. They cost, with general inflation, considerably more than the presbytery.

Reverting now to the situation in 1979-81 leading up to the Contract for the building of the new Presbytery, committee meetings had had continuing concerns about the cost. Interest rates were high, posing a financial risk, but on the other hand Fr O'Sullivan was also concerned about the current risk of unemployment amongst building workers. Further information should be gathered for consultation with the Diocesan Financial Secretary. Meanwhile other matters had proceeded, including car park extension and major maintenance of the Parish Hall.

Folk Masses began and were held at 6.00pm on Sundays. In 1980 preparations for the Liverpool Pastoral conference began. House Masses and Discussion Groups took place as a means of bringing all sections of the Parish together. In that year, the highest number of conversions to the church within the Clifton Diocese, (pro-rata to the size of the Parish), was achieved by Our Lady of Lourdes. The Annual General Meeting of 1981 also recorded the largest First Communion Class Milton had ever had. Preparations for the visit to Britain of Pope John Paul II were beginning.

The Folk Mass became a regular feature on Sundays and appropriate music and hymn books were purchased and PA equipment installed. The organ was provided with a new trumpet stop. The Parish Council with representatives from all groups continued to function.

The Bishop had suggested that for the Papal visit the Bishop hopes that preparation would include: the holding of a Mission in Lent 1982 in every parish; a Novena of prayer leading up to Pentecost; Holy Hour every Thursday beginning after Ash Wednesday; and further options to include, self-denial by fasting and abstinence on Fridays during Lent and special events for particular groups e.g. sick, handicapped, aged and children, and a drive for vocations. During Holy Week, Friar Francis returned to give another Parish Mission and a Mass for the sick was celebrated on the Feast of Our Lady of Lourdes. Many parishioners remember with joy the great welcome given to the Holy Father both at Cardiff and Coventry.

Fr O'Sullivan reported a loss resulting from the Holy Father's visit to Coventry. There was a big deficit re the sale of mementos and the debt to be shared. As well as the building of the new presbytery, a garage and store room was built and the whole car park was surfaced with tarmac at an estimated cost of £3000. It was agreed that this should not be done in stages.

New gas hot-air systems for the Church and Hall were planned and later installed. The altar rails were still in place and it was suggested that they should be removed to give more room at the front of the Church. The provision of Extraordinary Ministers of Holy Communion to assist at mass was mooted and gradually they were trained and finally commissioned. With Fr O'Sullivan distributing the hosts to the standing parishioners on the right-hand-side of the church facing, and the Extraordinary Ministers performing the same duty on the left, spelt the end of the altar rails, and they were soon removed to the workshop, where they still are.

Chapter 4

In July 1980, there was a possibility that a Leisure Centre might be opened in Worle. Fr O'Sullivan enquired whether there may be a vacant room in which he could say Mass. Nothing seemed to come of this, but in October 1990 he was unable to celebrate the monthly Mass in St Mark's Anglican Church in St Mark's Road, North Worle, owing to illness. This monthly Mass had been well supported by congregations numbering between 80 and 110. He resumed this when he had fully recovered from illness. At this time there was a request for a weekly Mass at St Mark's, but Fr O'Sullivan rejected this idea on the grounds that there was a shortage of priests in Weston, being only three, which in the future was more likely to be reduced to two. The monthly Mass continued in the 1990s but probably ended when the Masses were rationalised in 1996.

There was some story that the Friars held Masses in Worle and Fr O'Sullivan was not happy with this.

A Parish Finance Committee had to be set up by October 1984 in accordance with revisions of Canon Law. In his address to the 1984 Annual General Meeting, Fr O'Sullivan said parishioners were being encouraged to play a bigger part in the Parish. Parish councils were very useful in the life of the Church to advise and encourage the Parish Priest in his work. He also said, "We are in the business of the Salvation of souls and we can all help and encourage each other."

It was in the mid-eighties that three nuns, Sr Bridget Arscott, Sr Joan Lockwood and Sr Helen Dunn moved into a house in Worle to assist at Milton.

A high point had been reached. The financial stability of the Parish continued to be admirably maintained through the generosity of parishioners and the stewardship exercised by Fr O'Sullivan, ably assisted by an active and dedicated Finance and General Purposes Sub-Committee.

Sue Maguire 1986

Confirmation, by Bishop Mervyn assisted by Fr O'Sullivan in 1986, showing the East wall as it was after the altar had been moved forward as decreed by Vatican II.

Sue Maguire 1988

The altar on 8th September 1988 during the Golden Jubilee celebrations.
Miss Hussey's trademark little decorations are situated halfway up the candles.
She always reserved this for special occasions.

David Pluck 19th November 2010

The Forty Martyrs window: (1988) St Thomas More, St Margaret Clitherow and
St Cuthbert Mayne. The CWL paid for this window as
St Margaret Clitherow is their Patron.

Chapter 4

In 1986, a Summer School was held in Bristol from 21st July to 25th about the RCIA for which the Bishop required representatives from each parish. The Rite of Christian Initiation of Adults is the way in which we welcome and share with others our faith and way of life as Catholics. The RCIA is not a programme but the process by which we engage with others who seek the face of Christ. It involves the whole parish and is the responsibility of all baptised.

The 50th Anniversary of our Church was celebrated on the 11th February 1988. Several windows were in need of replacement to be substituted by the Forty Martyrs' Memorial Window on the right-hand side of the altar as seen by the congregation. It shows three saints: St Thomas More, St Margaret Clitherow and St Cuthbert Mayne. This was installed in commemoration of the 50th Anniversary at a cost of £2,369.40 plus VAT.

The redecoration in the same colours for the Church interior and the repainting of the Our Lord's and Our Lady's statues was organised, and the quotation for the Public-Address System was accepted for £2,139 plus 10% VAT. Other improvements included the replacement of the wooden gates by wrought iron ones.

The Garden Fête was held on 11th June, with the Golden Jubilee Celebration Ceremony on Thursday 8th September, which Bishop Mervyn attended. He visited the Parish again for the Confirmation Ceremony on Tuesday 27th September.

At the AGM on Thursday 14th September 1989 with Fr O'Sullivan in the Chair, the Mass for Holy Days of Obligation was settled at 7.45am. There were six Eucharistic Ministers: three Laymen and three Sisters. The Youth Club was formed with a junior section with Mr and Mrs Kingscote: one for ages 15 – 20 with Nicolas Simpson. There was a call for young people to join the SVP.

A Mission with the Redemptorist Fathers commenced on 25th February. The Sisters were helping with Parish visiting. Sister Moreen was inducted as Chairman of the Weston Council of Churches on 21st September.

In 1990 John Walcott retired as organist and Geoff Thornton took over in 1991, playing for the traditional Sung Mass with choir and organ. Geoff also initiated this Parish History and he retired in 2015. There was then a gap before another organist could be found. During this time the choir, wearing their blue robes except in very hot weather, sang (successfully) with only a few keynotes at the start of each hymn.

In October 1991 Fr O'Sullivan announced that there will be a rationalisation of Masses from 1992 so that there will be only three Masses on a Sunday in Weston. A census would be taken over the next 12 months where the attendance in each Mass would be counted, and from these figures a decision would be taken as to which Mass would be discontinued. Fr O'Sullivan assured the congregation that the three Parishes in Weston would work together to ensure that the best interests of the parishioners were catered for.

In the October meeting of 1991, Fr O'Sullivan added that the Mothers and Under-five Group would end at Christmas at the Convent in Walliscote Road and move to the Parish Hall. The two ramps installed for wheelchair use were satisfactory.

Chapter 4

In 1992, the attendance at the different Sunday Masses was 8.30am 80 – 100; 10.00am 130 – 140; Evening Mass 160 – 180; and Worle 60 – 90. It was felt more altar servers were needed for the 10.00am Mass and a suggestion was that girls should be invited to apply. However, this was not possible until the Holy Father granted permission. Fr O'Sullivan then gave a run-down on the Rite of Christian Initiation of Adults (RCIA), comparing the way in which converts were brought into the church nowadays as opposed to the old days, which was very different.

In 1992 a small room under a pitched roof, called the Parish Room, was added to the east of the sacristy. It was intended for children's liturgy and other small meetings. It was designed by Fr O'Sullivan.

O D Cope & Co Building Contractors' tender was for the Parish Room for £24,689, using face brickwork to match the existing, with roof trussed with felt baton and tiles matching the existing. All the new windows were brown uPVC with double glazing. The final account was due to be paid by 31st December 1992 but some money was withheld. The shrinkage to the plaster works was made good by 27th September 1993 and was paid by money held back from the final payment. The Chairman of the Finance Committee at the time was Ken Morrison. The final cost of the new extension with furnishings and VAT was £24,253 and the cost of the car park for 10 extra spaces was £3038.

This represented the last of the major changes to the fabric of the church for the time being, leaving only the mundane upkeep and maintenance to be carried out, important though that was. There were, however, other important changes.

The year 1994 was the first time that Communion under both kinds was mentioned, to which Fr O'Sullivan replied that this would be restricted to special Masses only. This is only possible at the discretion of the local Bishop. By 1989 only about a half of the parishes in the country offered the Chalice to their parishioners.

Sue Maguire October 2017   The Parish Room.

Chapter 4

The storm damage to the hall roof had been repaired under insurance by September. Mr Powell was responsible for keeping the garden tidy.

By September 1995 there was no Youth Club, but Fr O'Sullivan was going to speak to Canon Fitzpatrick to see if members from Our Lady of Lourdes could join Corpus Christi member, and on the ecumenical side, Mr M Greaney gave a talk on catechists' work with a view to a certificate in Religious Studies.

Mr Savage said that the new windows would be installed shortly in the nave. Both sets of stained glass windows were made by the local firm, John Baker Stained Glass Ltd, costing £7215.67 including VAT, £4,000.00 of which was provided from a legacy left by the late Mr Norman and Mrs Maud Wootton. Fr O'Sullivan said that he would prefer the window in the Lady Chapel should depict the Holy Family at a cost provided by a special collection.

Norman Wootton had been born on 28th October 1905 in Quarry Bank, Stourbridge, Worcestershire. He died in March 1982 aged 76. He married Maud Smith in the District of Stourbridge in 1948 when both were aged 43. Maud was born on 2nd October 1905 and died in September 1994 aged 88.

Fr O'Sullivan suggested that to help his work, the Parish Council should be revived. The trip to Prinknash Abbey was a great success so that next year a trip to Buckfast Abbey was suggested. They went there in 2000 and to Dartmouth the same year.

David Pluck 19th November 2010

The Holy Family window (1996).

Chapter 4

In 1996, the Holy Family window was installed in the north transept, and all the nave windows were renewed, replacing most of the original blue-green tinted nave windows with white cathedral glass with yellow crosses.

By September, Fr O'Sullivan had received the party sprung on him to celebrate the 40th Anniversary of his Ordination. He was absolutely delighted that people had remembered. Mr M Greaney was pleased with the Wednesday RCIA group meetings but wanted new members. Sadly, Ray Salt was leaving the Fabrics Committee, and Miss W Hopkins retired as Parish Treasurer. Mr Chris Simpson took over as acting treasurer. A Parish Executive Committee was formed with the first meeting on October 3rd. This was intended to help Fr O'Sullivan with his increasing duties and responsibilities. It was not only in the outside world that people were suffering under increasing workloads, demanding more of their time.

There were three Masses during 1996, 8.30am and 10.00am and 6.00pm. Later a Vigil Mass was introduced at 5.30pm on Saturday. Much later Bishop Declan told Fr O'Sullivan that he had to cut his Masses to a Vigil Mass and two Sunday Masses. This made him very unhappy because he knew that some of his parishioners would lose their favourite Mass. He canvassed the congregation as to which Mass he should drop, and chose to drop the Sunday 8.30am Mass. The children's Liturgy held at 5.00pm on Sunday was to be maintained.

In the Parish Committee Meeting Wednesday 9th October, the terms of reference of the old Parish Council were modified as follows:

to act as a consultative and liaison body;

to remove the burdens of material activities from the Priest; and

the original constitution objectives to be removed and new ones set up.

The meetings were to be more wide-ranging with members of the Committee able to bring up any particular subjects they wished pertinent to the Parish.

In the Parish Committee Meeting of Wednesday 13th November, Fr O'Sullivan asked for ideas for the Summer School on Collaborative Ministry held in Bristol, which was about parishioners using their skills and expertise for the benefit of the Parish. The purpose of the Parish Committee was to contribute to the "Mission of our Parish". Geoff Thornton suggested that we formulate a Parish Statement and Aidan Reynolds prepared a leaflet about the Covenant Scheme to encourage new contributors.

Fr O'Sullivan had been attending meetings of the Local Ecumenical Partnership led by the Anglicans and Methodists currently meeting at St Peter's. They would like Catholics to be involved with house-to-house visiting and census work. It was hoped to build a centre for a Parish Mission in the new development at Locking Castle. He asked for the Parish Sister, Sr Anne, to organise a visiting team.

In early 1997, as some people were worried about receiving communion in both kinds, Fr O'Sullivan gave some background about the introduction of the practice. After a vote he said he would introduce the practice at all Masses on Pentecost Sunday and possibly on the Feast of Corpus Christi.

Chapter 4

The fence was treated again by July but would need replacing within five years. Joyce became involved with the First Holy Communion class, and Fr O'Sullivan organised the renewal of the doors and front windows at a cost of £3000 by Southern Glass. The front and back windows of the hall were replaced and two walls were coated with preservative.

In the AGM on Thursday 22nd January 1998, the result of the vote on whether to accept Holy Communion in both kinds was that most parishioners were in favour. Holy Communion in both kinds began later that year. The Parish Sister, Sr Anne reported that five people were interested in following the course on RCIA.

In the Parish Committee Meeting of Wednesday 18th February 1998, John Savage reported on the new windows for the hall: there were two tenders; one from the small firm called Merlin of £4185 and another by Southern Glass of £4848. Merlin Glass was chosen. He also reported that some trees needed attention: a tree surgeon would cost £1000 but if some of the work were done by parishioners it would cost only about £300. In the end John Savage and Fr O'Sullivan pruned the trees.

After the hall windows were installed, Beryl Shaddick and John Parks redecorated the Hall. For years it had been a rule that any money paid out amounting to over £5000 had to be approved by the Diocese. Chris Simpson was unhappy because he believed it should be made higher after all this time.

In September, Dennis Furlong said that the SVP would help with the Harvest Supper, which would take the form of an American Supper, for which food parcels would be produced. This was the penultimate mention of the SVP. The last mention of the SVP was in 2002 when Fr Martin Queenan wanted to form a Congregation of the Society.

By January 1999, Ray Salt reported that the Hall had been redecorated with new windows and doors fitted. The reader's lectern had been altered by a local carpenter and a drape hung over the front.

Advice was taken about the redecoration of the church, the new Stations of the Cross and the changes to the lighting and sound system. John Savage, Aidan Reynolds and Fr O'Sullivan had met a consultant, Mr Haswell, from South Wales. He told the Committee to decide on a number points on the work to refurbish the sanctuary, such as the East wall for which John Savage was to mark on the floor the location of the new structure, and a decision had to be made on colour schemes. In the meantime, he would produce a black and white sketch to present to the Parish Council with comments on paint samples. The plan was to carry out the work in July and close the church. Services would be transferred to the hall.

At the Parish Committee Meeting of Tuesday 13th July 1999, there was a report on the tenders for the refurbishment of the church:

Building work - Stansell Ltd eliminated owing to insufficient detail and high price.

'P R J' and Noel T James also tendered but the painting price of 'P R J' was lower and so their tender was accepted. £19,973.10 including VAT.

Electrical work - three tenders but David Fear was recommended because his tender was lower and he had done work in the Diocese previously. £11,372.82 including VAT.

Audio equipment - one tender from a well-respected local firm was accepted at a price of £880.18.

Professional fees 10 – 12% of total cost but Mr Haswell would accept 9 – 10% because he was not conversant with the electrical element. £3383.

Planning supervisor £ 400 – 600.

Total cost £36,116 including VAT.

John Savage reported cost of a new carpet would be £1400 including VAT.

At the end of July, Chris Simpson said they had Diocesan approval. He also reported that he had been approached by Brian Cotter, who requested some sort of memorial to his grandfather, which he was willing to pay for, but this was not followed up at the time. The Youth Group at Corpus Christi, after reforming last year, was still running for the benefit of the youth from all three Catholic parishes of Weston;

Geoff Thornton reported on the Church History that he hoped to start, which preceded and fuelled the present project, saying that some materials were at hand to start the book intended for the New Millennium.

The interior of the Church had been completely refurbished and redecorated in celebration of the Third Christian Millennium in 2000 AD. The church was remodelled: arches were added to the sanctuary with pilasters down the wall, and the whole colour scheme changed.

Chris Simpson 1999

The Harvest Festival 1999.

Chapter 4

Sue Maguire

The Holy Water font at the entrance of the south transept to welcome in the New Century.

Sue Maguire

The sanctuary lamp.

The new Stations of the Cross were in place at a cost of £8,058.15 including VAT. A budget of £38,000 had been set aside for the cost of redecorating the church plus lighting and sound systems, which cost £37,966.

The Parish was directed to buy a computer – more expense. The first suggestion about buying a computer had been made over a year previously when Anita Bailey said that one could be bought for £100. (!)

Bishop Mervyn attended the Parish Dinner in 2000. John Savage displayed a wooden bowl, which was officially presented to the Bishop at the Dinner.

Chris and Janet Simpson

The altar, after the false alcoves were built, showing Holy Mass celebrated by Fr Martin Queenan in about 2010. The hymn board has been moved to the left-hand-side. The sanctuary lamp is just to the right of the Tabernacle.

By courtesy of Weston Mercury 1967

Ashcombe House Maternity Hospital.

The sanctuary lamp, donated earlier by Miss Eleanor Hussey (Sacristan) in memory of her parents, was re-positioned near the tabernacle. Miss Hussey was for many years the Matron at Ashcombe House Maternity Hospital, The Drive, Milton Road, where probably at least half of the children of Milton and its environs were born. Miss Hussey lived nearby at 12 Baytree Road and she worked very hard for the Parish. Often she was accompanied to Holy Mass by her work colleague and good friend, Sister Eileen Bidmead. In 1983 Miss Hussey ran the Youth Club for a short time all through the school summer holiday, which was unusual. She was assisted by Mrs Wilson the following year and she also served as a Sacristan. Miss Bidmead was a devoted friend of Miss Hussey, and, when the latter was dying, she visited her every day and read the Bible to her.

The picture shows Matron Eleanor Hussey with staff: Sr Smith, Sr Eileen Bidmead, Sr Appavoo, N/N Mrs Day, N/A Mrs Hunt and N/A Mrs Blatchford on the occasion that 8 babies were born on Christmas Day 1966.

In the Executive Committee Meeting Wednesday 23rd February 2000, Denis Furlong was proposed as Chairman and Mrs Janet Lowther was elected as Secretary. The Stations of the Cross had been delivered and two of them were shown to the Committee. John Savage said that he would put them up by the end of the week. Donations of £7,600 had been received and a further £450 were required. Chris Simpson suggested a loop system be installed.

A Parish Pastoral Council Workshop on Saturday 11th March 2000 was held at the Friary in Clevedon hosted by Friar Declan OFM (Parish Priest) and conducted by Fr Austin OFM. This covered the areas: The role of the Laity in the Church; The purpose of a Parish Council; and Making a Parish Council. What had been discussed some time before was beginning to be implemented.

In the Parish Committee Meetings in May the main points considered were the status of a Secretary and the Parish History. The Committee agreed the purchase of a lockable beech cupboard fixed to the wall of the Parish Room. The Hewlett Packard computer would be for use of the people of the Parish. The computer was to be used for the preparation of rotas, notices etc. Rita Wilson Associates offered to provide free computer training and Keith Wilson gave some training to Denis Furlong on his own computer at his home. The Loop System was to be kept in the lockable computer cupboard.

Those who were declaring covenants for tax purposes were informed that the word "Covenant" had now disappeared to be replaced by "Gift Aid Declaration".

In 2001, the Mothers and Under-Five Group was still going strong, although not many of the families attending were Catholic. Nevertheless, the non-Catholics could get some inkling of what we were about. Sr Joan was generally present, but in 2003 she left to go to Burnham-on-Sea, during the time that Lynette McMillan had taken charge of the group. Lynette offered to bring her back occasionally to see the children. The Group changed its name to 'Parents and Toddlers Group'.

The Social activities for the previous year included an Outing, a Quiz Night, a Carol Service and a Parish Dinner; and forthcoming events consisted of a Harvest Festival, a Parish Quiz, a Christmas Fayre and the Parish Dinner. There was a suggestion of perhaps a different venue for this in 2003.

The CWL were asked to help in Women's World Day of Prayer. Teresa Thorne, taking over from Denis Coombe, was preparing a Ministers Rota and we had a new Bishop, Declan Lang, as Bishop Mervyn Alexander had retired to become simply Fr Mervyn, Parish Priest of St Joseph's, such was his humility. Sadly, John Savage, who had done so much for the Church was not in good health, and he died on 17th November 2001.

At the beginning of the year, Jan Greaney had pointed out that the fence in front of the presbytery looked very poor. Geoff Thornton raised the question of the commemorative plaque in the fence and indicated that the Council should be consulted in any changes. Before the year end, Larry McGurk presented a sketch to the Chairman and Committee of a proposed replacement wall. The rough cost would be £34,500 for a maintenance-free brick wall with iron railings on top. Donations to the new wall reached £4,200.

Sue Maguire October 2017

The chapel in the South transept showing the small wooden altar built by Fr O'Sullivan, and the entrance to the Parish Room.

Sue Maguire October 2017

One of the new Stations of the Cross (installed 1999): the 6th Station: Veronica wipes the face of Jesus.

With Aidan Reynolds in the Chair, Fr O'Sullivan said that we had been directed to adopt a Mission Statement. Thought was given to this throughout the year and in the meeting in December, it was reported that a Parish Mission Statement had been distributed to parishioners for approval.

*

With employment trends such an important part of the environment in which the Parish exists, there were some notable changes taking place at this time. The Airport had closed to commercial traffic, due to cost of runway surfacing, and Westland Helicopters took over the operation and the ownership of the Airport land, as military aircraft and helicopters did not need the high standards required for civilian passenger operations. With the end of the Cold War armed forces' requirements for military helicopters and for missile motors being much reduced, by 1990 Banwell was making many of its 800 jobs redundant and closing, while Oldmixon ceased aircraft production in 2002 and approaching another 2000 jobs were lost to Weston.

Also in 1999, the large RAF Locking Radar School was moved away to RAF Cosford and the site sold for housing development, (which provided only temporary employment, though over quite a long period). In another speciality, the Clarks' shoe factory in Locking Road shut in 1999 (500 jobs) and the work moved to Portugal, although the site fairly soon was turned into a technical college employing teachers to raise skill levels.

With something approaching an employment crisis, North Somerset Council produced a plan for the Airfield site, which they had long regarded as a barrier to the expansion of the town of Weston. This coincided with the sale by Westlands of most of the airport land to Persimmon Homes, though a relatively small area would go to the Helicopter Museum Charity, which could fulfil its educational mission by helping with technical training for new industries.

Persimmons engaged with the Council to promote commercial or industrial activities on part of the site, so that jobs there could be early available to the new residents. The same Council policy was also applied to the area called Weston Gateway near the M5/A370 traffic intersection. The emphasis of work in Britain was switching away from manufacture and in this respect Weston-super-Mare was no different. Fortunately, there was plenty of work in Bristol, but it was more expensive to live there than in Weston – hence the growth in housing.

*

Noting the above, the Committee's review of the parish continued. It was seen how these policies were attracting people of a wide variety of origins and skills to the parish. At least a dozen original nationalities were represented in the congregation; later when a regular Mass in Polish was begun at St Joseph's church, it had the benefit of relieving the overcrowding in Our Lady of Lourdes church which had been occurring on Sundays.

The 2001 trip to Weymouth was successful and it was the best ever Quiz Night and Chris Simpson, the Chairman, continued that the Carol Service was very good too. Bob Gibbons was thanked for the children's Folk Mass. A kind offer was made for a new window displaying the Sacred Heart of Jesus. The year had ended on a good note.

In 2002, the would-be donor of the Sacred Heart window had been asked if he would donate a chalice instead with a picture on it of the Sacred Heart as none of the windows needed replacing. He accepted this suggestion and took away some appropriate catalogues.

Planning permission for a new brick wall was received and tenders were coming in for it. In the Executive Committee Meeting on 1st May 2002 with Chris Simpson in the Chair, it was reported that the building of the wall had been approved by the Diocese. The best offer was by O D Cope Ltd of £33,059.80 including VAT. The Chairman of the Fabrics Committee, Larry McGurk, felt that the tender was excessive and he renegotiated a price of £31,012.23 including VAT. Donations of £7,267.00 had so far been promised.

Chapter 4

By July, Chairman Mr Larry McGurk and Mr Ian Brough met regarding the church wall. Fr O'Sullivan revealed two letters received by Larry McGurk from one of the tenders, Cooke & Co, to say the work would commence at the end of September. There was some concern regarding the existing plaque in the present fence. Mr McGurk wrote to the Council and had a reply from Mr Russett, the Archaeological Officer. Fr O'Sullivan suggested that Mr Russett should come to Our Lady of Lourdes to see for himself.

More importantly, the Family Buffet was cancelled due to the Football World Cup.

The Retirement of Father Michael O'Sullivan

In 2002, ended the fruitful ministry of our faithful pastor, Fr Michael O'Sullivan after 30 years of very dedicated priesthood among us. He retired to his birth place in a little village, Boherbue, outside Cork where his family still live. During his stay in Milton he had been a Governor at Corpus Christi Primary School and an Assistant Chaplain at the town's hospital. His housekeeper, Joyce Deakin, retired at the same time, after being housekeeper to his predecessor and him for 35 years. Fr Michael was presented with two cheques, one from the parishioners and another from the Catholic Women's League in recognition of his great help in their charitable projects. Joyce Deakin received a cheque in recognition of her 35 years of service as a housekeeper to the then Fr Dr Mervyn Alexander and to Fr Michael O'Sullivan.

During the long period that Joyce Deakin had acted as Fr Michael's housekeeper, they became good friends. Joyce regarded it as her duty to protect him from his parishioners as any faithful secretary would, and she cared for him very well, being especially vigilant with his diet. All through his stay in Weston he had suffered with his health, an excuse he always brought up whenever the bishop wanted to move him on. Hence his long stay in the same parish. He attended the parish functions with Joyce at his side. It was only on the Catholic Women's League functions, when the men would slope off together to have lunch, that he often escaped away from her, but soon he would hear a familiar voice behind him saying, "You shouldn't be eating that; it's not good for you."

In return, Fr Michael gave Joyce some very valuable advice that she should buy her house in Milton Brow and not continue to rent it from the Council. The Conservative Government had given that opportunity to people who had rented their council houses for a long time to buy them at a knock down price, but she nevertheless continued to pay her rent until the day she died. She lived in the presbytery, returning to her home occasionally to oversee that all was well.

They both retired at the same time in September 2002, Fr Michael to his home in Ireland and Joyce to her house in Milton Brow. After that they took it in turns to phone each other on alternate weeks between the regular visits she made to his home in Ireland, where his family treated her very well, grateful for all the hard work she put in over the years.

Chris and Janet Simpson

Fr Michael and Joyce's Retirement – September 2002 with Canon Gabriel Leyden, Canon William Ryan, Canon Timothy Barry, Joyce Deakin, Fr Michael O'Sullivan, Fr (Former Bishop) Mervyn Alexander. The short lady on the extreme right is Sr Joan Lockwood.

Marie O'Sullivan November 2017

Church of the Immaculate Conception, Boherbue, where Fr O'Sullivan said Mass and had his Requiem Mass.

During Joyce's weeks alone, she had many visitors for she was popular in the parish - she was recognised for all the work she had done – and, as she grew older and became increasingly frail, people would run her to and from church. As mentioned previously, many years ago Joyce sadly lost her beloved husband, William. He was a Petty Officer Air Mechanic serving on the HMS Avenger. This escort carrier was torpedoed and sunk by German submarine U-155 just west of the Rock of Gibraltar on 15th November 1942. A total of 513 officers and ratings perished - there were only 12 survivors. Joyce's and William's only child, Allan William, was born shortly afterwards. Joyce never re-married but dedicated her love and time to her son, Allan, and the care of Fr Dr Mervyn, Fr Michael and the Parish. (Sadly, Allan, preceded his mother in death, passing away in 2011.)

Joyce Deakin died on 22nd June 2015 (aged 95), followed a few days later on 5th July, by Fr Michael O'Sullivan (aged 84). Fr Michael regarded his most important duties, if he did nothing else, were to deal with young people and visit the sick. Fr Martin Queenan conducted the Requiem Mass for Joyce at Our Lady of Lourdes on 7th July. Immediately afterwards he travelled to Boherbue in County Cork to represent the diocese at Fr Michael's Requiem Mass on the following day, 8th July.

During his 30-year tenure in the parish, Fr Michael "helped many men and women for three generations find the Church and find their place in the Body of Christ". His successor, Father Martin Queenan, said. "Father O'Sullivan walked every path and street of this parish (reminiscent of Fr John Lyons when he was Parish Priest of St Joseph's). He greeted. He chatted. He comforted. He welcomed. He sought out the lost sheep, every day.

*

Pope John Paul II was instrumental in the formal establishment of the Divine Mercy devotion and recognised the efforts of the Marian Fathers in its advancement in a Papal Blessing in 2001, the 70th anniversary of the revelation of the Divine Mercy Message and Devotion.

Miss Patricia Igoe donated the Divine Mercy picture in the side-chapel. She was from Callow in Ireland, but came to Weston via Birmingham, where she had worked as a district nurse. Geoff (then the organist) and Maureen Thornton had the picture framed and Patricia paid for it. They used to visit Patricia after she became housebound.

Another generous doner to the Parish to be remembered was Miss Mary Hynes.

Chapter 4

Sue Maguire October 2017

Plaque inscription on the left-hand side of the small wooden altar made by Fr MichaeO'Sullivan, pictured on the left, below. You can ust see part of the brass plate under the white cover.

Close-up of the Divine Mercy picture hung over the altar.

Before leaving the little side-chapel containing Patricia Igoe's gift, we ought to explain a little of why Pope John-Paul II introduced the Chaplet of Divine Mercy. This devotion to the Divine Mercy was based on the Christological apparitions of Jesus to

Chapter 4

Sister Faustina Kowalska (1905 – 1938), known as the Apostle of Mercy, who was a religious sister of the Congregation of the Sisters of Our Lady of Mercy. She was canonised in 2000.

She told how she had received the prayer through visions and conversations with Jesus, which she noted from the start in her diary. Jesus asked her to pray the Chaplet and encouraged others in doing so. The Chaplet's prayers for mercy are threefold: first, to obtain mercy: second, to trust in Christ's mercy; and, third, to show mercy to others. She reported that all who recite this Chaplet at the hour of death or in the presence of the dying, will receive great mercy. Jesus reportedly said that He will stand between His Father and the dying not as the Just Judge but as the Merciful Saviour.

She was born in Glogowiec (Lodz region), the third of ten children in a poor Catholic peasant family. She was given the name Helena at her baptism. She distinguished herself by acts of devotion, her love of prayer, hard work, obedience and tremendous empathy with human misery.

She left home in Aleksandrów at sixteen, taking a job in Lodz as a servant to support herself and her parents. During this period, she was eager to join a convent, but her parents were against it and Helena tried to suppress this desire.

She wrote in her diary that one day when she was with her sisters at a dance, she suddenly saw Jesus at her side, Jesus racked with pain, stripped of his clothing, covered with wounds, who spoke, "How long shall I suffer and how long will you keep deceiving me?" The charming music stopped. Any company vanished from my sight, with Jesus and I remaining there. Helena slipped surreptitiously away from the dance and entered the Cathedral of St Stanislaus Kostka. She begged the Lord to be good enough to allow her to understand what she should do next. "Go at once to Warsaw, you will enter a convent there."

Finally, after many disappointments, Helena, on August 1st 1925, applied to the Congregation of the Sisters of Our Lady of Mercy, where she was accepted. Before she could start, she had to put together her outfit, but first to earn the money to pay for it, so that she took a job in Warsaw as a housekeeper for a family with several children.

She took the name Sister Mary Faustina. She completed her probation in Krakow, and, in the presence of Bishop Stanislaus Rospond, she took her initial vows, and five years later, she took her perpetual vows of chastity, poverty and obedience. She worked in various houses of the Congregation working as a cook, gardener and a doorkeeper. She faithfully kept all of the monastic rules and devoted herself to her duties, but her fascinatingly rich mystical life was hidden to all, both inside and outside of the Convent. She was silent and focused, yet natural and cheerful, quietly displaying a great unselfish love for those around her.

Her busy lifestyle coupled with exhaustive fasting took its toll of her wellbeing, forcing her to seek medical treatment. During the last years of her life she suffered two several-month periods in hospital. Her health deteriorated significantly, developing tuberculosis, which attacked her lungs and gastro-intestinal tract. By the time she died, she was physically wrecked, but maturely, mystically and spiritually united with God. She died aged only 33 in Krakow-Lagiewniki on October 5th 1938.

4.5 Fr Martin Queenan – Parish Priest 2002 – 2015

By courtesy of Weston Mercury 25th April 2003

The year 2002 marked the arrival of a new Parish Priest, Fr Martin Queenan. A native of Sligo where he began a career as a bank official; he studied for the Priesthood in Rome at the Beda College from 1994 to 1998 and was ordained at Sligo Cathedral (1998) for the Diocese of Clifton by Bishop, Dr Mervyn Alexander. After temporary appointments in Salisbury and at the Church of St Gregory, Cheltenham, he celebrated his first Mass with us on Monday 11th September 2002, exactly a year after the twin towers in New York were destroyed.

Beryl Shaddick helped when Fr Martin was moving into the presbytery and later she carried out odd tasks such as contacting the Authorities regarding the Safeguarding of children and vulnerable adults - something newly introduced by the Government. This involved setting up Police checks, then called the CRB check and now called DBS. She had held a number of high-level administrative positions in her career and was an excellent organiser. Until Beryl left the Parish she was very popular on trips and at times quick and witty. But occasionally she was unusually quiet.

Fr Queenan's first meeting was the Executive Committee Meeting of Wednesday 30th October 2002. His contribution was that he wanted to re-start a St Vincent de Paul Congress and have a Welfare Group. After this he had to take over the problems associated with the wall. On the good side was that the amount promised for the wall had reached £7,557, but this was in the face of the 3rd quarter of this financial year indicating a deficit of £1,191.00 by the end of the year due to the Diocesan Levy.

Moreover, the wall in front of the presbytery was in a dangerous condition and had to be included in the project. A new planning application had to be submitted at no extra cost. The wall would be at the same height as the commemorative stone but the railings would be higher along the side of the church for extra security. There were to be two new gas meters and three new matching sets of gates of a similar design to the railings. The quotation from the builder was £5363 + VAT and £982 + VAT for the meters. Mr McGurk was going to renegotiate the figures, which seemed too high. Larry McGurk then handed over future negotiations to Chris Simpson. By the end of 2002 a total of £7,557.00 had been promised and when the building started the donations would be requested. The wall, railings and gates were designed by James Barattini (Winscombe), built and installed by Rob Wadsworth (3 Gillmore Road, Milton) and P W Engineering (Kewstoke).

Chapter 4

Fr Queenan was quite different from Fr O'Sullivan in several ways: Fr O'Sullivan dealt with the money himself whereas Fr Martin, despite having worked as a bank official, did not; Fr O'Sullivan was a particularly thrifty person who worked on the principal, "If it ain't broken don't fix it." This extended to decorating the church, and had it not been for the Parish Council the church would have been decorated far less frequently. On one occasion when the Parish was brimming with money, he cancelled the Summer Fête as we had no need to canvas for more cash.

Whereas Fr O'Sullivan delayed over such changes, depending very much on the guidance of Chris Simpson, his successor, Fr Queenan, went around the grounds noting all that should be done, and he set about doing it. He also proved to be very good at obtaining money.

Fr O'Sullivan vacillated over replacing the wooden fence so that by the time eventually came for it to be replaced by a wall, the Council rules had changed and a wall of "a one-brick thickness", as originally intended, had now to be a wall of a two-brick thickness. The wall was finally built with a two-brick English Garden Wall bonding and iron railings. This work was undertaken by Fr Queenan at a considerably higher cost, approximately £65,000. The wall incorporated the old tablet commemorating the building of the new Milton Road towards Worle in 1914.

On the surface, it was believed that the cost of the wall was greater than that of the presbytery. The reason for making this little study is to compare the price of building the presbytery (just over £41,000) in 1982 and the cost of the wall in 2004, which was £65,000. Allowing for inflation between 1982 and 2004 gives the cost of the presbytery as £95,500, which is still very cheap. However, this value does not include the price of the land, which was the land given to us by Daniel Cotter in 1923. If we had had to buy that land in 1982, it would have been as building land not cheaper agricultural land. Allowing for all this would give a realistic 1982 price. What it does show is that it often pays to buy agricultural land and leave it undeveloped for many years. Many big concerns have done this. The land bought in 1933 for £560 at agricultural rates is where the present church stands.

The double thickness of the wall proved very sturdy, so that when a car glanced off it with a loud crash, it was left unscathed, but the car was less fortunate. Perhaps the Council's change in the rules was fortuitous. This occurred during a Friday evening choir practice in 2017 when we were temporarily without an organist, but that night with some deafened members of the choir.

Because we had a new Parish Priest, the Diocese had to check the fixtures and fittings. Their report highlighted the following:

- the pointing and external windows needed attention;

- the organ needed attention;

- a wiring certificate was required;

- the ramps into the church were too steep;

- there were no toilets for the disabled.

Chapter 4

In the Parish Hall under Health and Safety:

- the toilets and kitchen were not user friendly; and
- the emergency exits should have handrails outside.

The Parish Room needed the gas heaters changing and the presbytery needed upgrading, redecorating with a shower added.

The care of the grounds was good thanks to Michael Waters for cutting the grass regularly.

This was occurring at one of the few times the Parish had a deficit.

Unlike Fr O'Sullivan, Fr Martin was very fond of dogs and bought a Rhodesian Ridgeback puppy called Hintza soon after he arrived (2002). In Rhodesia (now Zimbabwe) these dogs are used for hunting lions, but, nevertheless were very calm and friendly, just like their master. When examining the Minutes of the Parish Council these reflected that they were much less formal than those earlier times but still thorough.

Hilda Wallby was very good with the dog. Moreover, as Fr Martin was the first of our Parish Priests without a live-in housekeeper, she took him under her wing, inviting him for quite a few dinners and doing his laundry, freeing him more time to carry out his priestly duties. Fr Martin's mother regularly came over from Southern Ireland for a holiday. Both she and Hilda were approaching or in their eighties. They got on very well. Fr Martin's Induction Mass was held on Thursday 21st November, and then he set about changes. He changed the times of the weekday and weekend Masses from 10.00am to 9.30am. This enabled him to have more time to carry out his parish work, and to serve morning Mass at Corpus Christi after the Mass at Milton should the need arise. The agenda for the meeting of 14th May 2003 included discussions of Churches Together and Child/Adult Protection.

*

Sisilah Baker writes

I came to the UK in March 2000 and, initially, settled in Portishead for a period of two years before moving to Weston-super-Mare for good.

Whilst in Portishead, Chris and I went to St Joseph's as (we thought) it was the only Catholic Church in the area. When I eventually uprooted and moved to WSM, it came to my knowledge that there were three Churches to choose from. But, to my astonishment, one of the Churches was Our Lady of Lourdes. I was over the moon as, in Malaysia, I attended a Church of the same name since birth.

Although, I have been to the other two Churches, Corpus Christi and St Joseph, as in Malaysia, I still found my faith and strong spirituality in Our Lady of Lourdes. You may have, or may not, noticed that I am always sat at the same place on Sunday. This is because from where I am seated I can see Our Lady's statue, which brings an abundance of joy and love.

Father Martin Queenan was my first Parish Priest in OLOL, for whom I have so much love and respect. Now we have Father Alexander Redman, who is also deserving of love and respect. Both of them are reverend, kind and thoughtful in their own ways. As parishioners, we should be so grateful to have a Priest to lead us.

In November 2005, we went on a Pilgrimage to Rome, led by Father Martin, and during this trip we formed a close bond with Stella and the late Tom Caddick, Margaret and Brian Barraclough and Ann and John McCarthy, who have all remained close friends ever since.

Over the passing years we have gained and lost parishioners for different reasons. It is quite noticeable that we now have a number of parishioners from varied ethnic groups. We have from time to time held multi-cultural gatherings, with a wide variety of food from around the world, as well as, entertainment with multi-national influences.

Over the years I have lost several close friends, in the Church, through passing, which saddens me. However, we now have a number of parishioners from varied ethnic groups, who are very dear to me.

Since being in UK, I have greatly enjoyed the experience and embraced the culture. One of my greatest pleasures though, is being a member of Our Lady of Lourdes Church. I have met so many parishioners who have warmly welcomed me, and I now feel that I am part of a very large family, as everyone is so friendly, kind, considerate and caring. It really is a wonderful Church to be part of.

Sisilah Baker

Fresh from four years in the Holy City Fr Martin soon promoted a pilgrimage to his beloved Rome. In March 2003, he took a party of 42 from Milton and its neighbouring parishes, "eager to scurry across Rome's hallowed cobblestones where saints and pilgrims had trod for centuries." During the pilgrimage to Rome, Mgr Gabriel Leyden and Fr Martin Queenan were invited by Pope John Paul II to celebrate Mass in his private chapel. Since then several other pilgrimages have been arranged that were greatly appreciated and enjoyed, and are being continued by Fr Alexander Redman.

Mgr Gabriel Leyden (right) and Fr Martin Queenan recall celebrating Holy Mass with Pope John Paul II.

By courtesy of Weston Mercury

Chapter 4

In the Inaugural Meeting of the Parish Pastoral Council on Wednesday July 7th 2004, Fr Martin was confirmed as President, with Ken Morrison appointed as Secretary.

Fr Martin circulated a letter from Bishop Declan in September 2003 in which the Bishop felt that there were too many Sunday Masses in the Diocese, which "fragment a parish from being a true communion", and the possible shortage of priests also had to be considered. Corpus Christi had already stated that no change was possible because of the number of parishioners. The Bishop required a positive response to his letter by August 2004, with implementation by Advent 2004.

In the Second Meeting of the Parish Pastoral Council on Tuesday 14th September 2004, John Slattery accepted nomination to be the Chairman of the Council and was duly elected. The draft constitution was accepted. The document, "Guidelines for Pastoral Councils 2004", was circulated and discussed.

Fr Martin said that there were six active priests in the town a year ago whereas now there were only two: Fr Mervyn was in convalescence at St Angela's and might possible return to St Joseph's; Canon Ryan had finally retired; Fr Barry, after heart bypass surgery would need 6 -12 months rest; and, through bad health, Fr Stirrat was no longer available. Bishop Declan had urged Our Lady of Lourdes to reduce Masses from 3 to 2. A likely solution was:

	Saturday (vigil)	Sunday
Corpus Christi	6.00pm	10.30am
Our Lady of Lourdes	5.30pm	9.30am
St Joseph's	–	6.00pm

This would mean that our Parish would discontinue Masses at 11.00am and 5.30pm on Sundays, but only at a date to be determined.

As far as our Parish was concerned, the attendance at weekend Masses was 90/100 at vigil, 90/100 at 10.00am and 50/60 at 5.30pm. On Holy Days of Obligation, the 7.00pm vigil Mass would be re-timed at 7.30pm with the 7.00am Mass on the feast day being discontinued and the 10.00am Mass re-timed to 9.30am. On ordinary days the present Masses would continue. Our Lady of Lourdes working in conjunction with St Joseph's could make some changes to Mass timings in the event that the two parishes be combined under the pastoral care of one priest.

The constitution of the Parish Pastoral Council was discussed, and it was agreed that there would be 14 members with at least 5 meetings per year.

In the 3rd Meeting of the Parish Pastoral Council on Wednesday 17th November 2004, it was confirmed that the new Mass timings would be as shown in the table above. With the demise of the Sunday evening Mass, there was concern that the liturgy of the two remaining Masses would not suit all tastes. Geoff Thornton explained that at the 9.30

Chapter 4

Mass on the first Sunday of Advent (November 28th), he would be introducing a "Community Mass", which he felt sure would allay those fears. He with Bob Gibbons had been working closely to develop the new Mass.

In the 5th Meeting of the Parish Pastoral Council on Wednesday March 2nd 2005, John Slattery was in the chair and Ken Morrison was the secretary.

Julie Ottley resigned from the position of Parish Child Protection Representative and a replacement was sought. Fr Martin stressed the importance of this post, which involves the induction, within the rules of the Diocese, of catechists, helpers, carers, Ministers of Holy Communion and anyone involved on behalf of the Parish with members of the Parish.

Bob Gibbons, searching for budding musicians, met with a poor response, and it was decided to approach Corpus Christi for any of theirs for a once a month performance at a folk Mass.

The date for the sacrament of Confirmation was set for Tuesday May 3rd.

Sadly, on 2nd April 2005 Pope John Paul II died and Pope Benedict XVI was elected as Pope.

Fr Martin had a nasty shock too. A disturbing incident occurred when someone (down on his luck) knocked on the presbytery door asking for alms. Fr Martin gave him a few jobs to do during which time this man befriended the animal. Fr Martin paid him some money for his trouble; the stranger rewarded him by trying to steal more money. They grappled with each other in front of the presbytery. The dog, a Rhodesian Ridgeback, thought they were playing. The situation could have got out of control, but, as it was reported in the Weston Mercury, "…this was no ordinary priest …" Fr Martin fought back and called the police.

There was still a search for a replacement Parish Child Protection Officer by the time of the 6th Meeting of the Parish Pastoral Council on Wednesday April 27th 2005. Janet Simpson, a previous incumbent, stated that at a pinch she might return to that post.

Marita Muench reported that there were no parishioners requiring home visits from Parish visitors. It was suggested that when the Ministers of Holy Communion commence visiting the housebound and vulnerable members of the Parish, there may be a more favourable response.

Tony Inganni and his helpers had transformed the Parish Room, which now only required the new carpet to be laid. After this news, Fr Martin announced that during his holiday, Fr O'Sullivan would be returning to his old Parish to deputise.

In the 7th Meeting of the Parish Pastoral Council on Wednesday June 22nd 2005, Janet Simpson circulated a report of the Deanery Pastoral Council. The main points were:

1. Parishes are urged to be more welcoming;

2. St Joseph's Parish in Portishead is arranging a Pilgrimage to Walsingham in the spring of 2006;

3. Retreat Day for Eucharistic Ministers on June 15th;

4. St Francis's of Nailsea held its first public meeting on the theme of "Drugs in Society". About 40 attended.

5. A diploma course for catechists will be launched in Oct/Nov 2005;

6. Chaplaincy About Town (CHAT). A paid part-time chaplain will be appointed within the next few weeks. With volunteer support, he will be based in the town centre;

7. Results of questionnaires on Liturgy, Prayer, Healing and Spirituality are available in summary to attach to Parish bulletins;

8. Parish PCs are urged to hold joint meetings;

9. The next meeting of the DPC will be held at Our Lady of Lourdes on October 13th 2005. All members are welcome especially if they can help with the coffee!

No Parish Child Protection Officer had been found so that Janet Simpson took on that role.

It had emerged that, by invitation, some of the young people of the Parish were joining in youth activity on Sunday evenings at the Baptist Church in Baytree Road. Contact was made to determine if any help was needed from this Parish. There had been no further developments in providing our own youth activity.

The programme for next year's first communicants was to commence in September. Chris Simpson was thanked for providing excellent photographs of the children who made their first communion recently.

Fr Martin gave a detailed report of the two break-ins at the presbytery during which he was physically attacked. In addition to the considerable damage to the front door, some housekeeping money and a wallet were stolen. A man, who was known to Fr Martin, was arrested for questioning. Later the ungrateful thief was sentenced to 33 months in jail.

The 8th Meeting of the Parish Pastoral Council was held on Wednesday August 10th 2005, with John Slattery in the chair and Ken Morrison as secretary.

The children's liturgy was going to start soon under a new leader, Susan Turnbull. Fr Martin had received a request from Bob Gibbons to hold two folk Masses a month, but Fr Martin wanted more details.

Fr Martin gave an up-date on the break-in at the presbytery. He had recently attended an identification parade in which he had picked out the man who had confronted him. New doors had been fitted to the back and front of the house.

The next Annual General Meeting was scheduled for Sunday 18th September 2005 in the Parish Hall. John Slattery and Ken Morison were returned as Chairman and secretary respectively.

In the 9th Meeting of the Parish Pastoral Council on Wednesday October 12th 2005, with John Slattery as chairman and Ken Morrison was secretary, Fr Martin had four names of parishioners who would assume the formal role of Parish Visitors to the Sick at home or in hospital. Ministers of Holy Communion were meeting in three weeks' time for an instruction session before embarking on visits to take Holy Communion. They would only be taking it to those at home and not those in hospital. They would only be allowed to do this after they had been vetted and approved by the Parish Officer for the Protection of Children and the Vulnerable, Janet Simpson. To co-ordinate activities, a Parish Visitation Sub-committee was to be set up comprising Marita Muench, Jane Norris and Janet Simpson.

In the 10th Meeting of the Parish Pastoral Council on Tuesday 15th November 2005, there was a report by Janet Simson of the Deanery Pastoral Council held on October 13th, to which Jane Norris had also attended. The two points that emerged were:

1. CHAT (Chaplaincy about town) now had a part-time Chaplain with an office above the Wesley Owen bookshop; and

2. It was suggested that pilgrimages, although Parish organised, should be Deanery-based, leading to greater inter-parish involvement.

Fr Martin announced that he will lead a group of 22, mainly from the Parish, on a pilgrimage to Rome from the 20th to the 25th of November. Canon Timothy Barry was to cover for weekday Masses.

Fr Martin read extensively from a letter from Fr Danny O'Sullivan of the Parish of San Antonio in Peru. Following Bishop Declan's pastoral visit to Peru earlier in the year, the Diocese of Clifton had agreed to help fund the building of a new church. It was suggested that each parish should contribute £1000.

In the 11th Meeting of the PPC held on Wednesday 11th January 2006, with John Slattery in the chair and Ken Morrison as secretary, Fr Martin reported that the pyx had been blessed and six Ministers of Holy Communion would soon be taking communion to the housebound.

A Chaplain, the Rev Andy Sewell, an Anglican Priest, was appointed to CHAT and was seeking volunteer assistants who can be from all walks of life. Deacon Tom Moffatt of St Joseph's had already become involved.

In the 12th Meeting of the Parish Pastoral Council on Thursday 9th March 2006, with John Slattery in the chair and secretary Ken Morrison, the sub-committee had met Fr Martin to make a list of parishioners who wanted home visits. A strategy was being developed to initiate and proceed with home visits.

Fr Martin had agreed to allowing two folk Masses on the third and fourth Sundays of the month but more musicians and voices were needed, first to sing the praises in the Mass, and second to lead the congregation in hymn singing.

The 13th Meeting of the Parish Pastoral Council was held on Wednesday May 3rd 2006, when it was reported that Fr Danny O'Sullivan would visit the Parish on the 2nd September to celebrate Holy Mass at 5.30pm.

Visiting the housebound by Ministers of Holy Communion and Parish visitors were already functioning, and Fr Martin was arranging another training session. The first Holy Communion was planned for the 9.30am Mass on the 18th June, for which there were three candidates. Modest refreshments for the children and their parents would be served in the Parish Hall.

Fr Martin was very much in need of assistance both in pastoral and administrative duties. The secretary, Ken Morrison, said that such assistance had been discussed recently at the Finance and General Purposes Committee Meeting held on May 3rd, and Fr Martin had agreed to write a job description. Janet Simpson said that the Parish of St Gregory at Cheltenham, who employ three staff, was being contacted to advise on both headings.

Fr Martin was seeking suggestions of how the Parish should commemorate Fr Michael O'Sullivan's Golden Jubilee. It was agreed that it should take the form of a presentation to the Church, from the parishioners that would also mark the 30 years of dedicated service that Fr O'Sullivan had given to the Parish.

The last item was that Ken Morrison gave notice that he will be retiring from the position at the next Annual General Meeting.

The 14th Meeting of the Parish Pastoral Council was held on Wednesday September 6th 2006, with John Slattery in the chair and Ken Morrison as secretary for the last time.

Fr Danny O'Sullivan's homily told the parishioners of his work in Peru and of the church he intends to build. About £2000 was raised at the weekend in Our Lady of Lourdes special collection and donations to support Danny and his work. Later that day he gave a presentation at Our Lady Queen of the Apostles, Cheddar.

Prices were being obtained for two new credence tables for the Church to commemorate Fr O'Sullivan's Golden Jubilee. These were finally bought in 2009 from the Irish Contract Seating Co. for £2185 + VAT.

Fr Martin reported that the pyx had been blessed and six Ministers of Holy Communion would soon be taking communion to the housebound.

In 2007, Fr Mervyn Alexander retired, which meant that St Joseph's had no Parish Priest. Fr Martin discontinued the Sunday evening Mass at Our Lady of Lourdes so that he could celebrate Holy Mass at St Joseph's on alternate weeks in a sharing arrangement with other priests.

The funding for School Transport to Faith schools for those children in North Somerset not otherwise assisted had been terminated by the North Somerset Council owing to cutbacks. Initially, the Council wanted to stop the funding in 2007, but after persistent lobbying it relented and agreed to phase in the change. Nevertheless, the funding stopped in 2008. The financial assistance would then end except in special cases where the law required it, such as those who receive free school meals; those whose families are in receipt of income support; or those families in the highest level of working tax credits.

The cost to send a pupil to St Bede's Catholic College in Lawrence Weston, our nearest Catholic Secondary School, was estimated at £85 per annum (2010). For poorer Catholic families, this situation was eased by the formation of a charitable fund called "The Blessed Edward Powell Transport Trust", which in 2016 could help about a dozen North Somerset families with the cost of sending their children to the nearest Catholic Secondary School, St Bede's (http://www.stbedescc.org).

Chapter 4

In the Finance and General Purposes Committee 14th March 2007, Fr Martin said that a new Treasurer would be required on the resignation of Chris Simpson on 31st December 2006, although he did offer to continue for one more year. A piece of good news was that AV West Ltd had been unable to provide an after-sales service and had refunded £1,550.

*

After the job description had been drawn up and approved, Fr Martin's request for help was carried out by an appointed Administrative Assistant, Miss Barbara Smith, who started work in September 2007. Barbara was our first Parish Administrative Assistant. She was very efficient and knew everything that was going on in the Parish. If you wanted to know anything, you just had to ask her.

"Originally from the East End of London, I came to live in Weston-super-Mare in 1994 and became a Parishioner at Our Lady of Lourdes. The Parish was already known to me as I used to come and visit friends who lived in Worle. It took a long time for other parishioners to get to know me though as I worked in a boarding school as a Housemistress and was only home during the holidays.

As the years went by, I made friends and people were used to seeing me. Father Martin soon realised that I was capable of a lot more than minding other people's children and couldn't wait for July 2007 when I retired from Elmhurst Ballet School. I became the first official Parish Administrative Assistant and started my role in the Parish in September 2007 - working 12 hours a week.

It was a very satisfying job to do and included many roles. Although many were not in the job description, it was all part of the fun and I have many happy memories. I stayed with Father Alexander when he first came to the Parish but finally left at the end of May 2016 as my commitment as a Secular Carmelite needed to take priority."

Barbara Smith

*

Fr Queenan's celebration of the Liturgy was with great care and devotion and his provision of a Latin Mass every first Thursday in the month and every fourth or fifth Sunday in the month was welcomed by many. Following the retirement of Mgr Canon Leyden (Fr Gabriel) as Parish Priest at Corpus Christi parish, Fr Martin succeeded him as Catholic Chaplain to Weston Hospital, and he also became Dean of Weston-super-Mare Deanery, which includes the parishes in Portishead, Clevedon, Nailsea, Burnham-on-Sea and Cheddar. He was assisted in his ministry by a Pastoral Council; a Finance Committee; Extraordinary Ministers of Holy Communion; the Choir and Organist; Altar Servers; Readers; Children's Liturgy Helpers; Catering for social and welfare needs; Church flowers; and Church maintenance.

In 2008 we marked the 70th anniversary of the opening of Our Lady of Lourdes and there was a celebration in September in the Parish hall when Kath Reynolds baked and iced a splendid cake.

Kath Reynolds

Kath Reynolds' cake in celebration of Our Lady of Lourdes 70th birthday 1938 – 2008, held in the Parish Hall.

Fr Martin regularly visited the sick, both in their homes and in hospital. As they became increasingly infirm, Bernard and Wyn Bray went to the Cedars Residential Care Home, Weston-super-Mare. When Bernard was taken critically ill, he was admitted to Weston General Hospital where he died on 25th March 2009. Wyn went to St Joseph's Home, Cotham Hill, Bristol, living until she was nearly 103 years old. She died on 4th April 2011.

Sue Maguire October 2017

The Holy Water stoup in memory of Bernard and Wyn Bray.

Chapter 4

The Brays had lived in the Parish for many years and left a very generous legacy to the Church. They were welcomed to the Parish at the Parish Council on 20th September 1981. By 22nd September, Mr Bernard Bray was Vice-Chairman of the Parish Council and Mrs Wyn Bray was Chairman of the CWL. Mr and Mrs Bray were elected to the Council. On 24th January 1982 Wyn produced a comprehensive report from the CWL, while Mr Bray reporting for the KSC stated that there were now 33 members in the WSM Council with the hope of more. On 6th June 1982 Mr Bray reporting for the KSC said that the coaches had been organised for the Glastonbury Pilgrimage and Wyn Bray reported that the CWL, still meeting monthly, had arranged a trip to Worcester, a Wine and Buffet Fair, the first Communion Breakfast and the Summer Fête. The two of them were very dynamic. In November 1984 Mr Bernard Bray moved into the Finance and General Purposes Committee with Ken Morrison. Their memory and kindness is commemorated on a brass plaque on the Holy Water stoup in the narthex and a lovely rose bush which is planted in the border of the front car park.

May they rest in peace.

Sue Maguire October 2017

The rose bush planted in memory Bernard and Wyn Bray.

Fr O'Sullivan had intended to replace the gable end crosses, but had never quite got around to it. Fortunately, Tony Inganni (who by this time was training to be a Deacon) knew a stone mason who worked on Wells Cathedral. He was approached, readily agreeing to carve the replacement crosses for the two gables ends overlooking Milton and

Baytree Roads. They replaced ones that had been on the Church since it was first built. The new ones cost just over £3000. Bishop Declan Lang dedicated them in 2009.

Fr Martin visited Rose Wakley in Pine Lodge Nursing Home until she died. Rosina Wakley was widowed twice; first when Harold Macey, an Aircraft Inspector died in July 1971 aged 58, leaving her and three adult boys, Christopher, Nicholas and Paul; and second when William Wakley, who was a retired Travel Agent Clerk, died in 1982 aged 73. All that time she lived in Linden Avenue until she could no longer look after herself, when she moved into Pine Lodge Care Home, where she was regularly visited by Fr Queenan and friends. When she needed nursing, she moved into St Anthony's Nursing Home, where she died in 2007 nine days short of being 88. She had been a School Bus Supervisor, and had been a hard-working fund raiser in our Parish and for Corpus Christi school.

Our well-used Parish Hall continued as the venue for our varied social and welfare events including the "Passover" meal, Parish Dinners, refreshments after Sunday Mass, and individual celebratory parties. It was usually decorated in themes designed to fit the occasion.

The Fifth Annual General Meeting of the Parish Pastoral Council was held on 7th November 2010 at Our Lady of Lourdes, with Tony Inganni as Chairman and Barbara Smith as Secretary. Some of the parishioners had attended the People of Hope initiative at St Bede's, Lawrence Weston in October. The most significant proposal was that near parishes should seek closer ties with each other and a common way of supporting "Parishes in Communion for Mission". The three Weston Catholic Parishes had met at Our Lady of Lourdes a few days earlier.

Under the heading of Pastoral Activity, the Children's Liturgy Group, which met during Mass on Sunday mornings in the Parish Room, to experience the message of the Mass at their own level, was a great success and had been for some time. The result of their work is brought out by them at the Offertory and displayed on the Altar.

Under Ecumenical Works, collections were made at Sainsbury's in Worle with 13 collectors amassing a wonderful sum of £2,802.00.

The Social activities included a party to celebrate Joyce Deakin's 90th birthday, which touched her greatly for all the work put in; there was a Passover Meal towards the end of Lent and a Parish Dinner at New Year; there was a planned Christmas Bazaar.

Other headings included a report of a visit to Rome on pilgrimage in which Sybil Gwynne-Jones, Sheila Berry and Chris Press, newly joined via the Ordinariate, joined the group; there were two Parish Dinners held in 2011 and under the heading of Diaconate Formation, Tony Inganni was 18 months into a four-year study to the Permanent Diaconate.

Pope Benedict XVI visited the UK from 16th to 19th September 2010. It was the first State Visit by a Pope to the UK. He met the Queen, the First Minister of Scotland, Alex Salmond, the Archbishop of Canterbury, Rowan Williams, the Prime Minister and Leader of the Conservative Party, David Cameron, and leaders of the other main political parties. The highlight of the visit was the service for the Beatification of Cardinal John Henry Newman.

Chapter 4

On 19th September 2010, several parishioners accompanied Fr Martin to Cofton Park to share in the visit of our Holy Father. Pope Benedict's humility and common touch during his visit to England and Scotland was a revelation to behold, completely overshadowing the rather negative press broadcast prior to his arrival. The whole Beatification of John Henry Newman was televised and even through this medium the humility and Holiness of the Pope shone through brightly.

*

In 2010, two parishioners from Our Lady of Lourdes Parish felt called to join the Secular Order of Discalced Carmelites, Barbara Smith, who has been associated with a Carmelite community in France for many years, and Christine O'Rourke. Barbara had invited Christine to visit the French Carmelites and she had been so impressed by their welcome and life of prayer that Christine decided to explore a Carmelite life for herself.

The Secular Order (previously known as the Third Order) has several communities in England and is under the wing of Fr Matt Blake, a friar from the Carmelite Retreat Centre, Boars Hill, Oxford. Each canonically established community has a President and an elected Council, and there is also a National President.

In June 2010, Christine joined the Little Way community in Bristol and Barbara the St Luke's community in Wincanton. They were both received into formation (novitiate) in 2011 and made their first Profession in 2013. Christine then moved Parishes but made her final Profession in 2015 and Barbara in 2016.

Other parishioners have shown interest too in the Carmelite way of life. Sisi Baker is in formation in the Wincanton community. Three others (one in Bristol and two in Wincanton) have also shown interest but have not wished to continue.

Barbara Smith

*

It was on four Thursday afternoons during the long summer holiday that Christine O'Rourke started a little class for very young children, from about 3 years old to 7 or 8, in which she had prepared simple activities involving cutting paper and card, gluing and crayoning. Fr Martin usually came in briefly to talk to the children and Barbara Smith would read to them. These were ably assisted by volunteers taken from the Special Ministers of Holy Communion, all of whom had received their CRB (now called DBS) checks. After a couple of years these Thursday afternoons were reduced to two, and eventually stopped altogether when, sadly for us, Christine left the Parish to live with her sister. She was greatly missed as she carried out many other duties in the Parish.

Three years before Fr Queenan left, Hintza died on his 10th birthday (7th November 2012) and a few months later two more Rhodesian Ridgebacks arrived as puppies born on 3rd December 2012, Hintza II and his sister, Nandi, which caused some frustration by digging many holes in the lawns. Fortunately, she gave this up after what seemed a very long time!

Fr Martin had a brief but successful acting career when he was invited to act in a little scene by raising the Host as if in a Mass. It was in one of the episodes in the series "The She-wolves" on BBC 4. Dr Helen Castor wrote the book "She-wolves: England's Early Queens", which gave rise to this three-episode documentary in 2012. More scenes were taken than used for this series, some of which appeared in a further series by Dr Helen Castor, "Medieval Lives: Birth, Marriage, Death" shown the following year.

Barbara Smith

Hintza I 7th November 2002 – 7th November 2012.

From an unknown source

Fr Martin with Hintza II and Nandi 3rd December 2012.

The scenes were shot at the medieval Church of St Mary in Wedmore. A member of the film crew who was from Cheddar suggested travelling around the area, eventually settling on the medieval church in Wedmore as suitable for the scene. Latin Masses had been performed there. A parishioner from Corpus Christi asked Fr Martin if he would be interested. He took Paul Crook with him as an altar server.

A parishioner from Cheddar Parish, whose daughter was a researcher with Lamplight Productions, had known that he had taken instruction on saying the Latin Mass asked if he would be willing to assist with the Mass scene that was to be recorded.

Someone suggested that after the 9.30 Mass on Tuesdays, free morning coffee with biscuits should be available in the Parish Room. This proved very popular although, perhaps, fortunately, not all who attended the Mass came to coffee afterwards as there was only one table. This was an excellent opportunity for those who went to the Saturday evening Mass and those who preferred Sunday mornings could meet each other. The numbers coming to these Tuesday gatherings increased as time went on, especially when Hilda Wallby got bored at home because then she did her extra baking, and she made beautiful cakes or a large cake. No doubt she did Fr Martin proud with her cakes as well as her meals for him. This carried forward to when Fr Alexander Redman took over in 2015.

By arrangement with Fr Queenan, Barbara Smith and Christine O'Rourke used to give little mid-week services called, "Liturgy of the Word and Holy Communion" on days that he was away. These services comprised of the reading of the Lessons, various prayers

Chapter 4

and the distribution of the Host only. They were usually well attended. Had a priest been available, he would have come from Corpus Christi to celebrate Mass, but by this time Canon Barry had died and there was no available priest, such was the acute shortage of clergy.

In the Sixth AGM of the Parish Pastoral Council held on 22nd April 2012, under the heading "Parishes in Communion for Mission, Richard Austin of Corpus Christi had circulated a three-monthly magazine of news from the three parishes of Weston, 3CPWSM. The first edition was in November 2011 and the last was November 2012. It proved difficult to get sufficient contributions. Thereafter Richard produced the magazine just for Corpus Christi news until November 2013, when it stopped for ever, no-one wishing to take it on. There had been discussions of meetings of Ecumenical contacts between the Milton Churches, which had taken place often in the past, but this was now not quite so easy because the Milton Baptist and Church-of-England Churches had been re-aligned towards Weston Churches Together. Progress was reported in areas such as Children' Liturgy, RCIA, Prayer Link, Ecumenical Works, Liturgy, and School Transport.

In the planned visit by Bishop Declan Lang for the 12th and 13th May, it was hoped that he would bless the new Credence Tables and the Holy Water container (stoup). Memorial plaques to Bishop Mervyn Alexander and Wyn and Bernard Bray were being prepared along with the re-incising of the plaque for Fr O'Callaghan.

There were more details of changes that had been discussed for some years before, that the emphasis should be on helping the Parish Priest in going about his duties in improving the spiritual life of the Parish. The following were discussed: Called to be a People of Hope/Parishes in Communion for Mission; Deanery Meeting; Prayer Link; Children's Liturgy; Families in Church; Bishop's Visit; the Parish 75th Anniversary; and AOB.

By the Parish Pastoral Council of 5th February 2014, the date for Tony Inganni's Ordination Ceremony had been set for 15th November that year at Clifton Cathedral, after which a buffet lunch or dinner could be held in the Parish Hall the following day. Christine O'Rourke suggested that later in the year there should be a Retreat and Sue Inganni mentioned that Joyce Deakin, who had many years looking after Fr O'Sullivan, spent most of her time at home: Christine O'Rourke gladly agreed to visit her on a regular basis.

Discussions about pastoral guidelines had been held in the Diocese since 2006, and in the "Called to be a People of Hope" booklet produced by Bishop Declan in November 2008 available through the Clifton Diocese, 14 areas of work were identified for Parish Pastoral Councils to implement in the coming 5 years to improve pastoral care. The areas are: Prayer; Liturgical Prayer; Collaborative ministry; Adult education and formation; Ecumenism; Vocation; Youth; Family life; Catholic schools; Acting justly; A people of welcome; Rite of Christian Initiation of Adults; Environment; and Interfaith dialogue.

Much of these areas were previously being tackled in our Parish by the CWL, the SVP and the KSC, but the CWL had already collapsed through an inability to fill important committee vacancies for organisational processes by 2002, and the two other groups had folded even earlier. This did not mean that the sick, elderly and lonely were not visited, but it was not on a formal basis unless to take Holy Communion to those who could not come to church. The idea of studying these areas was to help parishes to put their pastoral work on a more structured basis so that areas of weakness could be identified with methods found to remedy them.

On 28th February 2013 Pope Benedict XVI resigned and the new Pope, Pope Francis I, was elected.

In September 2013, Bishop Declan produced "a Pastoral Councils Implementation Guide" through the Clifton Diocese to help the parishes.

By 8th October 2014, planning for Tony Inganni's ordination was complete. The first Friendship meeting had been well attended. Guidelines for visiting parishioners were set up and the CRB checks or DBS had been obtained for parishioners dealing with children and vulnerable adults. The altar servers would receive their Guild of St Stephen medals on St Stephens Day, 26th December.

The Guild of St Stephen

St Pope Pius X.

The Guild of St Stephen is an international organisation for altar servers. It was founded in England in 1904 by Father Hamilton McDonald in London at the Convent of the Sacred Heart. In 1905, St Pope Pius X gave his approval for the establishment of the Guild at Westminster Cathedral, which grew, and in 1934, Pope Pius XI enabled all Guilds of Altar Servers in the British Commonwealth to be affiliated with the Archconfraternity at Westminster.

The patron saints of the Guild are the Blessed Virgin Mary, St Stephen, St Thomas More and St Pius X.

The Guild Medal

In the centre, the letters XP are the first two letters of the name Christ in Greek. At the top is the crown of victory given by God to everyone who overcomes evil, especially those who die for him. At the bottom are the palm branches, traditional signs of martyrs who died for Christ. Around the edge are the Latin words of the Guild motto, which is CVI SERVIRE REGNARE EST (To Serve Christ Is to Reign). On the back, around the edge, are the Latin words SANCTI STEPHANI ARCHI SOLDALITAS (Archconfraternity of St Stephen).

Awards for Altar Servers
- The Bronze Medal - after 1 year's service
- The Silver Medal - after 10 years' service
- The Silver Medal of Merit - after 20 years' service
- The Gold Medal - after 50 years' service.

Objectives of The Guild of St Stephen

The objectives are:
- to encourage, positively and practically, the highest standards of serving at the Church's liturgy and so contribute to the whole community's participation in a more fruitful worship of God
- to provide altar servers with a greater understanding of what they are doing so that they may serve with increasing reverence and prayerfulness and thereby be led to a deepening response to their vocation in life
- to unite servers of different parishes and dioceses for their mutual support and encouragement.

The Guild of St Stephen Promise

I offer myself to God Almighty, to Blessed Mary ever Virgin and to our Holy Patron, St Stephen and I promise to do my best to serve reverently, intelligently and punctually, having the glory of God and my own eternal salvation as my object.

*

There were more routine matters discussed, but the implementation of the areas associated with the "Called to be a People of Hope" was complete.

By the Parish Pastoral Meeting on 15th January 2015, the Police Checks having been completed, the home visits were well under way. Regarding ecumenical matters, our contact at St Peter's was Jackie Mason, who would liaise with her husband Peter in arranging joint worship activities at Easter. In any other business, a representative from the Society of St Vincent de Paul had asked to give a talk. A date was to be decided.

*

The altar boys did not receive their medals as planned because they were not ordered in time. They arrived by the Parish Pastoral Meeting of 11th March 2015 and were presented on 3rd May.

Fr Martin spoke about a new directive called Proclaim 15, which was supported by the Bishops' Conference. This national initiative was intended to encourage new expressions of evangelism in parishes. A meeting in central Birmingham was planned for 11th July 2015 to equip parishes with evangelist aids for use from autumn that year. The vision for parish evangelism included small group sessions, with prayer vigils on 11th July.

Fr Martin outlined what a PPC should do, giving the answer from the Diocesan Implementation Guide: "The primary task is for members to ask themselves how members listen to God and to each other, to focus on the needs of the parish they serve. The group should be a listening group able to articulate its vision and to involve the wider parish community in decisions".

He summarised, saying that over the past two years the group's focus had been on spiritual developments while maintaining support for social occasions. To deepen our prayer, we now have two Lectio Divina Groups meeting monthly and the Divine Mercy Prayer Groups together with the Divine Mercy Candle, which can be lit as a memorial, seems to answer a need. A book for prayer requests is permanently in front of Our Lady's statue; the requests are prayed for at the Divine Mercy Meetings. A small library of books on the Faith is available in the church porch. In addition, Teresa Thorne organised a Taizé service attended by members of other local churches as well as members of our own congregation. Mary Studham reported on the development of the recent innovation of a Friendship Group, which was more aligned to spiritual matters than those of the past, which were largely social gatherings.

On the financial side, Jan Greaney, the Chair of the Finance Committee, reported on the financial aspects associated with the daily running of the Parish, including the group of people who organise the social events, which raise money for CAFOD and other organisations. The events in 2014/5 included the Christmas Dinner, the Passover Meal, the Good Friday Frugal Lunch, an International Day and more.

There were pilgrimages to Knock, to Lourdes and to Rome and in 2016, the Jubilee Year of the Mercy of God, a pilgrimage to Rome was being planned.

Looking at this summary given by Fr Martin and various committee members, it may be seen how the recent switch from a Parish Committee to a Parish Pastoral Council had changed the focus away from the bricks and mortar of the church towards the more spiritual and social aspects of Catholic life. This is not to say that before we were not spiritual and social, but the needs of our parish in previous years were concerned with building up and improving the church and its outbuildings. This had largely been carried out under the watchful eye of Fr O'Sullivan and completed by Fr Martin. This situation was probably true of most other parishes, so that Bishop Declan Lang's spiritual directives were more appropriate and timely to the needs of the diocese as a whole.

On a more personal note, Fr Martin knew that he was being moved on to the Church of St George in Warminster. This was discussed in July 2015 when decisions about the redecoration of the church had to be made.

Everyone was very sad to see him leave and he was very sad to go, but he said that the time was right: it is essential for priests to move on as they need to develop further in their work.

Our Community was appreciably increased with new members, many of whom have moved into our Parish as new houses had been built. These include people of many nationalities, thus enriching our parish life (does not "Catholic" mean "Universal"?). These people who have had the impetus and courage to leave their own native countries, and, in some cases, have had to learn a new language and a completely different culture, have rejuvenated the Catholic Church. Many take a full part in parish affairs and some have taken on key positions in the organisation. Fr Martin said that 17 different languages were currently spoken in the parish. On Pentecost Sundays in recent years we have celebrated International Lunches with excellent food, singing, dancing and costumes from the various national groups - all hugely enjoyed by everybody.

Our children too, enjoy their liturgy in the Parish Room prior to the Offertory of the Sunday morning Mass, when their entrance completes our parish family. Sometimes, the older ones read at Mass or sing the responsorial psalm.

We have also welcomed a number of former Anglicans who belong to the Ordinariate of Our Lady of Walsingham, promulgated by Pope Benedict XVI, who have made their home with us. They enjoy our liturgy, we like and appreciate their company and fellowship, and admire their youth and energy.

*

Sisilah Baker writes

The Parish of Our Lady of Lourdes consists of people from different walks of life. This is what prompted me to organise a Multi-Cultural gathering, encouraging everyone within our denomination to attend this social event. The first gathering was held in May 2013, followed by another in 2014 and one more in 2016.

To our utmost surprise everyone greatly supported this event; the young and old. The parishioners were welcomed to wear their traditional outfits representing their country. It was colourful, bright and brought a whole new ambience.

The food that was displayed was plentiful, spoilt for choice, scrumptious and titillated our taste buds.

For the first two consecutive years, the event was hosted by the talented Bob Gibbons, who injected fun and laughter amongst us. [He played the guitar during the Saturday evening folk Masses.]

Some of our parishioners also came up with entertainment, which showcased their ethnic diversity; River dance, a performance by the Philippines, Indian dance, Malaysian Dance, theatrical performances by our local parishioners, Jamaican song, a Polish number and many others. There was so much that we could share, and broaden our spectrum on the ever-growing culture in our parish church. It was definitely an experience, which will remain with us, and we acknowledge that we are blessed by the rich diverse ethnicity.

We care for and love one another, as God's people.

Sisilah Baker

Chapter 4

Sisi Baker 2017

Food preparation for the first Multi-Cultural Gathering in the Parish Hall.

Sisi Baker 2017

The Multi-Cultural meal seems to be going down very well.

Sisi Baker organised the first Multi-Cultural Gathering in 2013 for Pentecost Sunday in which there was a variety of food, music and dancing. She arranged another in 2014. After that it was decided to organise them biennially for June/July time, a little later in the year than originally. The pictures are from the first of these celebrations.

Sisi Baker 2017

The Feast of Our Lady of the Rosary with all the candles lit.

The image of Our Lady, situated in the side chapel of our Church, is a focal point for everyone. She stands humbly and invitingly and has an aura of tranquillity, which is infinitely full of grace.

Our Lady is not an ordinary Mother. She is the most perfect of Mothers, because she is the Mother of God. She is honoured and adored, lovingly, everyday especially on Saturdays and Sundays when many candles are lit and petitions are made. We not only honour Our Lady, we also ask for her intercession. As for the custom of lighting candles and placing vases of flowers before her, they epitomise our praise for the living Queen of Heaven, whom the image represents.

Each flame in Our Lady's side chapel is a symbol of our love and faith in GOD. She occupies a powerful place in our hearts. She has many faces and innumerable names; among them Our Lady of Lourdes, Our Lady of Fatima and Our Lady of the Rosary. She has appeared on occasions, mostly to children, or others, who are weak, helpless or in desperate need. She has, in some cases, procured miracles.

But, we believe all of the titles, and all of the miracles are considered to be as a result of Our Lady's close relationship with her son, Jesus. In addition to her special bond with Jesus, she also has a special relationship with the Church, and the Church belongs to her.

So that when we recite the Rosary, or bow our heads during the Creed, we are honouring Our Mother. Although, she is not GOD, she has earned our respect and devotion.

Our reverence for the Virgin Mary is greatly due to her response to GOD and her faith.

Sisilah Baker

Napoleon Almazan 2014

24th November 2014: a delayed Filipino celebration of Our Lady of the Rosary with Fr Martin Queenan in the background.

*

4.6 Deacon Tony Inganni

So far in this parish we have had only one Deacon, Tony Inganni, and this is his story, told by Sue Inganni:

"In the summer of 2009, Fr Martin approached Tony and asked him if he had ever thought of going forward for training for the diaconate. Our parish and its community had always been very important to Tony and he had thought for quite a while that there was something else calling him to do more. After much discernment and a long talk with Stephen Munday, who was ordained as Corpus Christi's first deacon and also one of Tony's closest friends, he asked Fr Martin to put his name forward for training for the diaconate.

That started a year of collecting together all the documents he needed. Tony's Dad was in the Royal Air Force and they travelled around a lot so that finding his Baptismal, first Holy Communion and Confirmation certificates proved difficult as some of the churches no longer existed, but eventually with the help of the

Chapter 4

Bishopric of the Sea everything arrived and along with an essay on, "What his faith meant to him", were sent to Bishop's House in Bristol. A few months later Tony and I were asked to attend an interview at the Education Centre in Bristol. There we met Tom and Fiona Douglas, Kevin and Annie Malone and Fr David Mills, who were the team responsible for student deacon training (Tom and Kevin are deacons). Tony was asked various questions about himself, our relationship, his family, his faith, the parish and what they would mean to him with regard to going forward for diaconate training.

About a month later we were asked to go and meet Bishop Declan at Bishop's House in Bristol. It was during this meeting that the Bishop told Tony he had been accepted for the next diaconate course to start that September. Before he could start the course, I received a letter from the Bishop asking for my permission in writing for Tony to undertake the diaconate course, which I was only too pleased to give.

The diaconate programme consisted of monthly meetings on a Friday evening and all day Saturday. He found the course both challenging and exhilarating. It made him look at various aspects of his faith, and with the help of some of the most amazing speakers (some of them I had the privilege of listening to) he found the whole experience wonderful, even with all the essay writing he had to do.

At the end of the first year Tom and Fiona, Kevin and Annie and Fr David stepped down and Fr Christopher Whitehead from St Bernadette's Parish in Whitchurch, Bristol, and Doreen Whyette from the Education Centre took charge.

Towards the end of his second year, Tony was diagnosed with Mesothelioma (asbestos-related cancer). But this didn't stop him, if anything it made him more determined than ever to finish his course and be ordained deacon. He even said this to his oncologist at their first meeting.

In October 2014, the preparations for the ordination began and with it came another letter for me from Bishop Declan asking for my permission for Tony to be ordained a deacon.

Sue Maguire

The Inganni Family Candlesticks presented by Samantha, Andrew, Marie, Michael, Jenny and Peter in loving memory of their father, Tony.

On 15th November 2014 in Clifton Cathedral, with many from our parish present, Tony was ordained Deacon of the Parish of Our Lady of Lourdes.

The sad thing about all this is that he never really had the opportunity to put his diaconate training into practice. On Ash Wednesday 2015 at 6.50pm in Weston hospice surrounded by all his family Tony passed away. Our Lady of Lourdes and its parishioners meant so much to Tony and he was very honoured to be ordained your deacon even though it was only for a short time. I know he would hope that one day in the future someone else will come forward to train for the diaconate and I am sure they will receive the same support, encouragement and love he did."

Sue Inganni

May he rest in peace.

Sue Maguire 2017

The decoration of the church was finished in September and the stained glass window in commemoration of Fr O'Sullivan's 30 years as Parish Priest, produced and installed by Wayne Ricketts Stained Glass, Bristol in 2015at a cost of £3500, paid for mainly by donations.

Departure of Father Martin Queenan

In September 2015 Fr Martin left to take over the Parish of St George in Warminster. He was always very relaxed and encouraging, and was greatly missed by the parishioners.

4.7 Ways of entering the Catholic Church

Geoff Thornton, our organist and choirmaster for many years, and instigator of this History of the Parish, writes about how he did it!

The Ordinariate is not the only way for people to enter the Catholic Church. It is only a recent innovation (and was really about closer ties between the Catholic Church and the Church of England) What did people do before? They simply called on the priest. Here is a story of a couple who did just that:

Our family was not a church-going one but we were always "packed off" to Sunday School on Sunday afternoon to the local Congregational Chapel. When the Chapel closed, we thought that we would no longer have to go anywhere again. No such Luck. The following Sunday we were "packed off" to none other than St Mary's – the local Anglo-Catholic Church (C of E). We did not know what to expect.

Chapter 4

What splendour met us as we entered St Mary's - Auntie Florrie's church!! – for the first time – what a contrast to the drab chapel we had gone to. The highly coloured and elaborate Sanctuary, with golden angels painted on the Altar front. Beautiful stained glass window, many statues of the saints with winking lights. A rood beam with Crucifix and figures of Our Lady and St John (I can see it as I write). We must have sat open-mouthed as the "Sung Mass" began with organ music and the robed choir coming into their stalls in the Chancel.

The magnificent High Altar was lit by 10 antique silver candlesticks with a larger silver Crucifix in the middle. Then began the procession round the Church with Cross, lights and embroidered banners.

The smoke and smell of incense filled the church. The organ pealed and the choir sang, "Hail thee festive day." The Mass continued and we were "hooked". We joined the choir; (boys and men) were later confirmed and took our first Holy Communion. Gradually, we became familiar with the Liturgy through the seasons of the Church's year. It was then that I fell in love with the music of the Church and started to teach myself the organ. Our whole lives were centred round the church; its services and social activities.

All was to change. At the age of 18 (1953), I was called up for National Service (RAF) and experienced a different kind of Church. The "C of E" Chaplains seemed to have different beliefs from St Mary's despite being "very good chaps". Our unit was posted to RAF Eindhoven, Holland, and I joined the Christian Fellowship there. Through the powerful Bible ministry of an American Bible Missionary I came into a "born again" faith.

When I was "demobbed" and no longer felt at home in my Anglo-Catholic Church, I went to several of our local churches and finally plumped for the Assembly of God Church, which was experiencing a revival. There I was baptised with the Holy Spirit and in water (full immersion). I enjoyed working in the Sunday School, Outreach and music groups. It was here that I met and married my dear Maureen (1962).

After a time, we were invited to serve in Evangelistic and Pastoral work in rural Lincolnshire where we stayed for four years. By then we had two lovely daughters, Helen and Stephanie, and needed a more secure living base.

We decided to move to Bristol (1971). A friend from the RAF days offered us accommodation while we looked for work. It was then relatively easy to find. I finally ended up working for Bristol City Council, seconded to their work for Community Relations and Racial Equality, mainly in the St Paul's and Easton areas.

During this we lived in Stoke Bishop (1971 - 1978). Our spiritual lives then were rather "on hold" but the break came when a free cottage with much needed extra room was offered in exchange for part-time duties as Verger at St Mary's, Henbury. It was a "bolt from the blue" and we were welcomed and appreciated for four lovely years. The cottage was literally next door to the 12th century Parish Church. Nearby was the beautiful Blaise Castle Estate. Our duties were very interesting and enjoyable. It brought renewal and healing into our lives. Through the local Ecumenical Lent Group, we started going to the Charismatic Prayer Group at St Teresa's, Filton. At this time Maureen had completed her B Ed Degree at Redland College and started teaching at various schools.

After four happy years at Henbury we decided to find a home of our own at nearby Westbury (1982). Meanwhile, we were finding our involvement at St Teresa's more and more absorbing, and one night we were coming back from the Prayer Group at Filton, I said to Maureen, "Do you think the Lord is calling us into the Catholic Church?" She said, "I have been waiting for you to say that for the past six months." And so we were received into the Church in 1983.

In 1986, Maureen got a teaching post at Corpus Christi School and we finally moved to Weston-super-Mare. In 1991, I was asked to deputise as organist at Our Lady of Lourdes for six weeks during the sickness of the regular organist. He did not come back and I was still playing the organ there 24 years later.

We moved to Uphill in 1993 and now regard Corpus Christi as our spiritual home. Our appreciation of the fullness of Catholic Faith and teaching grows daily. Deo Gracias!

Geoff Thornton

4.8 The Parish Dinner

After many years of going out for our New Year Parish Dinner we decided, after asking Fr Martin, to do it ourselves. We were very fortunate that the husband of Joan Bentley was a chef, so Joan and her husband, Stewart, Jan and Brendan Greaney, Tony and I got together to organise the event. We tried to have a theme for each Dinner, decorating the Parish Hall accordingly and then the meal was planned around the theme. Here are some of the themes:

2003 – French Evening; 2004 – Italian Evening; 2005 – American Evening; 2006 – Winter Woodland; 2007 – Pirate Ship; 2008 – Roman Villa; 2009 – Circus Theme; 2010 – Seaside Theme; 2011 – Party Theme; and 2012 – Moroccan Theme.

These different themes were very enjoyable to put together, especially transforming the Hall from a plain room into a bit of magic, as displayed on the two following pages.

In 2013 due to Tony's illness, I stepped back from organising the Dinner and Barbara Smith, with Jan's assistance, came forward to carry on a much looked-forward-to Parish event.

I would like at this point to thank the Parish for all their support and generosity in giving to the charity raffles. Many very good causes have received help due to your kindness. In the first 10 years, you raised nearly £4,000.

I am really pleased to be able to say that the Dinner in 2018 will once again be held in our Parish Hall and I am sure everyone who attends will have a great evening.

Susan Inganni

Chapter 4

Themes at the Parish

Tony and Sue Inganni

Tony and Sue Inganni

Tony and Sue Inganni

Jan Greaney

The American Night.

There was always a raffle at the Parish Dinners, which was where most of the money was raised. The number (not the ages!) attending these dinners varied, averaging about mid -70s. The cumulative total raised by 2012 was £5901.72. Money also came from Cream Teas and Quizzes, such that by 2016 the amount was £807.10. We usually tried to choose a different charity each year.

Jan Greaney

4.9 Fr Alexander Redman - Parish Priest 2015

Fr. Alexander like Fr Martin before him has studied in Rome; he also had a period in a monastery in London and has been a prison visiting chaplain, which he has taken up again in Bristol. We know this from his homilies. He has already continued the tradition of leading pilgrimages for parishioners. Beyond this he has expressed a preference for keeping a low personal profile for the time being, which we can understand and respect. He has however strongly supported this History of the Parish, and the Events organised by the Parish.

On 1st November 2015 Geoff Thornton ended his spell as organist and choir master on Sunday mornings after 24 years' service (1991 - 2015). The choir would have to sing unaccompanied until a replacement could be found. The problem was that organists were in great demand on Sunday mornings. The organist at St Joseph's, whose Mass was at 6.00pm Sunday evenings, was unable to help at that time.

On 4th November 2015 Fr Alexander Redman opened his first Parish Pastoral Council meeting. The redecoration of the church had been finished in September and the stained glass window commemorating Fr O'Sullivan's thirty years as our Parish Priest had been installed. The Christmas Bazaar was planned for Saturday 28th November: Sue Inganni served the lunches and snacks from the kitchen; there were several stalls, such as Barbara Smith's Cake Stall, Gifts, Tombola, Grand Raffle, Repository Stall, but no Card Stall and no Santa that year. Douglas Chamberlain donated money for the Grand Draw cash prize. Doug Chamberlain and his colleague, Vincent Travers, were prominent over many years as ushers at Masses and funerals. Money raised went towards two replacement Repository glass cabinets to be placed either side of the windows in the porch. There was to be a special stall for CAFOD with money going to the Ebola Crisis.

A special party was planned as a surprise thank you for Geoff after a Sunday Mass when Geoff and Maureen next attended. Fr Alexander's Induction was arranged for Tuesday 17th November at 7.00 pm, with a get together afterwards in the Parish Hall, where Barbara Smith organised the catering and a list of attendees from Nympsfield and Dursley. Fr Martin's Induction was organised for Wednesday 11th November in Warminster, and a coach was arranged.

The launch of the 27th Year of Mercy was on Tuesday 8th December until the Feast of Christ the King, 20th November 2016, with the opening of the Holy Door by the Pope at St Peter's Basilica. The Jubilee would be celebrated in all local churches around the world, with Holy Doors open in each diocese in the main cathedral or in a local historical church.

After Fr Martin left, Barbara Smith, the Parish Administrative Assistant, retired in May 2016, when the new Parish Priest, Fr Alexander Redman had settled in. Eventually our new part-time Parish Administrator, Mrs Maricris Magbanua was appointed and began settling in to her office in the presbytery. Her background story follows:

Chapter 4

Victor and I started going to the Church of Our Lady of Lourdes in March 2004, when I joined him here in the UK. We are originally from the Philippines, where we were both brought up in the Catholic Faith. As the years passed, we have been blessed with two children, Denzel (altar server) and Kelly Anne (choir). We go to church every Sunday as a family. I believe that my job now is God's plan because it never crossed my mind to become more involved. Being a stranger to this country is different, but our church makes us welcome: everyone is friendly and helpful, especial our Parish Priest. I do enjoy my job and being part of our community.

Aba Ginoong Maria (The Hail Mary in Tagalog)

Aba Ginoong Maria, napupuno ka ng grasya.

Ang Panginoong Dios ay sumasaiyo.

Bukod kang pinagpala sa babaeng lahat
At pinagpala ka naman ng iyong anak na si Hesus.

Santa Maria, Ina ng Dios

Ipanalangin mo kaming makasalanan

Ngayun at kung kami'y mamamatay.

Amen.

Maricris

Fr Alexander planned to hold a children's Mass in which they would be participating throughout by doing the Readings, dividing the Psalms between them, the Bidding Prayers, Offertory Procession, Offertory Collection and a children's choir. Regular Latin Masses recommenced on the first Sunday of March 2017.

The church was still without a professional organist and choir-organiser until 23rd July when normal service resumed with Frances Ball from St Joseph's, who is our organist at the 9.30am Mass on Sunday and for St Joseph's at 6.00pm on the same day. She had been asked previously but wanted to retire from work before taking up the appointment in September. The appointment is an official one with the Diocese of Clifton.

*

Chapter 4

Napoleon Almazan

Some of the Filipino Community with Fr Alexander Redman in the background celebrating 1st November 2016, All Saints' Day.

In recent years we have had an influx of parishioners from the Philippines who take a lot of photographs and organise various functions. The pictured one was held in 2014 to celebrate the Feast of Our Lady of the Rosary.

On Saturday 7th October 2017, the Feast of Our Lady of the Rosary, a celebration was held, beginning with a recitation of the Rosary at 11.30am followed by Holy Mass at 12.00 noon, after which the Filipino Community organised a lunch in the Parish Hall.

*

The summer fêtes have always been a tradition in our Parish, starting as a shared affair with Corpus Christi Parish, but for many years we have organised our own. The year 2017 was no exception, although perhaps a little different and certainly more colourful.

Sue Maguire 2017

A warm welcome to exotic foods at Our Lady of Lourdes Summer Fête 2017.
Mrs Rose Thomas, her son George and Jaiden Biju.

Stalls at the Summer Fête 2017.

Chapter 4

Sue Maguire October 2017

Chris Press and Mary Studham at their Flower Stall - Summer Fête 2017.

Sue Maguire October 2017

'Tug of War' – The Summer Fête 2017.

Chapter 4

La Retraite Sisters

Below are the Sisters who are in the Parish. They worked at the La Retraite schools in various places teaching the children and young adults, the next generation and the future of our Parish and parishes all over the world. That was their lives' work. Now they have retired and are cared for in their retirement. We thank them greatly for their devotion, example and care of such a valuable part of our Parish. Now that their work is over it is left to our own parishioners to undertake that crucial teaching role.

Name	Order	Location
Sister Jean Daniel *	La Retraite	Walliscote Road
Sister Eileen Healy *	La Retraite	Walliscote Road
Sister Pauline Mahony *	La Retraite	Walliscote Road
Sister Patricia Talbot *	La Retraite	Walliscote Road
Sister Dorothy Kerr *		Sandford Retirement Village Extra Care Home, 2 Hapil Close, Darlisette, Sandford, Winscombe BS25 5RF. The Monica Wills Trust.
Sister Patricia O'Connell *		Sandford Retirement Village
Sister Bridget Arscott		Sandford Retirement Village
Sister Winifred McCoy		Sandford Retirement Village
Sister Sheila Toal		Sandford Retirement Village

Their house at 11 Walliscote Road closed and was put for sale. The Sisters marked with a star moved to the Monica Wills New Care Complex in Keynsham, Bristol in November 2017. The three Sisters not marked needed more nursing and remained in Sandford.

Apart from their teaching work at Corpus Christi school and other schools during their working lives, they assisted with Holy Communion and were involved with youth work. Since they retired from teaching they visited the sick, ran the Catechisms, ecumenical groups, workshops for the deaf, quiet mornings or afternoons, with perhaps a talk with questions afterwards followed by a cup of tea, organising weeks of guided prayer in the Diocese and numerous other duties required by the Parish Priests and the needs of the Parishes in Weston. They have always kept close links with Corpus Christi School. Did they ever really retire? Their house has functioned as a centre of apostolic outreach in the local Parishes and beyond.

Although their move to Keynsham was delayed, their Thanksgiving Mass was held at Corpus Christi Church on 10th October at 7.00pm, followed by a lovely reception in the school hall attended by many parishioners and friends, including representation from France. An interesting exhibition about the La Retraite order was also on display and a celebration cake was kindly made by Sonia Breffitt, a Corpus Christi parishioner. We wish the Sisters happiness and good health in their retirement and we thank them for all they have done for us in many different capacities, especially their work with the children and young adults.

La Retraite was the inspiration of Catherine de Franchville and her confidence in God's saving love. Claude-Thérèse de Kermeno joined Catherine and with her was one of the founders of La Retraite. Claude-Thérèse returned to her native Quimper to open a retreat house there.

Peter Ottley 2017

From left to right: Sister Jean Daniel, Sister Pauline Mahony, Sister Patricia Talbot and seated Sister Eileen Healy.

Sue Maguire October 2017

The Sisters' Celebration Cake made by Sonia Briffitt, a parishioner of Corpus Christi.

Sr Jean Daniel

Symbol from the Breton Church where Claude-Thérèse de Kermeno received her first Communion. She was one of the La Retraite foundresses.

Chapter 4

By courtesy of Weston Mercury

The First Communion 11th July 1976, outside Our Lady of Lourdes in front of the confessional.

For our last picture, we have chosen a First Holy Communion group in 1976, to help us focus our minds on the children of the Parish, for it is they who are our great treasure, who hopefully will continue in the Faith and pass it on to the generations yet to come, a hope not only here but throughout every parish in the whole world.

The law of the Land requires that parents and the Catholic Schools provide certain aspects of education, but they answer to a higher law: the law of God. They start from the premise that each child is God's work of art and is made in God's image and likeness. Both the parents and the Catholic Schools try their utmost to bring children to their true potential, which is to be loving people and imitators of Jesus Christ who dwells in them and all of us.

We are in the business of the salvation of souls, the New Evangelisation urged upon us by His Holiness Pope Francis I is for us all to share our faith with others, so that they will enjoy God's love, joy and peace in the fellowship of His Church, in which we all rejoice. We welcome all with open arms. The grace of Our Lord Jesus Christ and the love of God and the fellowship of the Holy Spirit be with you all.

Amen

Chapter 4

Parish Priests of Our Lady of Lourdes

1964 -1967	Fr William O'Callaghan	Parish Priest successively at Stroud, Henbury and Portishead and appointed Canon. When he retired he could boast of a long period of good health until he eventually fell ill and died in 2003.
1967 - 1967	Fr Edward Hickey	Retired sick, then from 1969 was chaplain to Prior Park prep. school Cricklade, but his illness returned in 1972 and he retired to St Angela's Convent in Clifton, Bristol, operated by The Sisters of the Temple, where he died peacefully on 5th December 1977.
1968 - 1972	Fr Dr Mervyn Alban Alexander	Ordained as auxiliary Bishop of Clifton and lived in Bath, then became Bishop of Clifton. Retired in 2001 as bishop, he became parish priest at St Josephs, W-s-M until 2007, when he went to St Angela's Nursing Home in Clifton, Bristol, where he died on 14th August 2010, aged 85.
1972 - 2002	Fr Michael O'Sullivan	Retired to his birth place in a little village, Boherbue, outside Cork where his family still live. He died on 5th July 2015, aged 84.
2002 - 2015	Fr Martin Queenan	Left to take over the Parish of St George in Warminster, where he is now.
2015 -	Fr Alexander Redman	

For all those priests in the list above who have died may they rest in peace.

CHRONOLOGY

1964	On Sunday 18th October 1964, Our Lady of Lourdes, Milton, became an independent parish separate from Corpus Christi, and Fr William O'Callaghan LCL was appointed first Parish Priest. The original Presbytery at 253 Milton Road was purchased.
1965	Anglican Church of St. Peter's was being constructed. The first of the Men's Meetings recorded in the archives was held in the Parish Hall on Tuesday 5th October.
1966	In April Fr O'Callaghan announced the formation of the Society of St Vincent de Paul branch.
1967	Fr William O'Callaghan left and was presented with an oak lectern. Fr Edward Hickey became the new Parish Priest, but he was too ill to run the parish and stayed for only a couple of months.

	The late Mrs Edith Wright left a legacy to the church for the building of a new Parish Hall. The Erection of the Parish Boundaries was established in a letter on 4th August.
1968	The Youth Club was first mentioned on 5th July. Rev Dr Mervyn Alban Alexander became the new Parish Priest. The first mention of the Catholic Women's League (CWL) in Milton was in the Welfare Committee meeting of December. Fr Alexander shaped the administrative structure of the Parish Council with the Parish Priest as President, a Chairman and Vice-chairman, and each committee with a Chairman who reported to the Parish Council on progress since the previous meeting. In addition, there was an Annual General Meeting with a review of the year's work and future planning. The Sassoferrato picture was acquired
1969	The new hall was debated. As a result of the new liturgy and growing congregation, the money might be better spent on extending the church.
1970	The new Parish Hall was built for £6000 partly with the money bequeathed to the church by the late Mrs Edith Wright. Fr Dr Alexander was elected Vice-president of the Weston-super-Mare Council of Churches. Picture of the Blessed Virgin Mary in the new Parish Hall – origin unknown at this date (2018)
1971	The first Parish Council was held. Sisters from La Retraite moved into 11 Walliscote Road.
1972	Our Parish Priest Fr Dr Mervyn Alexander was appointed Auxiliary Bishop of Clifton on Friday 28th April. Fr Michael O'Sullivan became our fourth Parish Priest. Fr Michael O'Sullivan hosted his first AGM. The representatives for the Ecumenical Committee were Mr Basil M Fuller (Chairman), Mrs Williams, Miss McCafferty and Mr J Barber.
1973	The first mention of the Knights of St Columba is in the AGM of 2nd March under the section on Social and Fête Committee, and the start of the St Margaret's Guild, which was not mentioned again. There were 3 Masses on Sundays: 8.30 am, 10.00am and 4.00pm, with afternoon devotions (Stations of the Cross and Benediction) at 4.00pm. The times of weekday Masses varied from 8.00am to 10.30am with some evening Masses if there was no morning Mass at 7.30pm. There were no Vigil Masses on Saturday evenings. Confessions were on Fridays at 7.15pm, Saturdays at 11.30 m to 12.00pm, 3.00pm - 3.30pm and 6.30pm to 7.30pm.
1974	Auxiliary Bishop Alexander replaced the retiring Bishop Joseph Rudderham as Bishop of Clifton. The first summer fête at Our Lady of Lourdes in June showed Bishop Mervyn Alexander competing in activities with Fr Michael O'Sullivan. A gate was let into the fence opposite the presbytery, making a short cut to the Church, and a new door was fitted to the "Hut".

Chapter 4

	The Parish Mission conducted by Fr Francis OFM, a Capuchin Friar, took place from 9th to 20th October.
1975	Plans for an extension on the south side of the Church were discussed. The Executors of the will of the late Jack Kingston issued a bequest of £400 towards the Extension Fund.
1976	The south transept was completed giving a new side chapel and sacristy. Ken Morrison and the committee produced a prospectus for the Parish Hall with conditions of hire, and the income generated increased By September, the new altar for the side Chapel was ready.
1977	The reorganisation of the sanctuary and the decoration of the church were completed. This gave more seating in the south transept and the north transept, which became the Lady Chapel. Catholic education was being reorganised in the Diocese, which meant that the annual contribution to the Diocese was increased from £700 to £1600. An organ was bought from St Peter's Anglican Church, Burnham-on-Sea. There was an emergency meeting on 10th January to discuss the sudden resignation of Gordon Brooks, the Organist and Choirmaster, who was moving to Kent. On 22nd June the lime wood Crucifix cost £230 from Ormsby of Scarisbrick. The altar was moved forward by Stansell (Small Works) Ltd. of Taunton by September.
1978	The necessary work of re-siting the altar and re-positioning the Tabernacle and statues of the Sacred Heart and Our Lady of Lourdes was complete although the altar rails remained for a short time. The Solemn Consecration of the church by Bishop Mervyn Alexander was on the Feast of Our Lady of Lourdes, 11th February. The relic of St Cuthbert Mayne, one of the Forty Martyrs of England, was enshrined in the altar.
1979	On 13th January, the first meeting took place of a new Pastoral Council at St Joseph's. On Sunday 29th, April, there was a Day's Retreat organised for men at St Mary's Convent, Totterdown, and on Saturday 13th May the women had their turn at St Mary's with a Day of Recollection. Fr O'Sullivan arranged that Fr Francis Hinkman OFM would conduct a Mission from 16th to 23rd September.
1980	In April, the hedge by the hut was removed and the hardcore for a car park was delivered. Folk Masses began and were held at 6pm on Sundays. Preparations for the Liverpool Pastoral Conference began.
1981	The Annual General Meeting recorded the largest 1st Communion Class so far.
1982	When the Falkland Islands recovery operation began, it required much overtime and emergency working in our neighbourhood.

Chapter 4

	The visit of Pope John Paul II to Britain took place.
	The new Presbytery was completed.
1984	Parish Finance Committee was set up in accordance with revised Canon Law.
	The organ was provided with a new Trumpet stop.
1985	There was a trip to Prinknash Abbey.
1986	The last mention of the SVP and the KSC was in September.
	A Summer School was to be held in Bristol from 21st to 25th July about the RCIA for which the Bishop required representatives from each parish.
1988	The Golden Anniversary of our Church was celebrated on the 11th February.
	The Forty Martyrs window was purchased.
1990	John Walcott retired as organist due to ill health and Geoff Thornton took over in 1991.
	Fr O'Sullivan started saying Holy Mass at St Mark's Anglican Church, St Mark's Road, Worle.
	Bristol Aeroject Banwell was making 800 jobs redundant and closing.
1992	The small Parish Room was built east of the sacristy to hold 30 people.
	The attendance at the different Sunday Masses was 8.30am 80 – 100; 10.00am 130 – 140; Evening Mass 160 – 180; and St Mark's Anglican Church, Worle 60 – 90.
1995	Seven of the smaller nave windows were renewed, replacing most of the original blue-green tinted windows with white cathedral glass with yellow crosses. The stained glass windows were made by the local firm, John Baker Stained Glass Ltd.
	The Parish outing was to Prinknash Abbey.
1996	The Holy Family window was installed in the north transept made by the same firm as above.
	There were 3 Masses, 8.30am and 10.00am and 6.00pm. Later a Vigil Mass was introduced at 5.30pm on Saturday.
	In the late 90s the Church was remodelled: arches were added to the sanctuary and pilasters down the wall, with the whole colour scheme changed.
1998	The CWL's Big Sheep Outing was held in June.
1999	The Church was redecorated and the new timber Stations of the Cross were installed. A computer was installed and set up in response to Diocesan directives.
	The large RAF Locking Radar School was moved away to RAF Cosford and the site sold for housing development.
	A small wooden altar was made by Fr Michael O'Sullivan with wood salvaged from the Chapel of Holy Cross at RAF Locking.
	The Clarkes' shoe factory in Locking Road shut losing 500 jobs.
2000	Parish outings were held to Buckfast Abbey and to Dartmouth.
2001	Pope John Paul II was instrumental in the formal establishment of

Chapter 4

	the Divine Mercy devotion, and Miss Patricia Igoe donated the Divine Mercy picture.
2002	Fr O'Sullivan retired, and the new Parish Priest was Fr Martin Queenan. Fr O'Sullivan's housekeeper, Joyce Deakin, retired at the same time after being housekeeper to his predecessor and him for 35 years. The CWL closed. The Oldmixon factory ceased aircraft production with 2000 jobs lost. Fr Martin's Induction Mass was held on Thursday 21st November.
2003	Mgr Gabriel Leyden and Fr Martin Queenan were invited by Pope John Paul II to celebrate Mass in his private chapel.
2004	The highway boundary fence was replaced by a wall. The Inaugural Meeting of the Parish Pastoral Council.
2005	On April 2nd Pope John Paul II died and Pope Benedict XVI was elected as Pope.
2007	Fr Dr Mervyn Alexander retired, which meant that St Joseph's had no Parish Priest. Fr Martin discontinued the Sunday evening Mass at Our Lady of Lourdes so that he could celebrate Holy Mass at St Joseph's on alternate weeks in a sharing arrangement with other priests.
2008	The 70th anniversary of Our Lady of Lourdes church The funding for School Transport to Faith schools for those children in North Somerset was stopped owing to cutbacks.
2009	Bernard Bray died on 25th March. Bishop Declan Lang dedicated the new gable end crosses.
2010	The three Weston Catholic Parishes met at Our Lady of Lourdes to discuss "Parishes in Communion for Mission". There was a party to celebrate Joyce Deakin's 90th birthday. Members from the Ordinariate began to join our congregation. Pope Benedict XVI visited the UK from 16th to 19th September 2010. On 19th September, several parishioners accompanied Fr Martin to Cofton Park to take part in the visit our Holy Father, Pope Benedict XVI.
2011	Wyn Bray died on 4th April 2011. Two Parish Dinners were held during the year.
2012	The 75th anniversary of Our Lady of Lourdes church The First Meeting of the Parish Pastoral Council was held on the 1st May to discuss 'Called to be a People of Hope/Parishes in Communion for Mission'. Bishop Declan Lang visited the Parish on the 12th and 13th May. There was a pilgrimage to Rome in which some members of the Ordinariate took part.
2013	On 28th February Pope Benedict XVI resigned and Pope Francis I, was elected. In September Bishop Declan produced a "Pastoral Councils Implementation Guide" through the Clifton Diocese to help the parishes.

Chapter 4

	Sisi Baker organised the first Multi-Cultural Gathering for Pentecost Sunday in which there was a variety of food and entertainment.
2014	Tony Inganni's Ordination Ceremony at Clifton Pro-Cathedral was celebrated on 15th November. A second Multi-Cultural Gathering was held. On 24th November a delayed Filipino celebration of Our Lady of the Rosary was held.
2015	The DBS checks were complete and home visits had begun. On Ash Wednesday, Our Deacon, Tony Inganni died. On March 15th the altar boys received their Guild of St Stephen Medals; Fr Martin spoke about the new directive, "Proclaim 15"; a meeting in central Birmingham was planned for 11th to 15th July to equip parishes with evangelist aids for use from Autumn that year; and he explained what a Parish Pastoral Council should be doing. Teresa Thorne organised a Taizé service attended by members of other local churches as well as members of our own congregation. Joyce Deakin died on 22nd June (aged 95), followed a few days later on 5th July, by Fr Michael O'Sullivan (aged 84). The events in 2014/5 included the Christmas Dinner, the Passover Meal, the Good Friday Frugal Lunch, a Multi-Cultural Gathering and more. There were pilgrimages to Knock and to Lourdes. In July the decoration of the Church was completed. The stained glass window with its tribute to Fr O'Sullivan's thirty years as Parish Priest was produced and installed by Wayne Ricketts Stained Glass, Bristol. In late September Fr Martin Queenan left to go to St George's, Warminster, and Fr Alexander Redman became our new Parish Priest. Fr Alexander's Induction Mass was held on Tuesday 17th November. On 1st November Geoff Thornton ended his spell as organist and choir master. On 4th November Fr Alexander Redman opened his first Parish Pastoral Council meeting. The Christmas Bazaar was held on Saturday 28th November.
2016	A regular Mass in Polish was begun at St Joseph's church, which had the benefit of relieving the overcrowding in Our Lady of Lourdes Church on Sundays. There was a pilgrimage to Rome. Pope Francis I announced the Jubilee Year of the Mercy of God. Barbara Smith, the Parish Administrator retired in May. Eventually our new part-time Parish Administrator, Mrs Maricris Magbanua was appointed. The third International Dinner was held. Some of the Filipino Community held a celebration for All Saints' Day, 1st November.
2017	Regular Latin Masses recommenced on the first Sunday of March at 12 pm. From then they were held every Sunday. A summer fête was held on 24th June.

On 23rd July Frances Ball from St Joseph's became our new organist and choir master at the 9.30am Mass on Sunday.

In September Fr Richard Dwyer, Parish Priest of Corpus Christi Church, Weston-super-Mare, left to take up his new position in Bristol, and was replaced by Fr Kevin Hennessy.

On Saturday 7th October, the Feast of Our Lady of the Rosary, a celebration was held, beginning with a recitation of the Rosary at 11.30am followed by Holy Mass at 12.00pm, after which the Filipino Community organised a lunch in the Parish Hall.

In November the La Retraite Sisters left 11, Walliscote Road to go to the Monica Wills New Care Complex in Keynsham, Bristol.

BIBLIOGRAPHY

Abram, L. and Carver, A.T. (Revised edition), *1974, Uphill and its Old Church.*

Alexander, Rt Rev M., (2004). Canon William O'Callaghan JCL 1925 - 2003, Clifton Diocese Directory.

Anon. (1980). *The Parish Church of Weston-super-Mare, Guide.*

Appleby, C., (1979). *La Retraite: Origins and Growth.*

Beisly, P., (1988). *Weston-super-Mare A history and Guide,* Alan Sutton Publishing Limited, Brunswick Rd., Gloucester.

Beisly, P., (2001). *Weston-super-Mare Past,* Phillimore & Co. Ltd, Shopwyke Manor Farm, Chichester.

Birch, J. S. *Weston-super-Mare Parish Church of St John the Baptist 1221- 1960.*

Bishops of Clifton (2016). *Mervyn Alexander, Eighth Bishop of Clifton,* Clifton Diocesan Directory. P 158.

Bizley, J., (1958). *The Church of St Martin,* Worle, Somerset.

Clifton Diocese, (2008). *Called to be a People of Hope.*

Clifton Diocese, (2013) *Parishes in Communion for Mission.*

Clifton Diocese, (2013). *Pastoral Councils Implementation Guide.*

Cobb, P., (1990). *Walsingham,* White Tree Books, Redcliffe Press Ltd.

Cook, R. Amberly Publishing.

Corpus Christi Church. *Golden Jubilee 1929-1979.* Corpus Christi Church Weston-super-Mare.

Corpus Christi Church. *Corpus Christi Church History,* Corpus Christi Church Weston-super-Mare.

Corpus Christi Church (2004). *75 years 1929 -2004.* Corpus Christi Church Weston-super-Mare.

Doorbar, Rev. J.H.H., *Guide to Kewstoke Church and Village.*

Gibbons, P., (2015). *Clifton Diocese Directory.* Clifton Diocese.

Hallaway, H.R., St Joseph's Catholic Church Weston-super-Mare. Weston-super-Mare (Weston-super-Mare Library Archives Frederick Wood Room).

Harding, J. A., (1999). *The Diocese of Clifton 1850 – 2000.* Clifton Catholic Diocesan Trustees, Bristol.

Hogarth, G., (2015). *Three Priests, Barron, Buchanan and Bickerstaffe-Drew.* The Downside Review.

Jones, G, (2011). *Locking through the Ages.* A series of articles published in the St Augustine's Parish Magazine, 'Crosslinks'.

Kemm, W. St John, *The Story of Berrow and Brean.*

Knight, R. *Kewstoke Church and Parish.*

Knight, F. A., (2013). *The Seaboard of Mendip.* The Classics US.

Lyons, Canon J., (1934). *How the Second Spring came to Weston-super-Mare.* Corpus Christi Parish.

Morrissey, T., (1978). *Rev Edward Hickey, RIP,* Clifton Diocese Directory.

Obbard, E. R., (1995). *The History and Spirituality of Walsingham,* The Canterbury Press, Norwich.

O'Flynn, T., (1958). *The Centenary Celebrations of St Joseph's Church, Weston-super-Mare,* Heritage Magazine, Vol IV, No. 4, p. 113 - 115 and 142, July. The Heritage Press Ltd, Broadwater House, Tunbridge Wells; 66 St James Street, London, SW1.

Poole, S. (2004). *The Book of Weston-super-Mare,* Halsgrove, Tiverton, Devon.

Poole, S. (2012). *Weston-super- Mare then and now,* The History Press, Stroud.

Ratzinger, J. (2007). *Jesus of Nazareth,* Bloomsbury, London, New Delhi, New York and Sydney.

Queenan, Rev M. (2016). *Fr Michael O'Sullivan - 5th July 2015,* Clifton Diocesan Directory. P 178.

Rendell, S. and Rendell, J. (1998). *Steep Holm: The Story of a Small Island,* Alan Sutton Publishing Ltd., Phoenix Mill, Thrupp, Stroud, Gloucestershire.

St Joseph's R.C. Church (2008). *St Joseph's past and present: 150th Anniversary Memento.*

Solemn Consecration of the Church of Our Lady of Lourdes Baytree Road, Milton, (1978).

Terrell, S. *Milton and Worle a Peep into the Past,* Vivlia Ltd.

Thomalin, D.J. and Crook, C. (2007). *Woodspring Priory,* The Landmark Trust.

Tuncliffe-Smith, F., Doorbar, Rev. J. H. H., Overy, J and Knight, F.A., *A Guide to St Paul's Church,* St Paul's Church Parochial Council.

Newspaper Articles

Bristol Evening World (1961). *The rally of the forty Martyrs,* 30th June.

Bristol Evening World (1961). *Weston Catholics tackle a bill of £46,000,* 7th Jan.

Catholic Herald (1961). *A flood of miracles,* 4th Aug.

Catholic Times (1958). *Weston holds 2-fold celebration,* 31st Oct.

Daily Telegraph (1959). *Painting said to be a Pittoni,* 15th April.

Evening Post (1958). *£1000 appeal for Weston church restoration,* 7th March.

Evening Post (1958). *Relics from Rome sealed in altar at Weston Church,* 3rd Oct.

Evening Post (1958). *Relics from Rome sealed in altar at Weston Church,* 28th Oct.

Evening Post (1959). *Old picture in Weston church is a Pittoni,* 15th April.

Evening Post (1959). *Photographs sent to the National Gallery,* 10th Dec.

Evening Post (1961). *Ready to start on school,* 11th Jan.

Evening Post (1961). *Franciscan fathers on Weston mission,* 30th Sept.

Evening Post (1970). *Weston 'Pop' Mass priest for Bristol,* 23rd Sept.

Evening Post (1972). *Parish Priest to become a Bishop,* 14th March.

Evening Post (2000). *'Gentle' Stephen to be ordained deacon,* 14th July.

Evening Post (2002). *Priest leaves after 30 years,* 5th Sept.

Evening Post (2002). *Father Michael calls it a day after 30 years,* 10th Sept.

Evening Post (2004). *Congregation prepares for pilgrimage,* 17th May.

EW (1957). *Weston Council to sell site to R.C. church,* 21st Jan.

EW (1958). *Colourful centenary Consecration ceremony at Weston church,* 23rd Oct.

EW (1959). *Old master 'found' in Weston church,* 15th April.

EW (1961). *Weston Catholics tackle a bill of £46,000,* 11th Jan.

Irish Independent (1959). *Unusual memorial.*

Midweek (2017). *Weston's Station listed by Historic England,* 13th Dec.

St John's Parish Church Magazine (1883). May.

Universe (1959). *Rector's find will be his memorial,* 24th April.

Universe (1972). *Auxiliary Bishop for Clifton,* 17th March.

Universe (1972). *Bishop,* 28th April.

Western Daily Press (1965). *The New Church,* 9th Feb.

Weston-super-Mare Gazette (1883). *The old Parish Church of Weston-super-Mare,* 8th Sept.

Weston-super-Mare Gazette (1938). *Impressive Ceremonies Mark the Opening of Milton's New Catholic Church,* 3rd Sept.

Weston Mercury (1929). *New Church,* 8th June.

Weston Mercury (1934). *Consecration of Corpus Christi Church,* 9th June, Part 1, columns 2 and 3.

Weston Mercury (1938). *Another new Church,* 12th Feb.

Weston Mercury (1938). *The new churches,* March 26th.

Weston Mercury (1938). *Details of new Roman Catholic Church,* 9th April.

Weston Mercury (1938). *More gifts to the Roman Catholic Church,* 9th July.

Weston Mercury (1938). *The new Roman Catholic Church at Milton,* 23rd July.

Weston Mercury (1938). *Another Church nearing completion,* 23rd July.

Weston Mercury (1938) *Assistance for the Milton's new Catholic Church,* 23rd July.

Weston Mercury (1938). *"Corpus Christi a lame dog",* 23rd July.

Weston Mercury (1938). *£51 for Roman Catholic Church,* 20th Aug.

Weston Mercury (1938). *Milton's new Catholic opened,* 3rd Sept.

Weston Mercury (1946). *Passing of a Catholic Benefactor,* 27th April.

Weston Mercury (1958). *£1000 Appeal for Weston Church Restoration,* 7th March.

Weston Mercury (1959). *Canon Judge dies after nearly 50 years as priest,* 13th Feb.

Weston Mercury (1959). *Induction of new Parish Priest at St Joseph's,* 13th March.

Weston Mercury (1959). *Famous Artist's Painting at St Joseph's Church,* 11th Dec.

Weston Mercury (1960). *Westonian ordained at Corpus Christi Church,* 8th April.

Weston Mercury (1964). *Milton will be a Separate Catholic Parish,* 2nd Oct p20.

Weston Mercury (1967). *Ashcombe House Christmas Babies,* 29th Dec.

Weston Mercury (1970). *Milton Catholics open their £6000 Hall,* 8th May.

Weston Mercury (1972). *Milton Priest to become Auxiliary Bishop,* 17th March.

Weston Mercury (1972). Presentation Photograph only to Fr Alexander, 14th April.

Weston Mercury (1972). *To take title of Bishop of Pinhel,* 21st April.

Weston Mercury (1972). *Milton Priest Ordained Bishop at Clifton,* 28th April.

Weston Mercury (1974). *First Summer Fête,* 21st June.

Weston Mercury (1974). *Convent closes after 37 years,* 13th Dec.

Weston Mercury (1978). *Church to be consecrated,* 10th February.

Weston Mercury (1981). *The First Holy Communion,* 19th June, p2.

Weston Mercury (1981). *Father O'Sullivan Celebrates his 25 Years,* Section 2 p2. 19th June.

Weston Mercury (2002). *Father says final farewell,* 13th Sept.

Weston Mercury (2003). Mass with the Pope, 25th April.

Weston Mercury (2004). *Inspiring week to mark church birthday,* 28th May.

Weston Mercury (2006). *Priest dies on 93rd birthday,* 31st March.

Weston Mercury (2007). *Church info for Polish migrants,* 12th Jan.

Weston Mercury (2017). *Blue plaque for Olympian to be unveiled in March,* 2nd March.

Weston Mercury (2017). *Raddy's story: Olympic glory in water polo,* 30th March.

Weston Mercury (2007). *La Retraite sisters to leave town after being in Weston for more than a hundred years,* 21st Sept.

Weston Mercury Magazine (1984). Fri. 22nd April.

New Roman Catholic Church opened at Weston-S-Mare 2nd Sept. 1938.

The laying of the foundation stone by Bishop William Lee Bishop of Clifton 20th April 1938.

New Roman Catholic Church Opened at Weston -S-Mare Fri. 2nd Sept 1938.

New Catholic Priest for Milton 1967/8

Internet

Bernadette Soubirous, http://www.catholic.org/saints/saint.php?saint_id=1757 14/5/2017.

Biography - Saint Faustina – Diary, http://www.faustina-message.com/saint-faustina-biography.htm 21/3/2017.

Blessing in the Catholic Church, http://www.newadvent.org/cathen/02599b.htm 13/5/2017.

Cadoc, http://freepages.genealogy.rootsweb.ancestry.com/~llangattocklingoed/history/stcadoc.html 14/5/2017.

Canonization, http://www.newadvent.org/cathen/02364b.htm 13/5/2017.

Chaplet of the Divine Mercy, https://en.wikipedia.org/wiki/Chaplet_of_the_Divine-MercyMercy 21/2/2017.

Consecration, http://newadvent.orgcathen/04276a.htm 21/2/2017.

Corpus Christi Church, http://www.corpuschristiweston.org/history.htm 2/12/2016.

Cuthbert Mayne, https://en.wikipedia.org/wiki/Cuthbert_Matne 21/1/2017.

Doomsday Book, opendoomsday.org 9/7/2017.

Edward Powell, http://www.newadvent.org/cathen/14659c.htm 26/6/2016.

Gildas, http://www.heroofcamelot.com/docs/Gildas-On-the-Ruin-of-Britain.pdf 13/5/2017.

Giovanni Batista Salvi da Sassoferrato, https://en.wikipedia.org/wiki/Giovanni_Battista_Salvi_da_Sassoferato 24/1/2017.

Gordon Riots, http://www.nationalarchives.gov.uk/pathways/blackhistory/rights/gordon.htm 14/5/2017.

Gunpowder Plot, http://www.bbc.co.uk/history/british/civil_war_revolution/gunpowder_robinson_01.shtml 28/6/2017.

Hart, D. (2016). *A brief history of Worle,* Worle History Society. http://www.worlehistorysociety.net/5.html 7/12/2016.

History of the Christian Altar, http://www.newadvent.org/cathen/01362a.htm 12/3/2017.

How did Weston-super-Mare get its name, Weston Mercury (2006), 2nd March. http://thewestonmercury.co.uk/news/how_did_weston_super_mare_get_its_name_1306273 6/12/2016.

La Retraite, http://www.laretraite.lambeth.sch.uk/14/history-of-la-retraite 3/112016.

Legends of Glastonbury – Joseph of Aramithaea, http://www.britainexpress.com/Myths/Glastonbury.htm 21/4/2017.

Mervyn Alexander, http://www.cliftondiocese.com/diocese/past-bishops/mervyn-alexander/ 17/12/2016.

Ordinariate Questions & Answers, http://Ordinariat.net/q-a 9/3/2017.

Our Clevedon Friars, The Immaculate Conception Clevedon, https://www.google.co.uk/search?q=Our+Clevedon+Friars&oq=Our+Clevedon+Friars&aqs=chrome..69i57.6412j0j4&sourceid=chrome&ie=UTF-8 27/6.2017.

Personal Ordinariate, https://ordinariate.net/q-a 14/5/2017.

Poor Servants of the Mother of God, http://www.poorservants.org/archives.htm 17/12/2016.

Reverend Canon William Ryan, Clifton Diocese, http://archive.clftondiocese.com/reverend-canon-william-ryan 17/12/2016.

Reverend Canon Timothy Barry - RIP, http://archive.cliftondiocese.com/reverend-canon-timothy-barry-rip 23/1/2017.

Roman Catholic Relief Act 1829, https://en.wikipedia.org/wiki/Roman_Catholic_Relief_Act_1829#Agitation 10/12/2016.

Taylor, Philippa   http://www.answers@n-somerset.gov.org

The Elizabeth Files, www.elizabethfiles.com/plots-against-elizabeth-i/3509/ 23/4/2017.

The Laying of the Foundation Stone, https://www.catholicculture.org/culture/library/view.cfm?recnum=3661 12/3/2017.

The Right of Blessing a Church, http://www.liturgyoffice.org.uk 6/4/2017.

Taking Stock, taking-stock.org.uk/Home/Dioceses/Diocese-of-Clifton 6/4/2017.

Thomas à Becket, http://www.bbc.co.uk/history/historic_figures/becket_thomas.shtml 14/5/2017.

Weston super Mare brief history, http://www.weston-super-mare.com/newhistory/newhistory.html 2/12/2016.

Weston, Clevedon and Portishead Light Railway, https://en.wikipedia.org/wiki/Weston,_Clevedon_and_Portishead_Light_Railway 11/4/2017.

Worle, https://en.wikipedia.org/wiki/Worle 3/11/2016.